FORGOTTEN KING

Megaliths with animal figures at Lahusa Idano Tai in south-east Nias.

FORGOTTEN KINGDOMS IN SUMATRA

BY

F. M. SCHNITGER

With contributions by

C. VON FUHRER-HAIMENDORF

AND

G. L. TICHELMAN

With an Introduction by

JOHN N. MIKSIC

SINGAPORE
OXFORD UNIVERSITY PRESS
OXFORD NEW YORK
1989

Oxford University Press

Oxford New York Toronto
Delhi Bombay Calcutta Madras Karachi
Petaling Jaya Singapore Hong Kong Tokyo
Nairobi Dar es Salaam Cape Town
Melbourne Auckland
and associated companies in
Berlin Ibadan

Oxford is a trade mark of Oxford University Press

Introduction © Oxford University Press Pte. Ltd. 1989

First published by E. J. Brill, Leiden, 1939
Reprinted 1964
First issued (with corrections) as an Oxford University Press paperback 1989

ISBN 0 19 588905 3

Printed in Malaysia by Peter Chong Printers Sdn. Bhd.
Published by Oxford University Press Pte. Ltd.,
Unit 221, Ubi Avenue 4, Singapore 1440

TO MOECHTAR

Introduction

THROUGH Sumatran forests and mountains, men have cut trails for thousands of years, in search of resins that give off fragrant aromas when burnt; hunted elephant and rhinoceros to cut off their tusks and horns; cracked open rocks to get at gleaming yellow dust locked inside. With these materials, ancient Sumatrans built kingdoms whose wealth became proverbial across Asia.

As if the bounty of Sumatra's own soil were not sufficient, nature gave Sumatra two more, geographical advantages. Sumatra lies like a fallen log across the sea road from the Indian Ocean to the South China Sea, and to the Spice Islands of the Moluccas, so that mariners must sail near the shores to pass from one of these basins to the other. Nature also made Sumatra the meeting place of the monsoons. Wind blows from the west just long enough to take sailors from India to Sumatra, or Sumatra to China, before it reverses, blowing the ships back home. By the fifth century AD, Sumatra had become the nexus of a well-travelled route between India and China.

Sumatran cultures grew vigorously, greedily tapping the rich cultural and economic resources flowing through Asiatic maritime veins. Some have said that Sumatran kingdoms such as Srivijaya parasitized on this organism, but it would be more accurate to compare them to the heart of the beast, the pump which drove the circulatory system of trade and communication. During the first millennium AD, Sumatra provided much of the shipping, man-power, and technical expertise which moved goods and people around the Asiatic ocean.

Sumatra never has had a single culture, but the groups who inhabit the island have long preserved a form of unity consisting of a formal pattern of interaction with one another and with outsiders. This pattern of interaction was not static. At various times, the lens through which Sumatrans viewed the rest of the world has focused on India, Arabia, China, Europe, and Java. Relations between the people of the mountainous western and swampy eastern sides of the island have also been dynamic; sometimes the island's cultural identity has emanated from the agrarian hinterland villages, at other times the trading ports in the estuaries of the lowland have produced the arts and literature which other Sumatrans emulated.

Beneath the rippling surface of Sumatran life, other cultural currents continued to flow in the same course for millennia. These currents consisted of objects used in the daily life: the curved roofs of the Batak and Minangkabau houses, the earthenware water jars and cooking pots of the Malays, and the woven cloth and plaited basketry of various regions have preserved similar designs since prehistoric times, independent of the fluctuating mixture of foreigners in Sumatran ports and courts. In the early twentieth century, the rhythm of activity in such regions as Nias was determined by men's desire to construct monuments to themselves in the form of large monoliths, just as men had done twenty centuries earlier in Pasemah and, perhaps, Mahat.

This intoxicating blend of continuity and variation, isolation and exposure, wealth and energy, would seem likely to exert a potent attraction on professional investigators of ancient culture and artefacts. Reality confounds this expectation. The yield of archaeological research on Sumatra is a molehill compared to the great mountain of knowledge accumulated by legions of scholars who have studied neighbouring Java or even tiny Bali.

Several hundred students are enrolled in archaeology departments at universities in Jakarta, Yogyakarta, and Denpasar. No universities in Sumatra offer courses in archaeology. The Indonesian National Research Centre for Archaeology has not been able to entice Java-based archaeologists to move to Sumatra to open a branch for that island.

F. M. Schnitger's *Forgotten Kingdoms in Sumatra*, written over fifty years ago, is still the only book available to readers in search of a general view of remains from the island's classical age (which scholars of Schnitger's generation called 'Hindoo' civilization even though in Sumatra, the dominant religion was Buddhism). Several scholars have made important additions to subjects which Schnitger discusses in *Forgotten Kingdoms*, but the resources which have been devoted to archaeological research in Sumatra are far from commensurate with the island's size, historical interest, and potential as a source of discoveries. Schnitger's research on some problems has never been augmented by subsequent work, and in several instances will remain for ever the last word on the subject because the sites he explored have since deteriorated or been altered, or life-styles have changed, destroying continuity between ethnographic observation and historical inference.

Before Schnitger came to Sumatra in 1935, the major summary

of the island's archaeology was a travel report by the director of the Archaeological Service in the Netherlands Indies, F. D. K. Bosch (1930). This report has never been translated from the original Dutch. Sumatran archaeology during the colonial period was largely left in the hands of such individuals as plantation managers and government officials with an avocational interest in antiquities, who assembled collections of statuary culled from nearby ruins, provenances of which were often quickly forgotten. Some of these individuals were more intellectually inclined than others; a well-known example is L. C. Westenenk, who served in various capacities in Palembang, Fort van der Capellen (Batusangkar), and Bengkulu. Although these men undoubtedly destroyed much potential information through ignorance of proper techniques for research and recording, we must conclude that without their contributions, our knowledge of ancient Sumatra would be even poorer than it is.

Friedrich Martin Schnitger arrived in Palembang in January 1935. He had previously shown interest in Javanese antiquities and traditional dance, publishing several articles on these subjects between 1929 and 1934. Part of his work was funded by the Royal Netherlands Geographical Society, in whose journal he published several accounts of his discoveries.

Schnitger, who was not a Dutchman, remained an outsider in colonial Indonesian archaeology; he never joined the Netherlands Indies Archaeological Service or the Batavian Society for Arts and Sciences (Bataviaasch Genootschap voor Kunsten en Wettenschappen), the organization which supervised museums in the Dutch colony, although he did donate books to the Royal Institute for Linguistics, Geography, and Ethnology (Koninklijke Instituut voor Taal- Land- en Volkenkunde) in 1942 and 1943, according to the minutes of the administrative meetings of that organization ('Bestuursvergadering', BKI 102: xi, 5 December 1942, and xxvii, 27 March 1943). His last articles about Indonesia appeared in 1943.

It is characteristic of the history of archaeology in Sumatra that the first systematic series of excavations was conducted by a man who was not part of the official establishment (although he had permission for his research). He also started the first museum in Sumatra, in Palembang, himself taking the title of Conservator. Between 1935 and 1938, he shuttled between Europe and Sumatra. In January 1935 he excavated at Palembang, including the sites of Geding Suro, Kedukan Bukit, and Bukit Seguntang; in March he excavated at Muara Jambi; in April, Muara Takus, in Riau; in

June–July and September, he was in Padang Lawas, North Sumatra; in October, Sungai Langsat, Tanah Datar, West Sumatra. He was in Tanah Abang, Lower Lematang, where he did a trial excavation, in February 1936; in Muara Jambi in March; Leiden in August, Vienna in 1937, and Nias in 1938, although he was back in Leiden by October that same year.

Schnitger holds the honour of having written the first doctoral dissertation on Sumatran archaeology. He obtained his Ph.D. from the University of Vienna in 1937. The archaeological sections of his dissertation were published under the title of *The Archaeology of Hindoo Sumatra* (1938); in the foreword, he credits N. J. Krom as his guide to 'Hindoo-Javanese antiquities', W. Koppers and W. Schmidt as his instructors in ethnology, and R. von Heine Geldern for introducing him to prehistoric studies. This intellectual milieu clearly influenced Schnitger's interpretations of his discoveries in Sumatra; the Viennese school of that period is well known among anthropologists and historians for its emphasis on the study of diffusion as a means of explaining the distribution of cultural traits and artefacts.

Schnitger's publications in English and other languages (French, German, and Dutch) are not theoretical or analytical. He wrote in a manner which is partly descriptive, partly impressionistic. His unorthodox (some would say unsystematic) style may have kept him on the fringe of the Dutch scholarly community. N. J. Krom, in a review of *The Archaeology of Hindoo Sumatra* (1938), complimented Schnitger for being successful where others had been defeated by difficult field conditions, but he also criticized Schnitger for not focusing on his primary data instead of wandering through a range of related subjects ranging from prehistory to modern art.

F. H. van Naerssen, another important historian of early Indonesia, in his review of *Forgotten Kingdoms*, was more charitable, referring to the book's 'variegated but not inharmonious composition'. He finds other points to criticize, however: deficient references to published sources (he notes that the chapter on 'Putting Fish under a Spell' is 'very close as to structure and content' to an article on this subject by Wilkens in his *Verspreide Geschriften*, Vol. III, pp. 346–8); the fact that many of the graphic designs in the book (at the end of some chapters) were not Sumatran; and the awkward language of the original edition.

Other archaeologists have criticized Schnitger's work because he did not publish such important information as the precise locations of his excavations, their stratigraphy, or the contexts of small finds. He did, however, compile and publish architectural plans and profiles of temples which are now invaluable because in many cases, such as Bara in Padang Lawas, the temples no longer stand. Modern archaeologists, however, cannot help wincing when he refers casually to emptying temples of their 'rubbish'. At Bara, he dug a trench across 'the whole temple-site'. When the diggers hit a bronze object, Schnitger finished unearthing it with his hunting knife.

In his historical chapters, for instance those on Thomas Diaz and Tongku Tambuse, he gives no sources, and does little more than rewrite Dutch scholarly articles in a popular style. The chapters of the book are a succession of vignettes rather than a continuous narrative. Despite these shortcomings, *Forgotten Kingdoms* is still useful for specialists as well as laymen. Schnitger obviously felt deeply about Sumatra and some of the more unusual characters in its history. Perhaps they attracted him because they were somewhat tragic like himself, an outsider. He was criticized for being a popularizer, but he had undoubted energy and commitment, qualities which do much to make up for his technical failings. No one since has done as much to further our knowledge of classical Sumatran archaeology.

The book's opening passage on Palembang introduces a narrator who refers to himself in the first person, who speaks from a rather melancholic and detached viewpoint. Schnitger first addresses us not on history or archaeology, but through an evocation of the natural and human characteristics which define Sumatra's unique and variegated nature.

The story of archaeology at Palembang since Schnitger worked there is a mixture of success, failure, and unsolved questions. The great inscription from Telaga Batu of which Schnitger wrote that 'only a few words are decipherable' has been successfully translated by J. G. de Casparis (1956), who has also analysed the thirty inscribed stones found at the site by Schnitger in co-operation with the Palembang Municipality. The true date of the Telaga Batu inscription is now known to be around AD 680–5, rather than the ninth or tenth centuries as Schnitger speculated.

Seven major inscriptions, including the Telaga Batu stone, are now known to have been issued by the kingdom of Srivijaya, and the large granite Buddha from Bukit Seguntang which Schnitger thought must date several centuries earlier now has also been shown to date from the seventh or eighth century (Nik Hasan

Shuhaimi, 1979). Nevertheless, these advances have not resolved the controversies associated with that kingdom.

After *Forgotten Kingdoms*, the next significant account of Palembang archaeology was a record of survey by a team from Jakarta (*Amerta*, 1955). The next excavations did not take place until 1974, when a team dug at several locations within the city but did not discover any sites older than the thirteenth century (Bronson and Wisseman, 1979). Recently, however, archaeologists using aerial photos have found an important early site at Karanganyar, on the western border of the modern city. Ceramics, beads, and bricks also have come to light near Bukit Seguntang (Edwards McKinnon, 1985). However, no major sustained excavations have been undertaken, so that it is impossible to produce a much more connected picture of Palembang archaeology than Schnitger's.

In the Batang Hari valley Schnitger dug at Muara Jambi, which is usually associated with the kingdom of Malayu. Schnitger's account of the site contains several defects; for example, the names of Candi Gumpung and Candi Tinggi were reversed, and the chamber of Candi Gumpung is not as large as Schnitger reported, so that it is not the largest in Sumatra.

Important discoveries have been made at Muara Jambi during restoration of the temples, which began in 1976. Some of the major new finds include a beautiful Prajnaparamita statue found in 1978 at Candi Gumpung which dates from the thirteenth or fourteenth century and a bronze gong with a Chinese inscription dated 1231 at Candi Kembar Batu. One of the most significant discoveries has been the recovery of 11 deposit chambers at Candi Gumpung; these support the theory that at least some of the temples were designed as mandalas, and enable us to infer that the temple was built between the late ninth and early tenth centuries, and underwent at least one reconstruction in the eleventh or twelfth century (Boechari, 1985). No complete report of the research and restoration work at Muara Jambi has yet appeared, but the preliminary results already allow us to go beyond what Schnitger was able to tell us.

By contrast, no research has been performed at Sungai Langsat, where the great Bhairawa image was discovered, since Schnitger excavated there in October 1935.

The Muara Takus site on the Kampar River, which forms the subject of Schnitger's next chapter, has also been recently restored by the Indonesian Directorate for the Preservation and Protection of the National Heritage. The restoration has unfortunately not provided any further discoveries which might reveal which kingdom constructed this isolated site, or its precise date.

Schnitger's most important contributions stem from his research in the Padang Lawas area of North Sumatra. No new excavations have been made in that region although Biaro Bahal I has recently been restored. Many temples in the region have suffered greatly since Schnitger recorded them, and much of the sculpture has disappeared or been severely damaged. Schnitger's accounts, incomplete though they are from the point of view of modern archaeology, will be the best record we will ever have of many of these buildings. We have made no progress since his time in solving the mystery of which kingdom built these temples, and why they were located in such an inhospitable and remote area.

Schnitger's account of the 'prehistoric monuments' of Aur Duri, on the Mahat River, a tributary of the Kampar, has been extended by a recent series of archaeological studies. The Mahat valley is as beautiful as Schnitger described it, and even more remote than it was in his day. The road to the valley from Payakumbuh was passable by motor vehicles in the late 1930s; a spot by the roadside is still known as *kandang oto*, 'automobile pen', by the residents. The ruins of a *passangrahan* or Dutch-period government rest-house can still be seen at Aur Duri. No doubt Schnitger made use of it during his research on the area.

Now, however, the road is often passable only by horseback. The valley's inaccessibility retarded research into the sites which Schnitger reported until the mid-1980s, when a series of expeditions found that the valley was thickly strewn with groups of standing stones of various types. Many of these sites have now been mapped, and some excavations performed.

The study of 'megaliths' has undergone significant conceptual change since Schnitger's time. No longer do we assume that a single megalithic culture once existed in South-East Asia, nor would anyone venture to conclude that the Nias people migrated from the Irrawaddy valley, nor that the Palembang, Jambi, Kampar, and Batak megalithic cults came from Tonkin. One of the major criticisms levelled at the Vienna school of diffusionism is that some of its practitioners drew up a list of locations where superficially similar elements or traits are found, such as the portrayal of elephants, and assumed that similarity always denoted communication, diffusion, or migration. Today we are much readier to grant the possibility of independent invention of similar traits, and the importance of the local use of a symbol which happens to have been imported from another group as opposed to the emphasis which earlier archaeologists placed on the creation of a symbol as a feat implying superior intellectual ability.

Another principal change in our view of 'megalith builders' of the recent past, such as those of Nias or Assam, is that they do *not* necessarily give us a picture of life 2,000 years ago. The idea that any groups, such as the Tasaday or the Kalahari Bushmen, represent survivors from the prehistoric era is no longer taken seriously. No human cultures have maintained similar ways of life as integral systems for such long periods. Now we consider that we can benefit from the study of such cultures as examples of the way in which certain groups in different periods reacted to their environment and contacts with other groups, but we cannot assume that the specific symbols and meanings attached to them have persisted unchanged for millennia.

It is now acknowledged that the use of large stones is a simple trait which does not provide useful data on chronology, patterns of communication, or migration. Research now is oriented toward specific cultural centres, some of which happen to have megalithic monuments; the nature of the relationship between one centre and another can seldom be inferred from the monuments, because they have too few stylistic traits to tell us whether similarities in the use of stone monuments are due to communication, independent development, or descent from a common ancestral tradition. Little research has been conducted in any of the areas in Sumatra where megalithic monuments exist since Schnitger's time; no archaeology has been conducted in Pasemah or Nias. The Mahat valley has, however, been the subject of two recent archaeological expeditions from the Indonesian National Research Centre for Archaeology as well as other anthropologists and archaeologists. Excavations at one site, Bawah Parit, demonstrated that some stones were burial markers; several of them were found to stand above the skulls of skeletons interred in extended position. The skeletons were, however, highly fragile, and could not be recovered, and no artefacts were discovered associated with them. Thus we cannot judge whether Schnitger's estimate of 2,000 years for the age of the site is accurate (Miksic, 1987; Tim Peneliti Tradisi Megalitik Sumatra Barat, 1985).

Schnitger's impressionistic account of Bengkulu also has been amplified by subsequent research. This chapter contains a minor error; Fort Marlborough was *not* built after Fort St. George was abandoned. Fort St. George was the East India Company's headquarters in Madras. Schnitger has confused Fort St. George with an earlier structure in Bengkulu named York Fort, built in 1685 after the Dutch evicted all other European merchants from Bantam, in West Java, and evacuated in 1714 when Marlborough was built. Several studies of Bengkulu history have been written (e.g. Bastin, 1960), and York Fort has been excavated 1987 and 1988; a report is scheduled to be published in 1989.

Schnitger's interest in Bengkulu was perhaps excited by the tragic history of the settlement, and particularly the experiences of Sir Thomas Stamford Raffles there. Probably Schnitger was speaking for himself as much as for Raffles when he wrote, 'At all times mediocre specialists have thwarted genial diletants' [sic]. Schnitger was not a man to be thwarted, as his record of excavations and research in many parts of Sumatra shows. Despite 'Schnitger's shortcomings as an analytical archaeologist, his book has lasting merit. It is a sensitive inquiry into the link between Sumatran antiquities and traditions at the end of a long historical epoch, just before many threads which ran far back in time snapped.

National University of Singapore   JOHN N. MIKSIC
November 1988

I. References

Amerta (1955), 'Kissah Perdjalanan ke Sumatra Selatan dan Djambi', *Amerta* 3.

Bastin, J. (1960), *The British in West Sumatra*, Kuala Lumpur: University of Malaya.

Boechari (1985), 'Ritual Deposits of Candi Gumpung (Muara Jambi)', *SPAFA Consultative Workshop on Archaeological and Environmental Studies on Srivijaya*, Bangkok: SPAFA, pp. 229–43.

Bosch, F. D. K. (1930), 'Verslag van een reis door Sumatra', *Oudheidkundig Verslag*, pp. 133–57.

Bronson, B. and Wisseman, J. (1979), 'Palembang as Sriwijaya, the Lateness of Early Cities in Southern Southeast Asia', *Asian Perspectives* 19/1: 220–39.

de Casparis, J. G. (1956), *Prasasti Indonesia II (Selected Inscriptions from the 7th to the 9th Centuries A. D.)*, Bandung: Masa Baru.

Edwards McKinnon, E. (1985), 'Early Polities in Southern Sumatra: Some Preliminary Observations based on Archaeological Evidence', *Indonesia* 40: 1–36.

Krom, N. J. (1938), 'Review of F. M. Schnitger, *The Archaeology of Hindoo Sumatra*', *TKNAG* 55: 300–1.

Miksic, J. N. (1987), 'From Seri Vijaya to Melaka: *Batu Tegak* in Historical and Cultural Context', *JMBRAS* 60/2: 1–42.

van Naerssen, F. H. (1939), 'Review of F. M. Schnitger, *Forgotten Kingdoms in Sumatra*', *Cultureel Indie* 1: 125–6.

Nik Hasan Shuhaimi (1979), 'The Bukit Seguntang Buddha, A Reconsideration of Its Date', *JMBRAS* 52/2: 33–40.

Tim Peneliti Tradisi Megalitik Sumatra Barat (1985), *Laporan Penelitian Kepurbakalaan (Ekskavasi) di Situs Bawah Parit, Sumatra Barat*, Jakarta: Pusat Penelitian Arkeologi Nasional.

II. Publications by F. M. Schnitger

1929–30. 'Raden Mas Jodjana als danser', *NION* 14: 163–73.

1931–2. 'Een Hindoe-Javaansch Bhairawi-beeld te Leiden', *NION* 16: 257–9.

1931–2. 'Gadjah Mada', *NION* 16: 289–94.

1934. 'The Names of the Javanese King Jayanagara', *Acta Orientalia* 12: 133–5.

1935. 'Enkele oudheidkundige opmerkingen over het Tantrisme op Java', *BKI* 92: 149–60.

1935. 'Olifanten op Sumatra', *Algemeen Handelsblad* (22 December).

1935. *Oudheidkundige Vondsten in Palembang*, Palembang: Drukkerij Ebeling.

1935. *Oudheidkundige Vondsten in Palembang. Bijlage B, 1. Addenda en corrigenda. 2. Vondsten te Moeara Takoes*, Fort de Kock: Drukkerij Lie.

1936. *Oudheidkundige Vondsten in Palembang*, Leiden: E. J. Brill.

1936. 'Oudheidkundige vondsten in Padang Lawas. (Midden Tapanoeli)', *Elsevier's Geillustreerd Maandschrift* 9, 2/5: 289–309.

1936. *Oudheidkundige Vondsten in Padang Lawas*, Leiden: E. J. Brill.

1936. *Hindoe-oudheden aan de Batang Hari*, Leiden: E. J. Brill.

1936. 'De herkomst van het Krtanagara-beeld te Berlijn', *TBG* 76: 328–30.

1936. 'Vondsten te Moeara Takoes', *TBG* 76: 331–2.

1936. 'De tempel van Simangambat (Zuid Tapanoeli)', *TBG* 76: 334–6.

1937. 'Het grootste Hindoe-beeld van Sumatra', *TKNAG* 54: 570–5.

1937. 'A Great Ancient Image', *Asia* 37: 773.

1937. 'Beelden van Tjeta (Java)', *Tropisch Nederland* 9/22: 347–9.

1938. 'Unearthing Sumatra's Ancient Culture', *Asia* 38: 171–4.

1938. 'Prehistoric Monuments in Sumatra', *Man* 38, article 35, p. 41.

1938. 'Ancient Batak Tombs in Tapanuli (North Sumatra)', *Annual Bibliography of Indian Archaeology for 1936*, Vol. 11: 30–2.

1938. 'Een olifantsbeeld uit Zuid-Sumatra', *Tropisch Nederland* 11/2:

1938. 'The Archaeology of Hindoo Sumatra', *Internationales Archiv fur Ethnographie* 35 Supplement, 1–44. Leiden: E. J. Brill.

1939. 'Diervormige graven op Borneo, Sumatra en Nias', *Tropisch Nederland* 12: 215–19.

1939. 'Bataksche oudheden', *Tropisch Nederland* 12: 8–12.

1939. 'Diervormige doodkisten op Nias', *Cultureel Indie* I: 189–90.

1939. 'De symbolische verslinding', *Cultureel Indie* I: 302–3.

1939. 'Steenen monumenten van Noord-Sumatra', *De Natuur* 59: 217–21.

1939. *Forgotten Kingdoms in Sumatra*, Leiden: E. J. Brill.

1939. 'Monuments megalithiques de Sumatra-septentrional', *Revue des Arts Asiatiques* 13: 23–7.

1939. 'The Largest Image of Sumatra', *The Lloyd Mail* 9: 145–7.

1939. (with G. L. Tichelman) 'Die tanzende Gleiderpuppe der Batak', *Archiv fur Anthropologie* 25: 131–4.

1939–42. 'Les monuments megalithiques de Nias', *Revue des Arts Asiatiques* 13: 78–84.

1939–42. 'Les terraces megalithiques de Java', *Revue des Arts Asiatiques* 13: 105–12.

1940. 'Der palaeolithische Mensch von Sumatra', *Zeitschrift fur Ethnologie* 72: 372–3.

1940. 'Het ontstaan der rijken aan de Kampar Kanan', *TKNAG* 57: 397–403.

1941. 'Lieder von Nias', *Zeitschrift fur Ethnologie* 73: 34–9.

1941–2. 'Megalithen vom Batakland und Nias', *IPEK. Jahrbuch fur prahistorische und ethnographische Kunst* 15–16: 220–52.

1942. 'Schiffahrt und Neolithikum in Indonesien', *Asienberichte* 13/14: 30–42.

1942. 'Tierformige Sarge in Asian und Europa', *Paideuma* 2: 147–50.

1943. 'De beteekenis van den naam Sumatra en van enkele ander namen in Nederlandsch-Indie', *TKNAG* 60: 111–14.

1943. 'Madagascar en Indonesie', *TKNAG* 60: 397–406.

1943. 'Die altesten Schiffsdarstellungen in Indonesien', *Archiv fur Anthropologie* 28: 141–5.

Abbreviations

NION	*Nederlandsch Indie Oud en Nieuw*
BKI	*Bijdragen tot de Taal-, Land-, en Volkekunde*
TBG	*Tijdschrift van het Batavaasch Genootschap voor Kunsten en Wettenschappen*
TKNAG	*Tijdschrift van het Koninklijk Nederlandsch Aardrijkskundig Genootschap*

The author in front of a prehistoric relief in Pasemah, South Sumatra.

Preface

LAST year, when my *Archaeology of Hindoo Sumatra* was published, many friends in England and America wrote to me saying how beautiful the photos were and how tiresome the text, and some urged me to write a popular book on the same subject.

Now I must confess that nothing is more unpleasant than to write a book.

It is wonderful to wander through the jungle in rain and in sunshine, to laugh and play with primitive, friendly people, to bathe in the foaming waters of a cool mountain stream or to watch the sun setting in a sea of scarlet behind the vast, silent mountains. It is glorious to drift for hours in a canoe among reeds and ferns, to play a tune on a bamboo flute or to watch the graceful movements of fish in the clear water. It is something one never forgets—the song of mysterious birds singing in the fathomless jungles of Kampar, the red orchids blooming on lonely hillsides and the moon sailing out like a silver boat over the vast blue of the evening sky.

But it is terrible to write a book.

And yet—an island that is always kind and hospitable places one under obligations. And so I take up my pen once more.

This book gives a few sidelights on the wilderness of Sumatra, with its attractive people and remarkable animals, with its ancient, vanished civilizations and forgotten kingdoms, the tragic ruins of which lie buried in the jungle. It tells something about Hindu antiquities, continues with the megaliths of Nias and Samosir, and ends with prehistoric monuments. Here and there it touches on legends, folk tales and ethnological details. In this way attention is called to problems which may have been neglected in a systematic description, such as the well-known book of Professor Loeb.

It seemed to me a good idea to devote a few chapters to people who deserve more recognition than has been given them by history. In the jungle, footsteps are obliterated by every shower. The woods are full of unknown graves, and that is why I hope these people will continue to live in the following pages.

Moreover, I could not resist the temptation to tell something about the life of the elephants, since reliable information on this subject is very scarce.

In writing this book, many people have been helpful to me. Dr J. H. Maasland and M. A. Bouman have contributed valuable information, of which I have gratefully made use. They gave such hearty co-operation during my exploration of the Batak Lands and Nias that without their help this book would never have been written. To Dr P. Voorhoeve, also, I express my hearty thanks.

I also received help from Messrs. A. W. Bokma, Rudolf Bonnet, G. A. Bosselaar, N. J. de Bruin, F. H. Deys, Dr A. van Doorninck, S. Eman, Dr H. J. Friedericy, Professor R. Heine Geldern, W. Hoetagaloeng, Wm. S. B. Klooster, Professor Wilhelm Koppers, S. Kortleven, Dr V. E. Korn, J. C. Lamster, A. J. de Lorm, Dr E. P. Pflugbeil, S. H. Pruys, M. J. Ruychaver, G. L. Tichelman (who wrote chapter 9), G. J. Westerink, and T. G. Woudstra.

Dr C. von Fürer-Haimendorf was kind enough to contribute a review of the Naga megaliths in Assam, from which the reader may observe how very much they resemble those of Nias and Sumatra. I hope to go more deeply into this subject in another book.

In conclusion, I wish to thank the Royal Netherlands Geographical Society, which has given financial support to my explorations. Professor J. P. Kleiweg de Zwaan, Chairman of this Society, did pioneer work 30 years ago, in his anthropological studies in Nias. His approval has been the greatest reward for my work.

Leiden, October 1938.

Contents

Palembang

THE Musi River comes from deep in the interior of Palembang and has its source in the mysterious Barisan Mountains. During its long journey to the sea, many leaves, branches and trees fall into the stream. Weary of life, they drift calmly along to the mighty ocean. At night these fallen giants glide past Palembang, looming vast and black in the moonlight. Now they are almost at their journey's end and need only to pass the delta. Sometimes a branch brushes against the shore, filling the air with the mystic incense of the jungle, so that one is seized with a feeling of mingled joy and sadness.

Europeans commonly say that all the rivers of the East Indies are the same, i.e. grey and monotonous. I cannot share this opinion. On the contrary, if one wanders about for a long time in Sumatra, one sees that every river has its own character—some are old and slow, others young and playful.

The Musi is broad and complacent like an aged man, the Kampar glittering and full of jubilant bird songs. The Batang Hari is a cruel, white-hot pool of fire and the Panei is like a mysterious serpent, silent and beautiful.

Every river has a voice of its own, and often in sleep one hears it singing, like a muted choir.

On moonlit nights, young Malays of Palembang hire a boat and go rowing with their sweethearts. They glide past the Chinese houses, built on rafts. Inside, one catches a glimpse of red-enamelled altars, coloured dragons, and images of smiling gods. If anyone in the house has died, lilac candles are burning, their quiet flame reflected in the murmuring water.

As it is now, so it was a thousand years ago. Palembang then was a mighty kingdom, whose influence extended over a large part of the Archipelago.

Since 1918, when Professor Coedes, Dean of the French School of the Far East, published his amazing discovery that in the seventh century, a kingdom of Srivijaya lay in South Sumatra, an army of famous scholars have attempted to reconstruct this mysterious realm from ancient chronicles and travellers' accounts. They succeeded in proving that Srivijaya originated about 683, subsequently extended its power over all South Sumatra, conquered the Malay Peninsula, and in the eighth century sent an army to Cambodia, where the king was taken prisoner and beheaded. After that time, the kings of Cambodia every morning bowed to the west in prayer, as a tribute to the Maharaja of Srivijaya. He owned a pool paved with silver and connected with the river by a canal. Every morning an orderly threw in a bar of gold, and at ebb tide, when all these bars of gold appeared glittering in the sun, the monarch looked out from his great audience hall and rejoiced in the sight.

In the ninth and eleventh centuries Srivijaya had monasteries in Bengal and South India. It was a great, flourishing town with more than a thousand Buddhist monks. Pilgrims from China, who wished to visit the holy land of India, lingered here for a long time in order to learn Sanskrit and to become imbued with the teachings of Buddhism. In 747 the town beheld two famous priests within its walls—Wajrabodhi and Amoghawajra, who brought the magic teaching of the Wajrayana to China. In the thirteenth century Srivijaya seems to have declined, and in 1377 it was conquered by the Javanese.

From the beginning, however, scholars have been surprised to learn that Palembang is so poor in antiquities. One could not imagine that there were so few temples in so large a town. For this reason, I decided to make a careful investigation a few years ago. Although these attempts were crowned with success, one cannot say that the antiquities found were in accordance with the importance which Srivijaya is supposed to have had. It must be remembered, however, that the ancient fields of Palembang have been plundered for centuries by the inhabitants. It is also possible that the rulers of this country had less inclination to build temples than had their contemporaries in Java and Cambodia.

When I came to Palembang, a great inscription had just been found in the eastern part of the town. At the top, it had a canopy of seven serpent heads.

This reminds of an inscription from Ligor in the north of the Malayan Peninsula (AD 775), in which the king of Srivijaya is called 'the patron of the nagas, their heads haloed by the streaks of the lustre of gems', as well of the statement of a Chinese, in 1225, that the kings of Palembang had sprung from the spawn of serpents. This gives reason to suppose that the inscription is Buddhistic. Alas, the writing is so weather-beaten that only a few words are decipherable, but from the form of the letters, one concludes that the inscription dates from the ninth or tenth century. Under the text there is a funnel, evidently intended for draining away the water which was poured over the stone during certain ceremonials.

An excavation made at this spot resulted in the discovery of about 30 rough, calligraphed stones. Nearly all bear the inscription 'jayasiddhayatra', and some in addition the word 'sarwwasatwa', and were evidently laid there by pilgrims, who had come to this spot in order to partake in certain ceremonials. It is plain, therefore, that the jayasiddhayatra initiation could be followed by that of the sarwwasatwa, giving the faithful an even greater beatitude. The expression 'Srivijaya siddhayatra' in the inscription from 683 might mean that the king in question had made a pilgrimage to Telaga Batu in order to celebrate a victory over Srivijaya. If this assumption is correct, the inscription cannot possibly refer to the founding of this kingdom. Peculiar, also, are two irregular blocks of hardened clay, with three of four lines of Sanskrit in late Pallawa writing. All these inscriptions were made from the sixth to the tenth centuries.

In the neighbourhood lies the tomb of Ratu Sinuhun, a Muhammadan princess, who grew famous by the giving of various laws; she died in the beginning of the seventeenth century. Her grave is the holiest of Palembang. At night, faithful Muhammadans see a column of fire arising from it. It contains marvellous woodcarvings. Perhaps the situation of both monuments on this place is not an accident. Telaga Batu may have been sacred from a very remote time.

About 100 metres west of the place where the inscriptions were found, on the opposite side of the road, are several heaps of brick rubbish, perhaps the remains of ancient shrines. At the present time, there are only Muhammadan graves here. Going in a southeasterly direction, one soon arrives at the group of temples at Geding Sura, which I discovered in January 1935. According to tradition, Geding Sura was a nobleman from Java, who fled to Palembang after the fall of Majapahit (about 1528), founding a dynasty there, which ruled until 1823. There is, therefore, some reason to surmise that the grave temples were built during the sixteenth century.

Formerly, each building was covered by a tiled roof, resting on wooden beams. Now there are only a number of brick walls, decorated with crosses and medallions. On the south side is a flight of steps. One of the temples was originally built of natural stone; later, an outer casing of brick was made with an entirely different ornament. Among the ruins lay a beautiful image, dating from the eighth to the tenth centuries, 1.18 m high, representing a standing god in festive dress, with ear ornaments, armlets, and necklace, a garment with loops on both hips and draperies reaching almost to the ankles; eleven strands of hair fall over back and shoulders; the left leg is slightly bent; head, arms, and feet are missing. Not far away lay a lotus cushion. A corner-stone of terracotta also came to light. A thorough search of the field revealed the trunk of an elephant, the fragment of an animal head, and the relief of a parrot within a garland.

North of this group of buildings, on the hill Mangkubumi, lie two more brick monuments.

About 140 m westward is the shrine of a certain Panembahan, which is similarly decorated with crosses and medallions. Here, also, some of the walls have been renovated, without taking into consideration the original plan. On the south side, two flights of steps have collapsed, so that loose stones lie scattered along the length of the wall. The floor of the tomb was broken open; at a depth of about 1.25 m a plank was found, but underneath lay nothing.

In a south-easterly direction, on the opposite side of the river, three beautiful bronze images were discovered in 1929, representing Maitreya, Lokesvara, and Buddha. They are related to the art of Middle Java and thus were made in the eighth to the tenth centuries. Maitreya is the Buddha, who in the future will descend on earth in order to save humanity. Lokesvara is the lord of the present world order and the special patron of the Buddhist church. In his crown is sitting an image of his spiritual father Amitabha, the Buddha of the West.

Among the most interesting discoveries in East Palembang is a four-armed bronze Siva image, 77 cm high, which also dates from the Middle Java period. Around the hips, the god wears a tiger skin. The upper hands hold a fly-flan and a rosary, the lower hand a little jar. From the left shoulder, a snake extends across the chest; his head is to be seen on the shoulder. The hair is dressed in tresses. On the forehead is a third eye.

This beautiful art object lay together with three other bronze images of a much later date (fourteenth- to fifteenth-century), representing Siva, Brahma, and Vishnu, and in various ways giving evidence of Javanese influence. The first god is standing on a lion, the second on a goose, and the third on a *garuda*. These are probably statues portraying dead kings. Who knows if they were not worshipped in the temple mausoleums of Mangkubumi or Panembahan? As early as 1225, Chau Ju Kua mentions golden statues of the kings of Srivijaya; perhaps he meant gilded bronze images. These four statues are now in the museum at Batavia, where is standing, too, the inscription with snakes.

A few kilometres farther west, there seems to have been a shrine at the place where now is found the Muhammadan grave, Candi Angsoka. At any rate, several terracotta corner-stones of a Hindu character were brought to light. There is also a great block of natural stone, with a triangular cavity in the upper surface. Could this have been a Buddhist altar with the triangular symbol of fertility (trikona)?

In the vicinity lay fragments of elephants; one of them carries a lion in its jaws. A rampant lion, badly damaged, was also found, the right half of a gigantic monster's head and two smaller, beautiful kala heads, all of terracotta and influenced by Java. A kala head of natural stone was included.

The most ancient relic of Hindu–Buddhist influence in Sumatra, so ancient that it antedates the era of Srivijaya's greatest power by at least three centuries, is a huge granite image of Buddha. Since granite is not found in Palembang, it must have been brought from elsewhere, probably from the island of Bangka. One can imagine how difficult it must have been to transport this enormous statue over the sea. It was discovered in fragments and, when I had succeeded in making out the head, was reconstructed in the garden of the Palembang Museum of Antiquities. The first morning after the head had been placed on the body, the image was surrounded by white flowers and cakes brought by the Malay villagers. It was pleasant and rather moving to see how, after fourteen centuries of oblivion, the Buddha was suddenly restored to honour and, as it were, awakened to new life.

We had the head fastened to the torso with bronze pegs. For this purpose it was necessary to chip small holes in both parts, to be filled later with molten metal. It was a difficult task, since the granite naturally offered a good deal of resistance. Moreover, the coolie entrusted with this work was very superstitious. One morning he looked very downcast, and when I asked, 'Ali, what is the matter?', he replied: 'Oh, Tuan, this night I had such a terrible dream. I saw the image walking through the town with his head under his arm. Maybe it would be a good thing if we had a chicken slaughtered for him, don't you think so?' Well, of course I agreed, because I am very superstitious myself!

A kilometre to the south, at Bukit Seguntang and vicinity, lay the left half of a very large Malay inscription and a golden plate with the Buddhist articles of faith. At the same place were found several decorated natural stones and bricks chiselled with e-formed letters, probably guild signs. Very interesting are the fragments of a bodhisattva image, originally almost life-size. The features are full and gentle, the hair is dressed in tresses, confined in front by a band with rosettes; at the back may be seen a cord. From the left shoulder, a broad band extends across the chest. The lower part of the body is dressed in a smooth garment, fastened around the waist by means of a flat girdle, which is tied in front, a loop and the two ends hanging down together with a portion of the drapery.

Remarkable is a bronze Buddha head with a twisted bandeau with rosettes. To the south-east, on the northern bank of the river Kedukan Bukit, the well-known inscription of AD 683 was found. It announces that a king has set sail in order to attain magic power (*siddhayatra*). He left Menanga Tambang with an army of 20,000 men. He came here and founded the city of Srivijaya on a place, which formerly was called Malayu. The present inhabitants of Palembang still know that the rivulet Tatang, not far from here, formerly was called Malayu. A district, Tanah Malayu, lies up-stream on the Musi. Between this patch and Palembang is an island, Pulu Wijaya, reminding of the famous city of Srivijaya.

The excavations at Kedukan Bukit produced a god's head and a pedestal. Formerly, there was a second stone with inscription. Perhaps it contained the word '*siddhayatra*' and this spot was as sacred as Telaga Batu, where, in January 1935, I found a copy of the document of 683, consisting of 6 lines and chiselled on a rectangular stone.

Downstream, also on the north embankment, lay a great heavy pedestal, while the inhabitants also tell of a seated bodhisattva image, which has, alas, sunk into the mud.

About 5 km to the north-west, a 14-line sandstone inscription was found at Talang Tuwo. It announced that in 684 a park was made by order of a certain Jayanasa.

The trees planted here must be a blessing to all creation, thereby awakening the thought of the Buddhist faith and recalling the mystic body of the Diamond (Wajrasarira).

In former times, the Bukit Seguntang included at least four Hindu shrines—one at the summit, one at the west base, one at the base of the hill to the south-east, and one about 2 km farther north, where the great Buddha image was found.

Evidently, this hill country was sacred long before the coming of the Hindus, for Malay legends relate that a descendant of Alexander the Great (Iskander Zulkarnain) descended on the Bukit Seguntang. Two old widows, who had a field in these hills, one night saw the mountain enveloped in a fiery glow. On approaching, they saw a man seated on a white buffalo. He became the first king of Palembang and his name was Sri Turi Buwana. A few years later, he went across the sea and founded the city of Singapore, where he remained until his death. Perhaps we may infer from this that Srivijaya was transferred to Singapore.

The graves of Iskander Zulkarnain's descendants were still to be seen on the Bukit Seguntang a century ago. They were four heaps of stone, lying in a row, presumably from prehistoric times. Close by was the footprint of a certain Demang Lebar Daun.

On this same spot, a saint from Majapahit is also supposed to have lived. It was he who gave the celebrated hero Si Pahit Lidah supernatural powers by spitting into his mouth.

For centuries the natives of Palembang swore their most sacred oath on this mountain, and to this day, the graves on its summit are visited by pilgrims and strewn with flowers.

Downstream, on the right bank of the Musi, lies the Gunung Mahmiru (Mahameru), the sacred mountain which formerly overshadowed Palembang. But the ape Hanuman snatched off its top and hurled it at the wounded giant, Rawana. But he is not yet dead; his blood still flows and fattens the *sepat* fish of Singapore.

On the other side of the river lies the Batu Ampar, the ship turned into stone. It belonged to the trader, Dempu Awang, who became rich but disowned his mother, whereupon she changed him into the bird, *lang*. His ship was turned into stone. This legend is known throughout all Borneo and Sumatra.

Old chronicles give us interesting particulars concerning this kingdom. Thus they relate that on a small island is a large volcano, the summit and flanks of which are inaccessible because everything that comes into its vicinity is consumed by fire. In the daytime, it throws out great clouds of smoke and by night, a glowing fire. At its foot are cold and hot pools. Evidently, the famous volcano Krakatau is meant.

On a certain day, the ground opened in Sanfotsi (Srivijaya) and thousands of cattle appeared, which divided into herds and spread over the mountains. The inhabitants could take as many as they liked. Subsequently, the fissure was filled up with trees and bamboos. This story is still related in the Batak Lands. We heard it several times. Many places are also indicated where the cattle are supposed to have emerged from the ground. One such place lies between Ujung Batu and Ujung Jilok in Padang Lawas, to the left of the road. It is called Bulu Siparaongaong.

Whenever the king appeared outside the palace, he was carried on a golden couch, above which was a golden baldakin. Silken umbrellas protected him from the sun. He went sailing in a boat, which in the nineteenth century had a prow adorned with a serpent's head, while he was protected by guards armed with golden lances. His soldiers were unsurpassed in courage and contempt for death. When he mounted the throne, a golden image was made of him; and at his death and cremation, his followers leaped into the flames. In token of mourning, the people shaved their heads.

The king was only allowed to eat sago, because the consumption of rice would result in drought and poor harvests. He was also compelled to bathe in rose water, to prevent floods. Religious ablutions still occupy an important rôle among all the peoples of Sumatra, as they are thought to avert sickness, accidents, and evil influences.

A Chinese chronicle from the year 1225 relates, 'In order to protect the capital from attacks, there was formerly an iron chain stretched over the Musi. This chain could be raised or lowered by an ingenious device. Later, after many years of peace, when the chain was no longer necessary, it was deposited on the bank where for a long time it was an object of veneration among the natives.'

In the seventeenth century, a great cannon was also worshipped in Palembang. It was wrapped in red silk, strewn with flowers, and perfumed with incense. Here, also, we see the veneration of the magic power of metal.

Srivijaya also had a garden full of magic flowers, chiefly roses in many colours. No one was able to pick them, however, for then they would be consumed by a mystic fire.

Great trouble was caused by the numerous crocodiles. One day, an Indian came who declared that he could charm them. And, indeed, they did no harm to a man condemned to death, whom the king had ordered to be thrown into the river. Next day, the king announced that he would like to see the performance repeat-ed. When the Indian had put crocodiles under a spell, the king

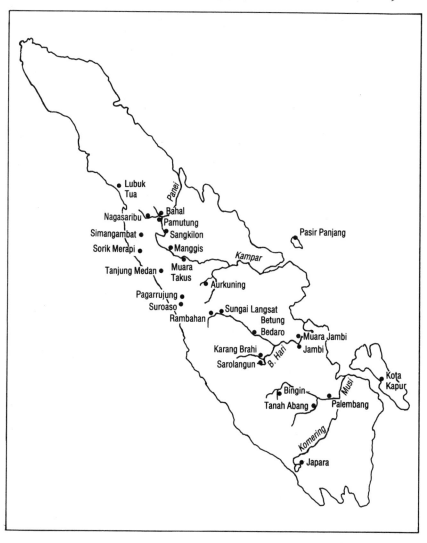

Hindu antiquities in Sumatra.

suddenly had him seized and beheaded. 'And since that time the crocodiles of Serira (Srivijaya) are entirely harmless,' concluded the tenth-century chronicle. Too bad that the writer did not prove the truth of his assertion by hurling himself among the crocodiles!

Throughout Sumatra, it is still believed that there can be a sort of friendship between human beings and crocodiles. Every man has a special crocodile which takes him on its back to distant places and protects him from possible dangers. During the annual rowing contests on the Queen's birthday, some Malays always beseech their guardian crocodile to give speed to their boats.

As the time of the Muhammadan fast approaches, the people are seized by a certain agitation. At sunset, many hasten to the Musi and gaze intently across the water. . . . And no wonder, for at any moment may appear the sacred crocodile with the scar on its head. And every child knows that this crocodile is really Raden Tokka, a noble from the court of Sultan Mansur (1704–22), who was commanded by his master to commit murder, but by a fatal accident struck the Sultan's own brother. He was then changed into a crocodile and lived henceforth in the churchyard of the Kebon Gede, west of the city. Once a year, however, just before *Puasa*, he swims down the Musi, as far as the Sekanak, ascends this river and pays humble tribute to the grave of Cinde Walang, the illustrious Sultan of Palembang.

Before concluding this chapter, we wish to call attention to a subject which certainly is deserving of further study, i.e. the woodcarving of Palembang. As early as 1349, Wang Ta Yuen mentions it with appreciation and also tells of the art of enamelled wood. Chau Ju Kua in 1225 and Ma Huan in 1413–15 also mention aloe and sandalwood.

Throughout the East Indies, it is quite common for woods to be more or less richly coloured, and also in Palembang.

The art of woodcarving has fallen into disuse, but if one makes a careful search, one may still find various doors, bridal chests, mirrors, boxes, oars, birdcages, weapon racks, seals, and plates with magnificent woodcarving, often gilded or covered with red enamel, painted with fine black lines. Lotus flowers and buds, conventionalized leaves, tendrils, spirals, and volutes occur in surprising variation, usually of a pronounced Chinese character. Ironwood (*tembesu*) is the favourite material.

Especially beautiful are the grave pillars still found here and there in old Malay cemeteries. They terminate in three points. The decoration consists of three pendants and a medallion, a motif which may only be used by the Sultan's descendants. Usually these graves are sheltered by a tiled roof, as may be seen over the grave of Njayu Betet, the favourite wife of a Sultan in Lemahbang. The little house has beautifully painted panels and under the ceiling is an arabesque of carved wood.

Now, however, all is decayed and destroyed by moisture. Here and there appears the vague design of pale gold flowers and leaves, but that is all. Now rich ferns surround the beautiful tomb, covering it with a soft, green pall.

Truly, the Muhammadan poet was right when he said, 'The world shall pass, the world shall not endure, the world is as a house made by the spider.'

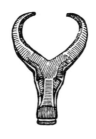

Batang Hari

THE English lieutenant, S. C. Crooke, who visited Jambi in September 1820, was the first to notice the antiquities of Muara Jambi, a few hours downstream. He writes,

Moeara Djambi is said to have been a capital town, and to have in its vicinity ruins of brick or stone buildings, containing images and other sculpture; but time was wanting to search for and examine these remains of antiquity; and nothing was discovered but a mutilated diminutive figure of an elephant, and a fullsized head in stone, having curly hair, in the style of a judge's wig, and a perfectly Caffre cast of features. This latter is sent with this report.

It is to be regretted that he does not say from which ruin he removed the Buddha head (for such it probably was) because the presence of a *nandi* (bull) tells us that Sivaism, also, was represented in Muara Jambi.

In March 1936, I made excavations and surveys there, which brought to light some new facts.

The sojourn in this little village with its primitive and kind inhabitants was very pleasant. In the beginning, I stayed at the house of the *pasirah*; it was, however, very noisy there, as in the dead of the night, people came who spoke and laughed aloud and sometimes even quarrelled. Moreover, it very often came to blows and, in the darkness, they threw at each other anything they could lay hands on.

Once, on such an occasion, a whole pan of rice landed in my bed, so that I thought that my last hour had come.

They were also in the habit of lighting big fires under the house at evening in order to keep the mosquitoes at a distance. Thick clouds of smoke surged through the floor-boards and made a further occupation of the large living-room unbearable. In no time we all had sooty faces; the soot also fell into the meal that had been prepared, but it seemed to annoy nobody. On the contrary, the *pasirah* then only felt quite comfortable and began to play a joyful little air on the mouth-organ that I had brought for him from Europe.

After a few days, I therefore decided to move to the school, which stood in the middle of the forest. In the evening many natives would call, desirous of making a careful study of the white *doktor batu* (stone doctor) who had come from the mysterious West—and to hear what he had to tell him. The stories from Europe were a source of never-ending surprise and delight. The visitors flung themselves with passion upon the illustrated magazines and asked a thousand questions bearing on the illustrations they contained. It was often difficult to answer them. How, for instance, could one make clear what an underground train was? 'A roaring fire-horse which spits flames out of its nose,' I said. 'Sometimes he dives into a large hole in earth and a hundred miles farther he comes out of another hole.' 'Something like the grotto near the waterfall?' someone would ask. 'That's right,' was the answer.

And what was snow? 'Hens' feathers, which fall from the heavens. Up there is a large hen, which sometimes shakes herself.' 'Why?' interrupted a boy. I confessed my ignorance. 'Perhaps because she is hungry,' murmured a compassionate girl. 'Or fleas,' supposed a more realistic old man. 'When it grows warm, all those feathers melt away.' Nobody could understand what made hens' feathers melt away like that. But the story of the fire-horse spread abroad with great rapidity and brought the whole countryside into commotion. From distant villages, people came flocking hither in order to hear it again and again. The simple school in the forest changed into a sort of Mecca, and the fame or archaeology spread far and wide.

Sometimes it was difficult to get rid of the people at 10 o'clock. But when this had been accomplished, all grew quiet; only the chirping of countless crickets filled the night. The Batang Hari rustled and through the roof shone the silver stars. In the school, there were coloured pictures of animals, bearing their respective names in large letters. When the wind blew outside, these pictures began to rustle, and by the uncertain light of the oil-lamp, took on ghostly forms; the animals seemed to come to life and their eyes began to glitter, they sprang about roaring inaudibly at each other.

When the lamp went out, it usually remained peaceful for a moment; and then suddenly a slight cracking was audible, a rustling noise of approaching steps and a soft squeak; the mice were on their rounds and, sniffing carefully, inspected the hammock. Who could that be lying there, they thought.

At night, at about half-past three, it usually began to rain,

incessantly for hours and hours. In the morning, a white mist
hung over the Batang Hari, which was then wider and deeper
than ever. Prolonged floods inundate everything here and the
houses and the fields are deeply submerged in the water. Large
branches of trees, pieces of wood, and sods of grass drift along the
river in an endless cavalcade; sometimes whole trees are carried
down to the sea serenely, stately, almost gently. The only creatures
that delight in all this are the ducks; quacking and screeching to
each other, they paddle around in the pools, happily beating with
their black wings or snapping at the smaller creatures with the red
beaks.

At about half-past ten it begins to clear up; a delicate blue forces
its way through in the dark sky, and children hasten outdoors to
see whether the fish-traps are already filled. A naked little girl
with a large yellow flower in her hair descends from the shore to
fill a kettle with water. A proa, manned by two women, sets out
to fish up as many pieces of wood as possible.

The current in the Batang Hari is extraordinarily strong. I felt it
when I went bathing in the afternoon. It required an extraordinary
exertion to swim 10 metres up and I even doubt whether a very
strong man would be able to do so easily. As the shore is very
muddy, a raft with a little house on it has been built and so by a
wooden staircase the water is reached; the small hut serves as
lavatory, whereas the raft as washing place. The first evidence of a
village on the Batang Hari is a row of such tiny white huts.

On the first afternoon that I went swimming, the whole village
came flocking out to watch this wonder. To a cry of loud and
prolonged cheers, I dived into the river, tumbled about, and
imitated the various coolies. 'His skin is as white as the belly of a
crocodile,' a woman cried admiringly. Children flung themselves
into the water cheering loudly and asking to be pursued in play. I
roared and snorted like a real crocodile and from underwater I
shot forth at the rascals, who, yelling loudly, dispersed quickly.
These performances gradually became a complete water ballet, for
everybody wanted to join in the fun and be 'devoured'.

The ruin near the school is a royal mausoleum, according to the
inhabitants, and therefore sacred. Excavations are not allowed.
The wall has a three-plane frame, casements, and an ogive; the
steps are undecorated. Although it has something of a Hindu
character, it is not impossible that we are concerned here with a
Muhammadan building.

Farther west, the temple of Gumpung was partially excavated. The entrance lies on the south side; the cella floor and the steps are badly damaged. A broad path extends about the building, becoming unusually narrow by the steps where there is a peculiar extension. The façade has double-bordered panels. The cella is 5.10 m square and is thus almost twice as large as that of Si Pamutung, Sumatra's largest shrine.

South of the steps lies a terrace, which is totally in ruins. The surrounding wall seems to consist of a double wall with a filling of earth or gravel. In the eastern wall, there was once a gate. The entire courtyard is paved with brick, truly an impressive piece of work.

Forty-three metres west of the south-west corner begins the north wall of Candi Tinggi's enclosure. The unusual arrangement of the walls is recorded in the ground plan. On the west side lie a temple and a terrace; in the east wall, a gate. The contour of these three buildings could be only vaguely discerned. The court, which measures 150 m from east to west and 155 m from north to south, is thus the largest in Sumatra and four times as large as that of Muara Takus. Farther west, there are three other temples. Probably they were built in the eleventh or twelfth century. If we may believe that the images found in Jambi are from here, some temples must be much older.

Among these images are a life-size standing Buddha, with garment around both shoulders, from the sixth century, two little standing Buddhas, a Buddha torso with garment fold around the left arm, the back of an entirely destroyed image on a lotus cushion, with plants springing from root bulbs, two elephants with diadem, four *makara* with standing demons in their mouths (one of them bears the date 1064), a *makara* with a *kinnara* in his jaws, a bull, a column in stupa-form, and a few fragments of lesser importance.

Batang Hari

West of the temple of Tinggi flows a rivulet called Sungai Malayu, reminding one of the famous Malayu, which was visited by the Chinese monk, I-tsing, in 671. Now it is not certain whether Malayu lay here or in Palembang. It is possible that it formerly lay in Palembang and in 683 was brought to Muara Jambi. We can even suppose that the ruins of Muara Jambi belonged to the well-known city of Srivijaya, and that here was the centre of the state, which conquered Palembang in 683, Bangka in 686, etc. Maybe Balaputra, who in the ninth century founded an abbey in Nalanda on the Ganges, was a king of Jambi. In 853, 871, 1079, 1082, 1088, and 1281, Tchan pei (Jambi) sent envoys to China. In 1024, it was conquered by the South Indian king, Rajendracoladewa. In 1292, Marco Polo mentioned it. From 1270 to 1293 the city must have presented a lively view through the presence of hundreds of Javanese soldiers. They formed the basis for the great expedition to the interior (Tanah Datar), where a second town of Malayu existed or was in the process of being built. This western town seems to have been destined to play a leading rôle; the eastern town probably has always had significance as a trading place.

Concerning the temples of Gumpung and Tinggi, the inhabitants tell the following legend.

Formerly, this place was called Bukit Singoan or Turunan. Here lived King Talanei, who commanded one of his slaves to plough the field. The work went so slowly that the king became furious and threatened to kill the slave if the field was not ready on the following day.

At night there came a mighty stranger, who spat in the slave's mouth. Thereupon he suddenly became so strong that he could tear whole trees from the ground, and next morning the field was finished.

The king now asked for the hand of a beautiful princess. She declared that she would be his wife if he would build a palace for her in one night.

The slave was put to work and made rapid progress. Towards the end of the night, when the palace was not quite completed, the princess secretly gave her servants the order to begin pounding rice.

When the king heard this, he thought day-break had come, and, in despair, he destroyed the half-finished palace.

It is very remarkable that in many of the legends of Jambi,

mention is made of wars with Siam, and that in various places in East Jambi, Siamese bronze images have been found.

The best-known legend relates that Muara Jambi was at one time a magnificent city, where ruled a prince named Sutan Talanei. When a son was born to him, there were storms and earthquakes. Alarmed by these manifestations, he summoned his star-gazers and asked the meaning of these evil omens. They declared that the prince would one day bring disaster to his father.

Sutan Talanei then put the child into a chest, with a letter, and threw him into the sea. The wind drove the chest to the coast of Siam and the king of that country adopted the baby as his own child.

When the prince became a youth, he asked the king why the princes always avoided him, and the answer was that his own father was the king of Jambi.

The prince then took a great army to Jambi, conquered his father, and killed him in a duel. All the people of Jambi were taken prisoner and brought over to Siam. Their own country became a wilderness.

To the north, in the Tungkal district, there are stories of a mighty ruler, Raja Gaga, who had a beautiful daughter. A Siamese prince came to ask for her hand but was refused. He then returned with a mighty army, built forts in several places, but was killed at Merlung, where his grave is still found.

East of the Sungai Assam, a small river which flows into the Batang Hari near Jambi, there lies a holy grave, deep in the jungle. The people call it Kramat Talang Jawa, because a certain Pangeran Tumenggung Puspa Ali, from Solo (Java), lies buried there.

This Pangeran had announced that he wished to be buried in this place. When the funeral was about to begin, there came a ship loaded with stones from Java and anchored at the mouth of the Sungai Assam.

Now a chain of 4,000 people was formed, extending from the harbour to the grave, and every stone was passed from hand to hand. A square was made, 20 × 20 m. The stones were not cemented, but were simply piled one on top of the other, making a wall more than three feet high.

Back of the grave is that of the Pangeran's wife and at the side are buried the cat and the dog, with which he used to play.

The Pangeran also had a son, and when he had reached the age when he had to be circumcised, this ceremony was attempted three times, but in vain.

When the boy saw that the operation was a failure, he told his father and the people that now he could not be a good Muhammadan and therefore it was better for him to go away. His father had no objection and so the son went away, no one knew where.

He went into the forest and was called Raden Alas. Tired at last with his wanderings and feeling ill and forsaken, he dug himself a grave and laid himself in it, until death made an end to his suffering.

This grave must be somewhere deep in the jungle.

The province of Jambi had no ruler of its own in the olden times, but was submitted to the Prince of Mataram to whom it had to pay tribute every 2½ years. The principal settlement was then at Tanjung Jabung.

One day, a man came from Turkey, called Paduka Berhala, who had four sons. The youngest, Orang Kaya Item, a brave and audacious man, made a plan with his brothers to keep back the next tribute with the purpose of freeing the country from Mataram. When the time came in which the tribute should be paid, the Prince of Mataram waited in vain. The generals and counsellors sent by him to Jambi were killed at the command of O. K. Item. At this, the three other brothers were much perturbed, but O. K. Item said to them: 'This country always belonged to our forefathers, princes of Pagarruyung, and so it also belongs to us, their descendants.'

Twice after this, the tribute was also held back and the ruler of Mataram, not wanting to investigate the matter any more, sent some brave warriors to kill O. K. Item. These people, too, were killed by O. K. Item. The Prince of Mataram realized that it was no use fighting against such a brave man, and ordered an astrologer from Pemalang to come to him, in order to learn from him how to kill O. K. Item. The astrologer informed him to have a weapon wrought of iron obtained from nine different places and derived from nine different objects whose names should begin with 'Pa'. The iron, however, should be got by theft. So some sly thieves went out, and were so lucky to hand to the monarch the desired iron. The astrologer commanded to send for some smiths from Pamaja Pahit, who should make the iron into a sword. These people were set to work by the Prince of Mataram in a deep pit, so that the people in Jambi nor anywhere else should know what was going on. Besides, it had been stipulated that the smiths were only allowed to do a stroke with the hammer every Friday.

When the sword was nearly ready, O. K. Item came to hear of the intentions of the ruler of Mataram, whereupon he decided to go to Mataram himself to take with him the tribute that had still to be paid. Before leaving, he ordered his brothers to break up Ujung Jabung and build a new fortress. Hereupon he embarked. Although this expedition was kept a secret by all the people who had joined, it was after all made known by Jambi traders sailing to Java. The ruler of this territory then declared that he should give his daughter in marriage to O. K. Item, but he really intended a stratagem. The Prince thereupon gathered his generals and officials to meet O. K. Item ceremoniously on his arrival, while at the same time he sent out people to find out if O. K. Item were coming or not. These men really saw the vessel, in which the tribute used to be transported, near the coast and they informed the Prince.

O. K. Item's boat met near the shore of Mataram a little fishing boat with one man inside. O. K. Item suddenly had an inspiration. He made an arrangement with the skipper of his vessel that he should order him to buy fish, but of a small kind. Thereupon he, O. K. Item, would buy big fish. And the skipper should pretend to be very angry and pretend to beat him to death. Further, the skipper should ask for the fisherman's help to bury O. K. Item's body on land. 'I want to investigate', said O. K. Item, 'whether the Prince of Mataram will really give me his daughter in marriage. To find out the truth about the making of the sword, I want to visit the place where it is made. As for you, before landing in Mataram, you must wait for news from me.' No sooner said than done. In bartering about the fish, a squabble arose between O. K. Item and his skipper, with the consequence that he beat him until he became unconscious and looked like a dead person. The fisherman grew alarmed, but with money and kindliness, the skipper persuaded him to bury O. K. Item's body on land. Before pushing off, however, the fisherman made the remark that the vessel altogether resembled the one in which the Jambi tribute used to be transported and that the skipper might get into trouble for slaying one of his people. The sailors then replied that it was indeed the boat and that the skipper really was O. K. Item, who had killed many people. The fisherman did not wonder anymore that O. K. Item should be the man who had held back the tribute, and he rowed off. Thinking on his way that

he might be accused of O. K. Item's death, he threw the dead
body overboard and went on. O. K. Item dived, swam ashore and
went inland, disguised as a beggar. From some children he learnt
the road to Meraja Pahit and heard from them that that name had
been changed to 'Pamaja Pahit', because the Prince of Mataram
had ordered a kris to be made there of iron from nine different
places whose names begin with 'Pa' and made of objects also
beginning with 'Pa'. O. K. Item then went on, looking for the
spot where the kris was being wrought.

The fisherman, who had landed, made it known meanwhile
that O. K. Item's boat had been near the coast, but had returned.
The Prince of Mataram hurried on the finishing of the kris, for he
did not trust O. K. Item's supernatural qualities.

If he was far away, he seemed near, and vice versa. The smiths
in the pit then worked on uninterruptedly and had almost
finished the kris when O. K. Item approached the pit. The smiths
called out to him: 'Hallo, beggar, what news from O. K. Item?'
O. K. Item told them that he could not even whisper it to them,
upon which he descended into the pit. He saw the kris, questioned
them about it, and they replied to his questions. They even gave
the weapon into his hands. O. K. Item wanted to examine then, if
the kris really had the properties ascribed to it, and stuck it
through the anvil which was split in two. Then he lifted the kris,
and shouting, 'I am O. K. Item!' he attacked the smiths, killed
them all, killing also the other people in the pit, 40 men all told.
He then stormed with the kris out of the pit and ran amuck in
Pamaja Pahit. The inhabitants fled to Mataram and informed the
Prince of what had happened. The latter cried, 'Now O. K. Item's
supernatural power has been proved; no one saw his vessel land.
And already he has run amuck with the sword in nine villages.' In
his frenzy, the Prince raised his army. Then the news came that
O. K. Item had already entered Mataram, which made the Prince
more anxious. One of his counsellors then approached him and
suggested to make an arrangement to prevent a big slaughter. The
Prince thought the man was right and went into the palace to
consult his wife. Thereupon his daughter, Putri Ratu, approached
him, saying, 'Oh, Father, allow me to marry O. K. Item, lest our
country should be ruined. He is a brave man, and if he behaves,
appoint him as chief in Jambi.' The Prince consented, and went to
meet O. K. Item with Putri Ratu and a whole retinue, preceded
by three priests and four counsellors. Putri Ratu was in bridal
attire. When they met O. K. Item, he said that he had wanted

to wait on the Prince, because he had heard that the Prince would make him his son-in-law. He was sorry to have run amuck and to have murdered so many people. The Prince addressed him and offered him his daughter as wife. The marriage was conducted there and then by the three priests. As wedding gift, the Princess declared that she wanted to receive the Jambi settlements. O. K. Item obeyed, upon which the whole crowd re-entered the prince's palace.

O. K. Item, being ashamed of his get-up, stuck, as a sudden inspiration, the kris in his hair as a kind of ornament, shouting three times in a loud voice: 'Let it be known to every Javanese that from this moment, the kris shall be called "Si Gunjai"!' So this is the origin of the name Si Gunjai, for 'gunjai' is the head ornament called for which O. K. Item used the kris.

Some days after this event, O. K. Item looked at the kris and made a plan to embellish it. He ordered a smith to come and told him to make five bends in the weapon and to forge in the upper end a dragon's head. Then he returned to Jambi with a whole fleet. During the passage, he occupied himself with the finishing touches of the kris, while all the workmen he had taken along bestowed themselves on making the lower part, in the work of which every one had a special share, as beautiful as possible. It was not long before the kris was quite finished. Not long after, the ships weighed anchor at Ujung Jabung.

A large feast was given lasting forty days and nights, and of which men and women, old and young, partook. When O. K. Item and Putri Ratu, dressed in full splendour, had taken their seats on the throne before the crowd, Putri Ratu commanded that the imperial ornaments, Si Gunjai and Si Nancan, should be brought forth, upon which Hulubalang Prabu Wirolang explained to the crowd in a loud voice the meaning of the imperial ornaments, announcing at the same time that O. K. Item and his wife had taken the place of the Prince of Mataram. 'The imperial ornament Si Gunjai', he continued, 'shall be respected by the whole Jambi nation: they shall pay tribute to it regularly and he who owns it, is our ruler.' Thereupon he took Si Gunjai out of the silver dish of tampui juice in which it was lying, paid homage to it and handed it to O. K. Item, whereupon the whole crowd paid homage to it. Some drank the tampui juice in which it had been lying, in consequence of which they tumbled against one another drunk, which convinced them of the sanctity of the ornament. Putri Ratu then announced to the people in a melodious voice the meaning of the other imperial ornaments they had brought along and when, after it, the Jambi chiefs had taken the oath of allegiance to the imperial ornaments, the ceremony was over.

It is told of the people who had become drunk after the tampui juice that they gave one another all sorts of titles e.g. 'Si Gunjai Mabok', which means 'the drunken Si Gunjai'. In this way, the story of the imperial ornament was made known among the people.

The princes of Jambi succeeded each other in the course of the years and the kris Si Gunjai and the lance Si Nancan have ever since remained the symbols of the imperial power in Jambi.

After O. K. Item's death, his brothers succeeded him. When they died, royalty passed on to O. K. Item's children, who bore the title of Susuhunan Pulau Johor. This remained thus for seven generations, until the grandson of the last Susuhunan Pulau Johor became ruler and bore the title of Panembahan. Five princes held this title. After the Panembahan of Muara Pijoan, the royal dignity passed into the hands of the grandson of the Panembahan of Bawah Sawah. He and his six successors had the title of Sultan. The last was Sultan Taha, named Saipudin, but in the Malay language and according to the adat: Sultan Agung Seri Ing Ngalaga.

One day when this Sultan was on a journey to Mangunjaja, he was shipwrecked near Muara Tembesi, at a place called Teluk Air Dingin. On this occasion, the kris Si Gunjai sank to the bottom. Thereupon all the Jambi subjects on the nine tributaries of the Batang Hari were gathered together at Teluk Air Dingin and were requested to dive after the kris. No one, however, got it because it had fallen between the coils of the Bidai Snake.

One day, however, someone came down the river in a proa and was stopped by the Sultan, as, since the moment that Si Gunjai had fallen in the river, no one was allowed to pass the spot, whether up- or downstream, without having dived for the kris. His name and descent were asked and the man replied, 'My name is Pah Sulung from Serampas and I am on my way to Kota Kandis to sacrifice at Orang Kaya's tomb to fulfil a vow.' He succeeded in getting back the kris.

A different reading of the legend says: When these provinces still paid tribute to Mataram, the country was called 'Kebonlado' and Jambi 'Grambi'.

At the time, there lived a certain Paduka Berhalo, a man gifted with supernatural strength; he lived at Pulu Berhalo, on the mouth of the Batang Hari.

Paduka Berhalo was ambitious and jealous of Mataram's power; therefore, he made up his mind to take possession of the above-mentioned tribute. He waited for the embassy which was to take along the tribute, murdered them all, and stole the tribute. The ruler of Mataram marched up against him, but was defeated.

He managed to return secretly to his country. Here he meditated revenge: he called for the help of the great and wise ones in the country, in order to obtain a weapon with which he should infallibly slay his enemy.

A kris was then made which, through supernatural influence, acquired extraordinary properties; a tree would fade immediately after it had been touched by the weapon for just one second; an animal in the neighbourhood of the place where the kris was hidden, would die immediately, too. Death and destruction were the least things it could cause. The reputation of that cruel weapon spread on the wings of the wind; from far and near, people flocked to behold it and everyone might see it without touching it, for only the touch would be deadly.

Paduka Berhalo also went on a pilgrimage to the Mataram kris: he went disguised as a beggar, so that one had no inkling of his person and his intentions when he approached the sacred object. Making use of his supernatural power, which was greater than that of the weapon, he got hold of it and threw himself amidst the dense crowd. In a moment, hundreds were killed; the prince himself managed to get away in time and escaped the atrocious slaughter.

Paduka Berhalo took the weapon with him and returned to Jambi, where he was soon proclaimed ruler.

At Sungai Langsat, on the northern bank of the Batang Hari, district Tanah Datar, residency Westcoast of Sumatra, a gigantic image was discovered. A terrifying figure, it represents the Malay ruler Adityawarman, with a knife and a skull in his hands, serpents twined about his ankles, wrists, upper arms, and in his ears, standing on a recumbent human body, which in turn rests on a pedestal of eight huge grinning skulls. The image, which was made in the middle of the fourteenth century, represents Aditya-warman at the height of his power. The king had spent his youth at the Javanese court of Majapahit, where he came into contact with the Bhairawas or Terrible Ones, a mystic sect of demonic

Buddhism, with Sivaitic elements, which had originated about the sixth century in the eastern part of Bengal. From thence it spread over India, penetrated Tibet, and advanced towards China, Mongolia and Japan, where it still exists in a degenerated form. It also penetrated Outer India and the Indonesian Archipelago, at first entering Sumatra, where it reached its culmination in the eleventh century, and spreading thence to Java. In the time of Adityawarman, its converts included the rulers at the Javanese court, a fact which in turn stimulated the final revival of demonic Buddhism in Sumatra. The Bhairawas sought their highest bliss in mystic union with their supreme god. In order to attain this, they sacrificed human beings, and, standing on the victim's bodies, allowed themselves to be initiated as gods. In this ceremony, the drinking of blood played an important role, since blood was believed to be a heavenly wine, which inspired them to ecstatic dances. Another part of the ritual was the rattling of human bones. The graveyards where these ceremonies took place at night were called by names such as 'the ever flaming', 'the eternally sombre', 'the filled by the sound of vultures'. Here Mahakala, lord of cemeteries, with his red, flaming hair, appeared to the faithful, in the midst of pillars of smoke, destroying all earthly ties. In 1370, Adityawarman was initiated as a god by the name of Kshetrayna, enthroned alone on a heap of corpses, laughing diabolically and drinking blood, while his great human sacrifice was consumed in flames, spreading an unbearable stench, which, however, affected the initiated as the perfume of ten million flowers, according to the inscription.

A few hundred yards north-west of the image lies a brick temple, which I excavated in October 1935. It turned out to be a structure twenty-odd yards square, with steps to the four quarters of the wind. An inscription found at the same place announces that Adityawarman had the building repaired in 1347, so apparently it had fallen into disuse. On this occasion, a dramatic performance was given, in which the king himself appeared as a dancer. He compares himself with Buddha, who descends from heaven to cheer humanity. He dances in a fragrant forest, resounding with the sweet song of birds and the lovely chant of heavenly nymphs, amid fountains where elephants disport themselves. Ordinarily, of course, the Bhairawa dances were not so peaceful.

Some time ago, the Netherlands Government decided to bring this image into the inhabited world. The silence of the jungle on the Batang Hari was broken by the sound of many voices. Ages ago, the colossal image had been erected for eternity; now three hundred coolies toiled to lower it with thick cables from the high bank. In the river below, a sturdy raft lay ready to receive the massive stone.

One's thoughts went back through the centuries to the time when an army of engineers and workmen pushed the sacred image to the river's brink. They must have been filled with a terrible fear at the thought that the statue might break and the angry god descend in a flaming cloud to destroy them all. It took many days before the colossus was rowed upstream from Sungai Langsat to Sungai Dareh. There it was loaded on a motor lorry and transported to Sijunjung. During the transportation, a terrible storm arose and a great tree fell directly in front of the lorry, almost crushing the image in its fall. It was as if the spirit of the departed king were protesting.

In Sijunjung, it was set up against a background of bougainvillea and the rosy colour seemed to penetrate the hard stone. Every evening at sunset, the image assumed a mysterious, soft glowing hue, as though it yearned to absorb the light. Some months later, it was decided to bring it to Fort de Kock, where there is a fine museum with a zoological garden. The strongest motor lorry was selected. First, the three-ton pedestal with the skulls was transported; then the four-ton statue itself. In the zoological garden, it was set on a hill facing Merapi, Sumatra's sacred volcano, mentioned in ancient legends. On its flaming summit once descended Iskander Zulkarnain, the first king of the Malays. Image and mountain now regard each other; there is a mystic communion between the two. . . .

The glory of Sungai Langsat has long departed; the great image has been removed, and the temple is fallen into ruins. Over the desolate jungle on the Batang Hari descends the warm Sumatran night with its multitude of stars in a clear sky.

Kampar

THE vast, silent night broods over us and from afar comes the sound of elephants. For a week we have been camping here in the jungle of Muara Takus, situated on the Kampar, a river which curves about the equator like the coils of a mighty serpent. It is lonely here; the full moon casts a strange, sinister light over the ruins.

'*Tuan*,' says my servant, softly, 'I am afraid.'

'Afraid?' I ask, astonished.

'Yes, when the full moon shines, the elephants cross the river and go to the holy temples. Then they gather in a circle around the high tower and fall on their knees as a tribute to the spirit of their dead king, who lies buried there. . . .'

Silent, majestic night; the crickets sing and their voices mingle with the murmuring of the river.

'And why shouldn't elephants drop on their knees to their dead leader?' I think. You hear such strange tales here in the East. But come, we are not here to dream but to excavate, and that is hard work. Tomorrow will be another busy day, for the gate which I have just discovered in the north wall encircling the temple buildings must be cleared and measured. And so I spread my sleeping mat on the ground and lie down. . . .

I drowse for a while. What a beautiful little log house we have, so near to the bank of the Kampar. A former governor had it built as a lodge for his hunting parties. Last year, the elephants played with it and turned it into a ruin! But the new house is stronger, and besides . . . the river sings me gently to sleep. . . .

It is well past midnight when I awaken with a start. Around me stand a group of natives. Midon, my best worker, bends over me. The fold of his white turban sweeps over my face. In his hand, he holds a large, old-fashioned musket.

'May the *tuan* pardon me. At first we did not want to awaken you, but now. . . .'

A muffled roar interrupts him, a sound such as I have never heard, which has the power to make the stoutest heart tremble, the voice of the jungle. . . .

'In the village, we heard the trumpeting and roaring of the elephants, they were descending from the misty mountain of

Suligi. They crossed the river, heading straight for the *tuan*'s house. Then we were afraid and remembered that the *tuan* was alone. . . .'

'Go on. Go on,' I interrupt, impatiently. 'Where are they now?'

'They are slowly coming nearer. In a quarter of an hour, they may be here. . . . We cannot escape.'

With an effort, I concentrate my thoughts and try to calculate the chances for escape. . . . If we were in the temple court, on top of the highest ruin, we would be safe. But how to get there? The distance from the house is about 100 m. If one ran hard. . . . No, impossible. In imagination, I already see the elephants running out from the underbrush!

But there is still another possibility. Near the lodge, the Kampar has a steep, abruptly descending bank. No elephant would dare to climb over the edge. If we can only reach this bank, we are safe. So said, so done. Stealthily as cats, we descend and wait.

A quarter of an hour later, the ground begins to tremble and a tremendous racket fills the air. The rumbling of an elephant's stomach may be heard for miles, but never have we heard it so near at hand. It is loud as a klaxon and is caused by the crackling of masses of young leaves and branches which the huge beasts strip from the trees with the greatest enjoyment. Meanwhile, they seem to talk and laugh in their hoarse voices, varied by shrill whistles and a trumpet-like blare.

Dear little elephant that I once met in the zoo at Fort de Kock, how often I have fed you with peanuts and lumps of sugar. You told me you had relatives in the jungle of Muara Takus, cousins and aunts and an old niece by marriage.

Well, they certainly made a terrific noise that night. All the time they remained playing and walking about the temple grounds and not until morning did they retire into the underbrush.

That morning I shall remember as long as I live. At sunrise, tired and shivering, I climbed up the high river bank and took a look over the forest. I did not meditate long, however, but took my tapes and notebooks and went over to the temple grounds. Come, I would measure the gate.

While I stood writing, there came a muffled sound, not far from where I stood. It was as if something heavy had fallen on the ground. For a moment I had a vague suspicion, but quietly continued my work. Soon the sound came again—it was as if someone were gathering firewood . . . and it must have been a tremendous worker, for suddenly the noise increased.

Instinctively, I dropped everything I held in my hands, hurried over to Candi Tua, the largest ruin, flew up the steps and crouched behind the central tower. For a moment nothing happened; for a moment, deadly silence. Then, with a thunderous roar, a tree crashed down precisely on the spot where I had just been standing; the whole gate was covered by its branches. At the same time, another crash resounded, branches were broken, the underbrush was torn aside. Two huge elephants rushed into the temple court, fighting and screaming, striking each other with their mighty trunks; and then, as suddenly as they had appeared, they disappeared again into the woods on the other side.

My heart beat in my throat, for out of the forest now came a third elephant. He remained standing in the sunlight, spread out his great ears. Slowly, his trunk swung back and forth, seemed to search for something, and then remained still.

Apparently the animal scented danger; in the distance sounded the voices of workmen approaching. The elephant listened, then walked silently across the temple court. By the great tower he stopped, scratched himself against the wall, looked about for a moment, and then wandered pensively into the forest. . . .

At Muara Takus, on the right bank of the Kampar Kanan, lie a number of ruins from the eleventh and twelfth centuries. They formed part of a town, which was entirely surrounded by an earthen wall. The space enclosed measures about 1.25 km. The buildings are encircled by a sandstone wall, measuring 74 × 74 m. In April 1935, I excavated the brick foundation of a great gate, approximately in the middle of the north wall. Since the surrounding wall is built over this foundation on opposite sides, the latter must be of an earlier date.

Directly opposite the gate, on the south side of the courtyard, stands the best preserved building: the slender, graceful Maligai Stupa. The foundation has the form of a rectangle and measures 9.44 × 10.60 m. Inside, 52 cm behind the outer wall, is an older foundation decorated with pilasters. On the north side ascends a flight of steps, which have been twice rebuilt in the course of time. It is probable that at one time, they supported a parapet with two kneeling elephants. Perhaps the gallery also had a low retaining wall.

On the foundation stands a 28-sided pediment, decorated with blocks of yellow sandstone. From this pedestal ascends a round tower. As may be seen from the drawing, the body of the stupa

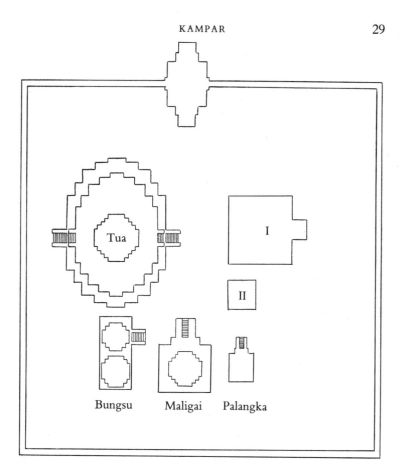

The antiquities in Muara Takus. 74 × 74 m.

rests on a double lotus cushion. Within this flower is an older
lotus. The crown of the stupa seems to have been 36-sided; on
four sides were placed sitting lions of sandstone. The 36-angled
section is followed by a regular octagon above which extends a
frieze with 16 lion heads. The dome consisted of a sandstone
lotus, which no doubt formerly supported a stupa. In the centre of
the tower was once a hole, about 2 m deep, in which rested a
wooden mast, bearing several sunshades, one above the other.
East of the Maligai Stupa lies a rectangular terrace, 5.10 × 5.70 m,
with an extension and a flight of steps on the north side. On the
outer wall are pilasters.

   West of this stupa lies a similar terrace, called Candi Bungsu. It
formerly supported a 20-sided foundation, with a stupa in a

wreath of smaller stupas. It recalls the upper terrace of the Borobudur.

At the later period, this brick terrace was enlarged on the north side by a sandstone stupa. On the east side ascends a flight of steps. On a high, 20-sided base rests a low 36-sided base which bears a lotus. In this lotus was found a hollow, filled with earth and ashes. Among the ashes lay three bits of gold-leaf and a golden plate, engraved with *vajra* and three letters. At the height of the 20-sided base lay a stone with nine letters and in the middle of each side a *vajra*.

Immediately north of Candi Bungsu stands Candi Tua, the largest (though not the highest) building of Muara Takus. The greatest length is 31.65 m, the greatest breadth 20.20 m. The ground storey shows signs of reconstruction; the processional path has a very irregular breadth. The second terrace is lower, but like the first is decorated with limestone pilasters. On the east and on the west sides ascend flights of steps with lions. The stupa proper rests on a 36-sided base. In the lotus, only an empty hollow was found.

East of Candi Tua, I excavated a sandstone foundation measuring 13.20 × 16.60 m, while south of these ruins, a foundation 5.75 × 5.75 m came to light.

The temples of Muara Takus are probably the graves of royal personages. Malays say that the Hindu ruler was transformed into an elephant, and for this reason great herds of elephants regularly visit the ruins to do homage to the spirit of their departed ancestor. Close to the temples is a shallow ford, which the animals cross whenever they descend from Mount Suligi to the plains. It is remarkable that since time immemorial the stupa court has been their favourite playground, where they walk about and disport themselves all night long by the light of the moon.

During the excavations of April 1935, we were able to verify this strange phenomenon from personal experience. When one considers the antiquity of animal trails in the jungle and the elephant's extreme conservatism, it seems likely that even centuries ago, the animals betook themselves to Muara Takus, and for this reason the place had an odour of sanctity. The Malays must have considered it a so-called elephants' dancing ground, such as are still known in India. This may also be the reason why the Hindus built their temples on this particular spot. As long as the city lay here, the elephants naturally stayed away; but after its destruction, the jungle reclaimed her rights and the Lords of the Wood retrod their ancient paths.

In the year 1003, the king Se li chu la wu ni fu ma tiau (Sri Sudamaniwarmadewa) sent two envoys to China to bring tribute; they told that in their country, a Buddhist temple had been erected in order to pray for the long life of the emperor, and that they wanted a name and bells for it, by which the emperor would show that he appreciated their good intentions. An edict was issued by which the temple got the name of Cheng tien wan shou (Candi Bungsu) and bells were cast to be given to them.

The oldest inhabitants of Muara Takus descend from the Princess Putri Seri Dunia, who came with her family from Pariangan Padang Panjang (Minangkabau). Her beauty became so famous that a Hindu ruler asked her hand in marriage. The princess accepted his proposal on condition that he should build a palace for her. This the *raja* did, and the remains of this palace may still be seen at Muara Takus. Then the *raja* returned to his own country to make preparations for the wedding.

In the meantime, a great Batak army marched on the city. A relative of the princess, named Sutan Palembang, wrote a letter to the Hindu ruler, giving the messenger a basket (*gantang*) of seed. As numerous as the seeds in the basket, so numerous were the Bataks. The Hindu ruler, however, did not return.

When the Bataks arrived at Muara Takus, they found the entire city deserted. Putri Seri Dunia, with her followers, had fled into the forest and married a *datu* from Minangkabau. She bore a son, whom she called Indo Dunia, and to this day, there is a place in Muara Takus called Galangan Indo Dunia. This youth later became lord of Muara Takus and was succeeded by Raja Pamuncak (Datu di Balai), known in history during the period when the country was converted to Islam.

Another legend is as follows. One of the last rulers of Muara Takus (or Takui) was named Raja Bicau. The city was then so large that a cat could wander from roof to roof for three months before reaching the last house. The king had only daughters. When the eldest was about to marry the Maharaja of Johor, all manner of people came to attend the feast and the cockfights.

Among the guests were the brothers Singa Menjadian and Singa Mendedean, who had just settled in Gunung Malelo (upstream) and who had come originally from Rau. Others, however, assert that they came from Palembang. One of them asked for the hand

Maligai Stupa.

of one of the king's daughters, but was refused because he had a hideous skin disease.

He now sent his sister's child (*kamanakan*) with a basket of grain and his own head kerchief to his brother, Singa Merdekeh, Raja of Kuamang (Panti), and asked him to send as many soldiers as there were grains in the basket. The Bataks now came with a huge army and attacked Muara Takus. In this battle, the last *raja*, Panjang Jungur, lost his life.

At Batu Besurat, the Bataks threw a calligraphed stone into the river and said, 'When this stone appears again above the water we, too, shall return.'

At Pamatang Gadang, however, they met with resistance. Here, great trees were piled up and hurled down upon them. Many corpses were crowded into the stream and their terrible stench gave it the name 'Sungai Sibusuk'. From here, the bodies came into the Kampar and floated past the place which henceforth was called Bangkai-inang or Bangkinang (Batak for 'corpse'). The name 'inang', meaning 'mother', was used for Batak, because when frightened or surprised, they always exclaim, 'Inang!'

It is told that in ancient times, there was an underground stream connecting the Kampar Kanan with the Kampar Kiri. The legend tells of a certain Indo Chatib from the *suku* Bondang, who once went fishing in the neighbourhood of Koto Air Tiris. He pursued a fish which had hidden in a hollow in the river-bank. But Indo Chatib kept a firm grasp on the line by which the fish was caught and so could easily follow the fugitive. At last, he arrived at the Kampar Kiri.

A more credible tale relates that formerly there was a stalactite cave near the village, Batu Balah. The water which trickled down formed a stream, which flowed underground to Gunung Sahilan.

Muara Takus was formerly called Si Jangkang (a plant) or Telago Undang. The name is said to be derived from Takut, the name of a tributary of the Kampar, so called because at this place the people began to fear the lords of Muara Takus (*takut* = fear).

This kingdom once ruled over all the surrounding country, and the recollection of this fact has not yet faded. To this day, the ruler of Rokan must make a pilgrimage to Muara Takus before his coronation to have his head annointed with lemon juice. And on the Queen's birthday, when all the *panghulu* in Bangkinang come to pay their respects to the Controleur, the *panghulu* of Muara Takus leads the procession, under a golden umbrella.

East of the temple buildings is the stream Ampamo, so called because the water is red as gold. Farther east lies the Bukit Katangka.

It is glorious to bathe here in the Kampar. The water streams over broad slate banks. One simply sits down and allows the cool water to roll over one's body. The high bank consists of red–brown and silver–grey cliffs, soft as cake, on which grow numerous graceful ferns. Squirrels, with amusing, upturned woolly tails, frisk about in the underbrush, looking with mischievous eyes at the intruder.

At sunset, the natives stand praying on the little promontory, the women entirely shrouded in white and purple veils. Countless prayers have been uttered on these banks in the course of the centuries. The evening wind is full of whispers, the dark river full of shadows. Gently they glide to the vast ocean. Night falls over the Kampar. In the endless jungle stands a lonely stupa. . . .

By full moon, a great natural phenomenon takes place in the Kampar. A mighty tidal wave rolls in 60 to 70 km from the sea, destroying everything that lies in its path. A boiling, roaring wall of water six feet high is seen approaching, which crashes against the bank with a noise like thunder, dragging whole trees into its seething whirlpool. How this *bono* originates is not known. It also occurs in the Rokan, but is not so high nor so dangerous as in the Kampar.

Formerly, there lived at the mouth of the Kampar, a tribe called Singo Bono. Near Tanjung Semayang is a holy place, where many people come to pray. When the *bono* approaches, there appears on the river a mysterious boat, rowed by invisible hands. The appearance of this spirit ship brings good fortune to the entire country.

In ancient times, there lived a great chief at Kampar, who had a lovely daughter. Her bosom was, however, half female, half male. Many men asked for her hand but in vain. The girl's only friend was a dog. One day, she became a mother and bore seven pups. Her father was overcome with shame and threw the animals into the river.

But every time there is a *bono*, the dogs can be seen returning, to seek their mother. They leap and growl and destroy everything in their way. But, always, they become exhausted and return again to the sea.

It is also related that the *bono* is caused by seven wild horses, which come up the river in a herd. Once a chief shot at them, and the *bono* stayed away four times. But the man became terribly ill and could never walk again. We mortals must be careful. . . .

At Koto Tuo, near Muara Takus, a number of golden relics have been preserved, of which the following legend is told. Datu Jalo Mangkuto once dreamed that he would obtain gold if he gave the *emas* the blood of a white buffalo. Then he made a black buffalo white with rice flour and slaughtered it, upon which the *induk emas* emerged from the river in the form of a tortoise. The *datu* bound him to the pillar of his house. But when the tortoise heard that he had been deceived with a whitened buffalo, he tore himself loose. A slave took away his shield. Then the animal went to the slave's mother to beg for his lost shield. She restored it to him and now he gave the gold to the mother who bought the freedom of her son from Datu Jalo Mangkuto.

In bygone days, there was a man from Jambi, who sailed up the Rokan, and in the land of Rokan he ended his journey and remained for several months. His name was Pendek Alang Berkokok. He liked only easy work; if there was a beautiful woman in the village, he made a conquest of her and every day he made a new quarrel. The Raja of Rokan wanted to drive him away or kill him and looked for someone in his own land bold enough to accomplish this deed.

Now, in Tanjung (Kampar), there was a brave man named Datuk Rangsang Kampar (D. nan Gadang Cincin), and Datuk Peduko Sangsamo was sent to bring him.

They met in the mountains between the *negeri* Pendalian and Sibiruang; there, the dogs barked at each other.

Sangsamo said that he was on his way to find Cincin. The latter, not wishing to betray himself, said that in seven days, he would bring Cincin to Rokan.

Then Sangsamo said, 'Where our dogs barked just now is the boundary between Kampar and the *luak* Rokan,' and to this day, the mountain range is called Bukit Kalaran Anjing.

Cincin returned to Tanjung, called his son, Si Juang Pahlawan, and six days later, went with him to Rokan. There he promised to help the ruler, after which he and his son found Berkokok and killed him.

Now, Cincin wanted as a reward something to which there would be no end. This wish caused great consternation in Rokan.

The Raja sent out messengers. One of them came to Pendalian and there he found a child which he brought to Rokan. The child said, 'Let this be the reward, that Rokan and Tanjung be united.' And so it was.

Elephants

THE oldest Hindu evidence concerning the elephant in Sumatra is a four-armed image of the elephant-headed god Ganesa, 56 cm high, which I excavated at Simangambat, South Tapanuli. One of the hands is broken off, but in the other three, he holds a hatchet, a tusk, and a skull; in the hairdress are the new moon and the death's head, symbols of life and death. This discovery proves that the temple of Simangambat was sacred to the Siva faith, thus comprising the oldest Siva document in Sumatra (eighth or ninth century).

Ganesa is the son of Siva, leader of the heavenly host. He is usually fat-bellied and well disposed toward mankind. He removes obstacles and in this capacity is the god of thieves. He also averts illness and is the patron saint of doctors. It is said that at his birth, his father, in a fury, struck off his head, but repenting later, swore to give him the head of the first being he chanced to encounter that morning. This happened to be an elephant, and so Ganesa was endowed with his present misshapen form.

However, this did not prevent him from becoming one of the most popular gods of the Hindu faith. Women, especially, honoured him and numerous images of him are therefore found in Java. In Sumatra, on the contrary, he is found only four times in stone and once in bronze. This is probably to be explained by the superior position there of Buddhism, which tolerated no gods of the Siva faith.

Yet the Buddhists, too, included the elephant among their deities, as is proved by the magnificent relief of a dancing pachyderm, which was excavated at Pulo, in Central Tapanuli. It reminds one of the prelude to *The Ocean of Stories*, the famous old Indian book of tales in which is told how Ganesa created the world, 'dancing in the twilight, while with his trunk he scatters golden stars over the firmament . . .'.

Strangely enough, this dancing of the elephants has lingered in the popular fancy and has served to inspire many beautiful and touching legends, such as that which is told in Jambi. In the full of the moon, they congregate in an open space in the wood, arrange themselves in a circle, stand on their hind legs, and greet the moon with their trunks.

Involuntarily, one is reminded of the story in Kipling's *Jungle Book*, in which is told how the slave boy, Toomai, is carried deep into the forest on the back of an elephant, to attend a gathering of the herd. He hears the clashing of great tusks, the sinister scrubbing of enormous flanks and shoulders, the restless swishing of their tails. . . .

'Then an elephant trumpeted and for ten terrible seconds all repeated the call. The dew from the trees spattered down like rain on the unseen backs, and a dull, roaring sound began. Not very loud at first and little Toomai could not tell what it was; but it swelled and swelled and Kala Nag lifted one forefoot, then the other, set them down on the ground . . . one . . . two . . . , one . . . two, like sledge hammers.'

As we see, the resemblance to the Sumatran legend is not complete, but anyone who has encountered elephants in the jungle feels that the description is true to life.

Another common belief is that the elephant causes lightning. In various parts of Sumatra, there are conflicting opinions as to how this is done. In the Batak Lands, it is declared that he simply hurls the lightning from his trunk. In Palembang, on the contrary, it is supposed to be caused by the sharpening of his teeth. In the Kampar, another story is told: as soon as a storm approaches, the elephants begin to tremble in every limb, their hair stands on end, the lightning flashes then proceed from these hairs.

Still more remarkable are the stories of their death. As soon as they feel the end approaching, they go to a lonely mountain; on it stands a tall tree, the death tree. Under this, they lie down to breathe their last breath. This mountain must be a terrible sight; here lie bleached skulls with hollow eye sockets and gaping jaws, enormous bones and long tusks. If anyone could collect these tusks, he would be rich.

But the road to the elephants' mountain is unknown. One day, a man walked through a great forest. Suddenly, he stumbled over a great tusk. When he pushed aside the underbrush, he saw still more tusks, and at once it dawned upon him that he had happened to find the elephants' cemetery. Joyfully, he lifted two tusks over his shoulder and figured out how much money they would bring him. It was strange, however, that he could not find his way back and continued to return again and again to the place from which he had started. Evening fell and he began to be very much frightened. At length he understood that he must lay down the tusks. He did so, and soon after, found his way back home.

Of equal interest is the discovery of a small, bronze elephant in the south of Tapanuli. In his trunk he holds a lotus bud; on his back sit two women. Apparently, the latter are portraits of the dead. According to superstition, after the soul leaves the body, it descends to the underworld on the back of an elephant. The oldest and most beautiful evidence of this is the wonderfully modelled stone elephant at Pageralam, in South Sumatra. On opposite sides of the animal kneel two men, each with a great pointed helmet on his head, a sword at his side, and a drum on his back. This portrayal of two warriors on their way to the kingdom of the dead is one of the most beautiful and original of all the sculptures in Sumatra.

Beginning with the ninth century, old accounts of travel mention that the elephant was used in battle. Especially the kings of Palembang and later those of Aceh had a formidable corps of fighting elephants. We do not know whether the animal is indigenous to Borneo, nor do we know whether it came originally from Sumatra. In the Padang Highlands, there is a legend that the elephants came originally from Melaka and that at one time there was a bridge between Melaka and Sumatra.

Many more stories might be told about elephants, but the usual hunting yarns may be omitted. Any man who has lived in the East Indies has a stock of them. Very few, however, have been able to observe this interesting animal in its own surroundings.

The author has only once seen an elephant which had been shot. It was in Central Jambi, downstream from Muara Tebo. It had been shot four days previously, and even from a great distance, one caught the putrid smell of the cadaver. It lay in a forest clearing; in the animal's horrible death struggle, everything within a distance of six feet had been destroyed. Now it lay on the right side, one forefoot drawn up, the belly yellowish-white, the head black with clotted blood. The setting sun cast a weird light on the lifeless body, not a sound disturbed the jungle's silence; over the fallen giant reigned the majesty of death.

A herd of elephants covers an extensive field, in which they continually wander about. The pasture of each herd consists of low marshes and high mountain regions. As soon as heavy showers cause the river-banks to overflow, the lowlands are flooded and the herd slowly retreats to the hill district.

The size of a herd depends on the extent of its habitat, so that the largest herds remain in the delta of great rivers, while the smaller ones live in the districts irrigated by small rivers, such as Bengkulu and North-west Sumatra.

The number of animals in a herd varies from 15 to 100.

The extent of the region occupied is at least 200 km and at the most from 1 000 to 1 200 km, while the boundaries are clearly defined. If the rainy season is long, the animals remain longer in the hill district, as a result, no wonder then, elephants are observed where they appear only once in four or seven years.

The number of elephants in Sumatra is, of course, difficult to estimate. In the south alone (Lampongs and south half of Bengkulu), there are at least 2,000. Formerly the natives had many firearms, but not at the present time. For this reason, elephants are now in less danger of being exterminated, and in the rainy season they regularly visit the rice fields and pepper gardens, where they feed to their hearts' content.

In the woods, they graze only on young twigs and leaves of various trees, especially those with soft fibre, such as *waru*, *dadap*, etc., the bark of which is torn off in strips. Even branches with the thickness of an arm are gnawed, after which they are usually thrown away. The tops of various young palms, such as *nibung*, *serdang*, and *pandan*, are also regarded as a delicacy. In addition, they eat young rattan creepers of all kinds, from very thin ones to those having the thickness of a cable, the crown of which is attached to the trees and dragged down by their trunks. In this way, heavy branches are sometimes torn off, falling to the ground with a heavy thud. Now and then, a dead tree trunk crashes to the ground. In extensive marshes, the elephants graze for days at a time on young reed shoots and grasses. In the hill country, slender bamboos, growing on the banks of small rivers, are dragged to the ground and stripped of their top and side branches. The wads of chewed fibre are discarded.

The herd remains all day in the same place, looking for food and moving only about 3 km at the most. Their trail is a network of tracks, crossing and recrossing continually and covering a breadth of 1 or 2 km. As the vanguard with the female leader always consists of females with their young, only a short distance is covered. The other elephants roam about in groups of three or four.

In following an old trail, it is always important to follow the trail of the young, as otherwise the chance of catching up with the herd is extremely small. Moreover, the vanguard, which includes the young, always follows the easiest track.

In districts far from the inhabited world, parts of the herd keep in touch with each other by means of signals (short trumpetings). Usually they collect directly after nightfall and over a front kilometres wide signals are heard, which cease after the animals have concentrated at one point. Here they rest for several hours. Toward midnight, a few trumpet squeals are uttered and the herd again sets into motion. During the night they remain close together. The track is only a few metres wide and runs without interruption over hills, rivers, and marshes. The distance covered during the night depends on the character of the ground and the number of young animals. A herd with many young covers only from 5 to 10 km.

From daybreak until 9 or 10 o'clock, the herds take a rest then spread out and continue their march. When they have been for a long time in a limited field, they begin to make a great deal of noise at night and continually they are heard romping and playing, snorting and squealing.

One asks how it is possible for them to notice in time the steep edges of ravines and other obstacles in the dark woods. For instance, if there has been a landslide, the trail of the herd makes a detour at a distance of 10 metres from the point of danger. In another place, the track is 1 m away from the edge of a deep ravine. During a night march, when they come to a deep river which they cannot cross, they change their direction, follow the edge of the forest for 1 km or more and then descend at exactly the most favourable point. The strange thing in this procedure is that they do not even approach the edge of the bank or slope, but turn aside at a distance of 15 m, follow the edge of the embankment at this same distance and then with a sharp curve come out at precisely the right place. In their most dangerous treks along steep banks and vast ravines, they leave a narrow trail, walking apparently in single file. The 'solitaire', who has only himself to look after, seems to take fewer precautions, climbing and descending much steeper slopes than the rest of the herd which moves in company. Evidently, the leader takes the less experienced animals into consideration.

When elephants are grazing in the daytime, one sees continually wild pigs and deer behind the herd and even in their midst. In the marshes, the company consists mainly of *bangos* (marabouts), occasionally herons; and more to the edge of the swamps, wild pigs and deer. The last two are observed only in the morning and afternoon. All these animals graze on the rattan fruits torn down by the elephants, while the wild chickens scratch at the heaps of manure.

In the vast reed marshes, which are entirely submerged during the rainy season, there are quantities of fish here and there, protected from the herons by high reeds. During the grazing of the elephants, the way is cleared for these birds, and they find a mass of trampled fish.

In the hill country, but never in marshes, one often sees tiger tracks behind the trail of the herd. Apparently the tigers follow this trail at night, hunting for deer or wild pigs.

Creeping up on the herd is very difficult for human beings, because sharp-eyed deer and especially birds and monkeys at once notice their approach. When a cry of warning is heard in the dense jungle, the nearest elephants stop grazing at once, standing dead still for several minutes, with their ears outspread. If the cries are repeated, the elephants quickly disperse and join another section of the herd farther on. When a part of the herd scents danger, they always give a short, shrill trumpet call, then join the advance guard, all the animals assembling directly and remaining remarkably still.

The behaviour of various herds after scenting danger varies greatly, depending on the leader's courage and strategy and the size of the young. A herd with very small calves will retreat slowly, and if the enemy continues to pursue, they will take a defensive stand.

After a long time, if the leader notices nothing unusual, she will turn back on the trail in order to investigate. She avoids making any noise, and after every 10 or 20 steps, she stands perfectly still for several seconds, continually sniffing the air. Sometimes she reconnoitres along several of the trails followed by the herd. If she finds nothing, she turns back and soon they continue to graze and to play as before, but more quietly and with greater caution. Again and again, the trunks are raised and all unnecessary noise is avoided.

When the leader detects danger, however, she announces her displeasure by growling and pawing the ground continually with one of the forefeet. Slowly, she returns to the herd, growling all the while. As soon as she has passed all the animals, she gives a short trumpet call, whereupon the whole herd gallops away, with a crash as of thunder. This headlong flight continues only for a few hundred metres, terminating always in dense cover (reeds, rattan, dense jungle or *bambu duri*), where they remain very quietly until nightfall, after which they increase the distance between themselves and their pursuers by a forced march. Further pursuit is most dangerous for the hunter. The leader is then in the rearguard, facing the enemy and at least 50 m away from the others. She makes almost no noise and stands listening, eating slowly, watching, dead still for minutes at a time.

To Central Sumatra in 1684

MORE than two and a half centuries ago, a Portuguese named Thomas Dias made a journey through Central Sumatra at the instigation of the Governor of Melaka. Accompanied only by a few Malays, he took the road to Minangkabau, straight through high and impenetrable mountains, and after enormous exertions succeeded in reaching his destination. He had the good fortune to win the king's favour and to establish trading relations with him. After a sojourn of two weeks, he returned by an easterly route.

History has not done justice to Thomas Dias. His name is not recorded in histories or encyclopaedias. He died poor and forgotten. Yet he was the greatest explorer of Sumatra, and that is why we wish to devote a few pages to him, as a small, tardy wreath on his lonely grave.

In ancient times, the trade of Central Sumatra was centred more on the east than on the west coast of the island, and the first contact of Europeans with Minangkabau was by means of the great rivers which flow into the Strait of Melaka.

In 1514, a Portuguese expedition sailed up the Siak River in order to meet the illustrious ruler of the kingdom. A few natives were sent in advance into the interior, reached the sultan and returned with a few articles of trade, including gold. Soon there developed a flourishing gold trade between Minangkabau and Melaka. Possibly the Kampar was followed for some distance, then overland to the Siak and along this river to the sea.

The inhabitants along the Siak River were Minangkabaus, while the lower tributaries were under the dominion of the Sultan of Johor. According to ancient chronicles, a brother of the Sultan ruled Siak in 1602. Apparently, trade languished under the rule of Johor, for when Joan van Riebeeck ceased to be governor of Melaka (1665), he declared that 'very little of interest' came from Siak. 'Only a few natives of Melaka sometimes remained for a long time in the interior of Siak in order to buy bezoar stones from a wild and savage people living there.' The East India Company itself had not yet come into contact with Siak.

The situation changed when tin mines were discovered in 1674, when the natives transported great quantities of ore to Melaka and the rulers tried to establish relations with the Company. The

Orang Kaya Bandahara of the village of Petapahan, deep in the interior on the Tapong Kiri, even sent his son to Melaka for this purpose. The governor of the town at once proposed that the Government should take action and even asked for reinforcements of vessels and crews so that he might seize the mines. But the Government had already had so much unpleasantness in exploiting their own mines elsewhere in Sumatra they thought it wiser to buy the mineral from the natives. However, instructions were sent to Melaka to make a more careful survey of the mines, as the sample of tin which had been sent was remarkably fine.

The tin mines were surveyed in 1675 or 1676. In the fall of 1676, however, the Government wrote that expectations regarding the mines had been disappointing. They therefore contented themselves with buying the ore skipped to Melaka and made a contract with the rulers who had appeared there, whereby it was agreed that the Company should have the monopoly of all the tin delivered. The following year, a little more progress was made by ordering Lieutenant Hendrick Themmer to sail up the Siak River and to buy the ore at the mines. Moreover, experienced workers were sent out from Melaka and the river closed to private individ-

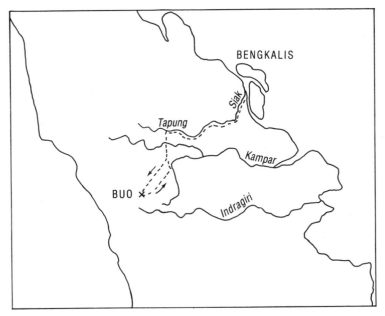

Journey of Thomas Dias.

uals, indications that the Company had decided to supervise the business. Further dealings with Siak, however, were broken off in 1677, when a revolt broke out among the Minangkabaus of Naning and Rembau, adjacent to Melaka. But early in 1680, peace was restored, and the people of Melaka began to think of re-establishing relations with Siak, all the more desirable because trade with Indragiri had been broken off, the Company station there having been attacked and plundered in 1679.

On 17 May 1683, Governor Cornelis Van Qualbergh sent a ship up the Siak River to deal with the Minangkabaus at its source. On this occasion, they succeeded in obtaining a store of gold and tin at Petapahan. Here Thomas Dias seems to have been left behind as a representative of the Company.

During the same year, a second expedition was made under the leadership of the Secretary of Melaka, Hendrik Van Roonhuijzen. He became suspicious of Dias, but the latter succeeded in defending his good name at Melaka, so that he was sent again to Siak with the order to force his way to the King of the Minangkabaus. As the Company's ambassador, his mission was to beg the king's help in various trade problems.

This was the first time that an European had met the ruler face to face. Yet the Company had been in touch with him earlier, for in 1665 two native dignitaries had been sent out from the West Coast with presents for the court, while the Resident of Padang, Jan van Groenewegen, had offered the Government to go there himself in order to encourage the gold trade. This plan was frustrated by the Resident's death. The sending of the first envoy, however, had made the sultan rejoice, because his importance was thus acknowledged in regions where his prestige had long been destroyed by the Acehnese. He therefore appointed the Resident as his viceroy and promised to direct the gold trade to Padang. Relations were thus friendly, but the journey into the interior remained a dangerous undertaking.

In June 1684, Thomas Dias sent a message to Minangkabau concerning the mission with which he had been entrusted. The sultan sent in return a favourable reply by a company of nine envoys. Hastily he collected the necessary coolies to carry his baggage and in only two days took his departure. A Minangkabau noble with his followers joined the expedition. The entire company consisted of 37 people. In order to avoid the suspicion of several interfering *raja*, they took a different road from the usual one.

At first they went south, through level ground, so that on the first day, they covered about 20 km and spent the night at Air Tiris on the Kampar Kanan. The inhabitants of this village showed the greatest astonishment when they heard that Dias intended to go to Minangkabau. The news was disagreeable to them, apparently because they feared that the expedition would result in the annexation of their territory. Dias therefore reassured them, declaring that he intended to go only two days farther and then to return.

The second day, only 15 km were covered, on account of the hilly country, and in the evening they arrived at Si Blimbing, situated on a tributary of the Kampar Kiri. Here, too, the inhabitants showed great surprise and uneasiness. Subsequently only a short distance was covered, and in the evening they reached Kota Padang. Here, however, the inhabitants were so suspicious that they would not even allow the travellers to sleep in their houses. Dias and his men were compelled to spend the night under a tree, while watch was kept by a few natives armed with muskets. In the morning they continued their journey, arriving at Paku in the evening. Their progress was unusually slow, we do not know why. Paku lies only a few kilometres from Kota Padang and we may assume with certainty that the inhabitants of Paku had already been warned concerning Dias. His reception was therefore not too cordial.

For this reason, the hardy Protuguese decided to march away before daybreak and to cross the great mountains which divide East Sumatra from Minangkabau. It was a bold undertaking which frightened even the brave Minangkabaus among his followers. They preferred the ordinary trade route along the rivers. In vivid colours, they depicted the wildness and solitude of the mountains, the numerous wild animals, lurking rubbers, etc. But in vain.

And so began an expedition which will be forever illustrious on account of the leader's magnificent courage and perseverance. A journey which, even now, 250 years later, is accompanied by some danger and is attempted only by a few Europeans. In imagination, we see Dias silently marching at the head of the troop, compelled to carry enough rice for three weeks, and therefore heavily loaded, so that progress was extremely difficult. Probably several pack-horses were included, to carry clothing, bedding, cooking utensils, presents, etc.

It was in the dry monsoon and the sun shone with all its power on the travellers. The heat of Sumatra was like a drawn sword which struck them speechless. In the merciless glare, all the colours of the jungle were faded.

Towards evening, they usually pitched camp in some forest clearing. Firewood was collected and soon the flames of many fires were seen flickering against the dark sky. The natives cooked their supper, ate some *ubi* (sweet potatoes) and talked for a while. But the day had been exhausting; conversation soon ceased and each went quietly to sleep on his mat. The fire burned lower and lower and then was extinguished. The night was filled with the chirping of crickets and above the vast mountains the stars appeared, aloof and sparkling. At such times, Dias must have felt unspeakably lonely.

But nothing of this appears in the sober, business-like letter which he wrote concerning the journey and which by some miracle has been preserved for posterity. Only those who know by their own experience the beauty and terror of the jungle can sense how much is omitted in this letter and how great must have been the power and the self-confidence of this remarkable Portuguese. If he had died in this green hell, his name would never have been known. All trace of him would have been lost in the wilderness, just as thousands of trails have vanished in the tropical jungle—traces of men and animals, as completely forgotten as if they had never existed.

After seven days, they reached a settlement of three or four houses. Here they rested for a whole day. Apparently, the march had tired them extremely. Several of the natives must have wounded their feet. Probably on this day, the horses were washed and the harness repaired.

Next day, they left early in order to avoid the great heat. In ten days they arrived at Minangkabau and rested at Ngungung, four miles from Buo, where the sultan lived. A delegation of nine men was sent to the palace to tell the ruler of Dias' arrival and to beg for an audience.

At once, the king sent a certain Raja Malio at the head of 500 men carrying yellow banners, to say that he was very pleased at the coming of Dias and asking him to proceed immediately to Buo. Raja Malio delivered this message, after having commanded the chiefs of Ngungung to give the travellers every assistance.

Early next morning, Raja Malio returned to escort Dias to Buo. Dias, however, asked to be excused, for suddenly he felt an overpowering weariness and all his limbs were stiff and painful—the reaction of his terrible exertions in the mountains.

The following morning, however, the audience took place. The king's two sons came at the head of 4,000 men to escort Dias. The sun glittered on numerous golden umbrellas and on gold and silver salvers, which were carried in the procession. One of the princes received the letter of the Governor of Melaka from a golden platter; while nobles carried the presents on silver trays. With a salvo of muskets, the prince mounted the palace steps. Dias remained waiting at the foot of the stairs.

The king had the letter read to him, then invited Dias to come into the palace. He handed his guest a great silver salver with betel, expressed his admiration for the journey which had been made, and then asked the object of the visit. Dias replied with Oriental courtesy that the Governor of Melaka had the greatest interest in His Majesty's welfare. The king was evidently rejoiced over this message and in turn expressed his friendly sentiments for the governor. He had a house prepared for Dias and gave orders that he should be supplied with anything he might need.

After two or three days, Dias again asked to speak to the king, addressing himself to several of the nobles. To his great surprise, they declared that this was impossible and that he must regard it as an unusual favour to have spoken to the king even once. Apparently, they were suspicious and wanted to keep the Portuguese away from the king.

There was no time to be lost. Suddenly Dias remembered that the mother of Raja Malio was lady-in-waiting to the queen. At once he requested her to take his message to the queen. She sent him betel and arak on a silver salver, covered with a golden cloth, and told him that in three days, he would be summoned by the king.

The promise was kept, for in three days, Raja Malio came with 12 followers with banners, to escort him to the palace. The first gate was guarded by 100 men armed with muskets; at the second gate stood four men, and at the third, only two. Within sat the king, surrounded by his *haji*. When he heard how the ambassador had been treated by the nobles, he was very angry. He praised the courage of Dias and said he would record the remarkable expedition in his journal, as he was the first Christian who had ever appeared in Minangkabau. Then he dismissed the nobles, with the exception of Raja Malio, his secretary, and the three *haji*, after which he descended from the throne, sat down on a bench near Dias, and asked what he wanted. As a special favour, he granted him the title of 'orang kaya sudagar raja di dalem astana'.

Next afternoon at 3 o'clock, Dias visited him again and was presented with a yellow banner, a musket inlaid with silver, a hallebard, and a brass ring. The king also gave him a sealed document, permitting him to trade in Siak, Petapahan, and Indragiri. He was also given authority to dispense justice in these harbours, to make slaves, and even to condemn people to death. And finally, the king gave him a beautiful horse, as a gift for the governor. The horse was named Gunung Layang, the Flying Mountain.

A day later, Dias took leave. The king gave him a letter for the governor and commanded him to leave the imprint of his seal ring on a plank of the house, so that later he might verify the seals of letters from Melaka. At the same time, he gave Dias a small box, full of pornographic pictures, with the words, 'This was sent to me by the admiral, with the request not to see you. Take it with you and let the governor see, so that he may know what disgraceful presents the admiral sends me!' With this diverting episode, the visit was concluded.

Dias then relates how a strange *haji* tried to turn the king against him, how his men recognized in him a drunken sailor whose bad conduct had resulted in his having to flee from Melaka to Riau. When the king heard this, he had the wretch beaten to death by 200 men.

Dias now left Buo, accompanied to Siluka by Raja Malio, who walked under a white umbrella with tassels, and 3,000 men, firing their guns continually.

In the river at Siluka, he saw gold being washed in wooden trays. Then he returned via Menganti, Sumpur and Ungan to the Mandiangin Mountains, with their gold mines. From here the journey continued to Air Tanang, Pangkalan Sarai, Tarusan, Kotabaru, Mariring, Merubiang, Tanjung Balei, Pasar Lama, Ujung Bukit, Domo, Padang Sawah, Kuntu, Lagumo, Lipat Kain, Paku, Kalubi, Kota Padang, Siblimbing, and Air Tiris to Petapahan.

So ended the boldest expedition ever made by a European in Sumatra. The amazing journey of Holloway and Miller to Padang Lawas in 1772 and that of Raffles in 1818 to Minangkabau fade into insignificance compared with that of Thomas Dias. In 1891, Yzerman made his famous expedition to Central Sumatra and in 1904, Commander Van Daalen made his magnificent trip through the Gayo and Alas Lands. Both these men, however, had a white man's equipment—generous supplies, excellent weapons, etc. But none of them had the sense of adventure, the brilliant courage, the diplomatic tact, and the amazing adaptability of the little Portuguese, who roamed, alone and fearless, for three months in a region where no white man had ever set foot.

Putting Fish under a Spell

SHAMANISM in Sumatra is found among the Bataks, the Sakais (in Siak), the Kubus, and the people of Pasemah. It also is practised by Malays on the east coast of Siak, on the Brouwer Strait or Selat Panjang, and on the island of Bengkalis. Here is the base for the *trubuk* fishery. By the light of the moon, great shoals of *trubuk* swim into the Brouwer Strait. Their presence is betrayed by tiny ripples on the water and by an occasional fish which leaps playfully out of the water. Sometimes they come in such numbers that an oar placed in the water stands upright—at least, so the Malays say.

Fishing is the principal means of subsistence in these regions. Now and then, however, it happens that the fish remain away for a long time and the people are threatened with famine. They therefore organize a great feast, for which a woman is temporarily chosen as queen, with the title Jinjang Raja. Four old village chiefs (*batin*) of Bengkalis act as her ministers and their wives act as ladies-in-waiting. The Jinjang Raja then invokes the 16 spirits of various capes and inlets of the Brouwer Strait, allows them to possess her, and to speak through her mouth. In this way, the people hear what sacrifices they must make in order to placate the spirits and coax the fish. A feast of this kind costs hundreds of guilders and is accompanied by a number of ceremonies.

When it has been decided to give a feast and the necessary money has been collected, two pavillions are built, one at Bukit Batu, on the shore, and one at the mouth of the little river of Bengkalis. These are decorated with leafy branches and yellow streamers. Then the Jinjang Raja is brought from her house and escorted to Bukit Batu in solemn procession with the four *batin* and their wives.

She is led into the pavillion and sits down on a chair decorated with the figure of a horse's head. She is draped in a silken garment and in her hand she holds a yellow kerchief with golden fringes. Outside the building, there is singing and dancing, gongs and other musical instruments are heard, while the four *batin* step forward to perform a dance with the Jinjang Raja.

Then a great brass salver is produced, on which lie incense, oil, and rice. A small stove filled with glowing coals is also provided and incense is thrown on the fire. The rice is strewn over the

Jinjang Raja, while she anoints her body with oil. Her eyes begin to glisten and to stare fixedly at one point. In a faltering voice, she tells what must be done in order to celebrate a proper feast and the *batin* carry out her instructions. Usually they specify the number of buffaloes, goats, and chickens which must be slaughtered, the making of cakes and the observance of certain formalities. The chief of Bukit Batu, who bears the title of admiral (*laksamana*), is compelled to pay strict attention to these orders. During the ceremony he has as little to say, as has the Sultan of Siak, except that both are allowed to sit next to the Jinjang and to ask her an occasional question.

It may be weeks and even months, however, before the Jinjang announces when they must go to the Bengkalis River to invoke the god Jangi. Sometimes she becomes restless, thrashes about wildly with her arms, and sometimes she falls into a deep sleep. Then another woman (*bidu*) makes her appearance, takes off the Jinjang's garments, and exchanges them for others. If this has no effect, she tries to restore consciousness with a peculiar, gentle song. If this has the desired result, the *bidu* supplies the Jinjang with food. In the meantime, the people wait in the greatest excitement, for as long as the ceremony lasts, no one is allowed to do any fishing.

But one fine day, the spirit announces that the people may depart, and at once there is the greatest excitement. The Jinjang is brought to the mouth of the river in a beautifully decorated boat, followed by hundreds of fishing boats. Such a procession is like a fairy tale. The Brouwer Strait, usually so quiet and lonely, is now a scene of intense activity. The Jinjang sits on a wooden horse, under a pole wound with leafy branches. The men surrounding her beat the air with knives and axes to drive away the spirits. One of them continually makes jokes, most of them very dirty. Chickens and grain are thrown into the sea, also an occasional coin.

When the procession reaches the festal pavillion, the second part of the ceremony begins. The Jinjang is brought in on her chair. Again she is strewn with rice grains, amid clouds of incense. The woman now has an attack of hysteria, screams, sings, and rolls on the ground. The *batin*, having drunk enormous quantities of palm wine, are now quite tipsy and act as if possessed by demons. Barking like dogs, they roll over the ground, walk on hands and feet, make obscene gestures, and throw filth at the bystanders.

The 'ladies of honour' now take the Jinjang by the hand and

lead her to a swing hung with golden bells. She sits down and now, one by one, the 16 spirits are invoked who rule the fish. Gently swinging, the Jinjang speaks to them and as no one understands the language of the spirits, the *bidu* translates their replies. They tell why the fish stay away and how they may remedy this evil. At this moment, a mighty cry of joy bursts over the water, a cry from thousands of throats. The natives pelt each other with rice cakes and perform sham battles.

In the evening, the Jinjang returns in a state boat. Decked with flowers, surrounded by dense clouds of incense and dozens of lights, she sails through the starry night like a goddess.

Then the plaintive song is sung of the prince from Melaka (the *trubuk* fish) who sought in vain the hand of the princess of Siak (the *puyu puyu* fish).

This is the story:

In the waters of Melaka, at Tanjung Tuan, lives the *trubuk*, apparently a young ruling prince. He has set his heart on the princess *puyu puyu*, who lives in a riverpool in the interior of the country near Tanjung Padang. Apparently, he knows her only by hearsay; the *kelasa*-fish, who has seen her, describes her beauty to *trubuk* and increases his passion. *Trubuk* proceeds to Tanjung Padang. Returned to Tanjung Tuan, he bids the mackerel call up the other fishes. His dignitaries and officers appear, and *trubuk* reveals to them that on a trip upriver, at the last full-moon, he has seen lady *puyu puyu* and cannot live without her. He asks for advice and help. His followers, sharks, dolphins, rays, mackerel, catfish, jewfish, the conger-eel and the mud-eel, the last two playing a rather dubious part, all offer to carry off lady *puyu puyu*, boasting of their courage, strength, and weapons. But the *siakap*-fish utters a word of warning; such an expedition should be prepared very carefully. He reminds them of the attack on Singapore by the swordfishes, which had been frustrated by a wall of banana-stems erected on the advice of a small boy, and adds that the inhabitants of the riverpool are already aware of the intended expedition and preparing for it. Questioned by *trubuk*, *siakap* replies that he is unable to name the traitor, as many fishes are coming and going there.

Lady *puyu puyu* is living peacefully in her riverpool, when the mud-eel arrives and informs the spiny eel of the intended attack. Spiny eel informs her mistress that 'the noble youth is now ready to come and devour her'; he is only waiting for the full moon. Lady *puyu puyu* is disturbed; she thinks that his coming will be her death, and bursts into tears; her ladies-in-waiting and maids hurry to her and ask what the matter is. She tells them that prince *trubuk* of Tanjung Tuan will come and carry her off by force if she does not follow him willingly. She asks all her servants what should be done. The ladies—all of them fresh-water fishes—have their say; some think that, being women, they cannot resist; others opine that they must try their luck in a fight. Lady *puyu puyu* declares that she does not object to the marriage, but is afraid that she will suffer later on. It is not that the youth does not please her; the trouble lies in the difference between their countries, which will lead to difficulties. His country lies in the West, hers in the interior, hardly coming to the public notice; he is of the sea, she of the land, and no good will come of a marriage, which therefore she must decline. She cries, and the other fishes say that she is right and must abide by her decision. Some swear that they will be captured together and follow their mistress everywhere; others trust that heavy rain or drift-nets will frustrate the attack. The *seluang*-fish suggests that they should flee into the forest-swamp.

While they are discussing the matter, conger-eel begins a frivolous dance. *Sekapar*-fish does obeisance and rises and knocks him senseless. When conger-eel recovers, he reproaches *sekapar* and sings a string of *pantun* describing the love of *trubuk* for lady *puyu puyu*. The audience rebukes him for jesting, but lady *puyu puyu* says that though danger threatens, that is no reason why there should not be some fun. And then she sits down by her duennas and has a good cry.

The rumour of lady *puyu puyu*'s distress reaches her insignia-bearer, who comes to pay his respects, accompanied by all the old servants and warriors of the state. They claim the right to fight for the princess, and each of them names the sea-fish he will single out for his adversary. *Kelah* (the carp) says that their only means of escape is to pray to God, as they will never be able to offer serious resistance to *trubuk*. *Kelah* claims to be clairvoyant; with the blessing of the gods, Allah will grant the princess's prayer. Lady *puyu puyu* is convinced that *kelah* is right; towards the evening, she begins praying and offering. She takes a ceremonial bath (*mandi berlimau*), withdraws into her palace, and prays until dawn, when a storm bursts, wherein her parents come down from heaven and bring a beautiful tree, which takes root in the middle of the riverpool. 'The appointed time having come', the princess jumps into the tree and climbs into its branches before her duennas have time to catch her. The fishes agree that *puyu*

puyu 'has found her place', and she appears in the story no more. It is said that, living on the tree, she resigns herself to never meeting her lover, and thinks of the *kelasa*-fish, whose fate it is to mate with a bird.

Trubuk has his warriors called up to storm the defences of drift-nets. When all of them have bragged of the great things they are going to do, he departs with them at the time of the full moon, selecting the various commanders from his trusted warriors. When they are near the shore, the wind rises and moves the drift-nets. At Bukit Batu the expedition stops and fishermen hurry to the spot and lower their nets. *Trubuk* escapes into the river and realizes that God does not will that he shall meet his beloved. He hears that princess *puyu puyu* has escaped into a tree; and returns to Tanjung Tuan and his own country, mourning for ever his unfortunate love. His love will never end, but

> If I should come to die, love, in my grief,
> Oh, bathe me in the water of your eyes,
> Give me as shroud a cloth which you have worn,
> And pay a weekly visit to my grave!

Tongku Tambuse

AT the beginning of the last century, nearly the whole of Sumatra was in an uproar. Muhammadan pilgrims had returned from Mecca preaching the severe religion of the Wahabites. As this sect wanted to purge the religion of Muhammad in Arabia from the many faults that had slipped in, the pilgrims in Sumatra also thought it their duty to establish purification of that dogma.

This caused much fighting and bloodshed. Full of their divine vocation, they tried to introduce the reformation with force and violence. Great was the support they obtained immediately, while daily, new adherents joined. However, greater was the number, who, averse to anything new, stuck to the old *adat* and would sacrifice everything for its preservation. The friction between two such opposite powers ignited the flame of war, and nearly the whole of the beautiful island became a prey to the wild passions in which the population indulged.

Near the confluence of the rivers Sosa and Siutam was at the beginning of the nineteenth century a large village, called Tambuse or Daludalu, the capital of Rantau Binuwang, bordering upon Sosa. It was the most important place in that district and its chiefs considered themselves descendants from Sultan Iskander Zulkarnain, or the Two-horned One, the Indian name for Alexander the Great.

Rantau Binuwang was a prosperous district because of its trade in wood products, which were bought by the Chinese and Buginese and transported to commercial towns like Melaka, Johor, and Riau. On account of this trade and the transit-trade of the uplands, Daludalu had become the most lively place of that part of Middle Sumatra. Through the large intercourse with other nations, many had undertaken the pilgrimage to Mecca. Since the beginning of the seventeenth century, Rantau Binuwang had been an Islamic land.

Among the pilgrims were also Imam Maulana Kadli and his son, Haji Mohamad Saleh, the later on so notorious Tongku Tambuse, also called Balejo. About 1820–5, they must have returned from Mecca and settled in Daludalu. They, too, had been present during the war of the Wahabites for the purification of Muhammad's religion. Altogether under the influence of that reformation, Imam Maulana Kadli opened a school. His reputation of being a deeply religious man, as well as his great zeal for the Muhammadan faith, soon gathered round him many pupils. The conversions were quietly carried out. But Imam Maulana died and his son, who succeeded him as leader in prayer and in the new dogma, did not possess his father's patience.

He insisted that the Yang Dipertuan of Rantau Binuwang should follow the regulations laid down by the Muhammadan religion and should force his subjects to adopt the new dogma. This man was, however, not to be persuaded to do this. But Haji Mohamad Saleh obtained in the meanwhile a great many followers and the Yang Dipertuan, fearing that his authority should be suppressed, chased the Haji out of Tambuse. Being the weaker, the Haji travelled round to gain satellites. Only when he was sure that his dogma would find supporters among the foremost people, did he venture back to Tambuse. The Yang Dipertuan dared not use violence against him, but when they began to take recourse to debauchery and it became evident that the fanatics would not spare his person, the Yang Dipertuan left his capital and settled in Tanah Putih.

This flight gave a free hand to the zealots in Tambuse. From a praiseworthy purpose, it became a religious strife, and when also the news of the many cruelties that fanatics had committed and still committed in the Padang Uplands was known, a civil war ensued between the adherents of the purification dogma and the others, which ended only after the conversion of the latter or after their emigration to Tanah Putih. They were safe there from further persecution. The only means of communication was the river and it was not likely that the war would be continued there with so little chance of flight, if the issue should be unfavourable.

It was, of course, not thither that the *padri* or *orang putih*, as they called themselves—from their way of clothing, consisting of a white shirt and a white turban—directed their view to find new food for their zeal. For, proud of the victory gained over their adversaries, they had become even more eager to continue their work of conversion elsewhere. Now it did not only concern the Muhammadans who were of another opinion but also the heathens. A much wider task; namely the spreading of Islam. All those who were not converted to this belief were infidels, of whom the great prophet had said that it was right to fight against them, whom he commanded to kill, wherever they might be, unless they showed repentance, and whom he ordered to extirpate that

God should reward those who fight for the true faith.

Crowds of bloodthirsty people went round through the districts situated in the Lubu River. They forced the population to adopt their faith, if they did not prefer death. From there, they went to the district of the Siutam and Sosa Rivers. Here it was the heathens who were to be extirpated; and the Bataks, not used to hard fighting, were soon subdued. They offered their submission. But when the condition was made that they should adopt Islam, and those who refused, because they did not understand it, were ruthlessly murdered, they fled into the forests and districts far away from their country. The chiefs of Sosa were converted and so maintained in their dignity. This conversion was only in name, for no sooner the savage hordes were out of the country than the just-converted Sosa chiefs abjured the new faith, gathered their subjects, made peace with the neighbouring chiefs of Ulu Barumon, and murdered the *padri* who had stayed behind.

Tongku Tambuse, meanwhile, had gone to the Sumpur territory, and so it was possible that this murder was not immediately avenged. In Rau, Tongku Tambuse had joined the fanatic, generally known by the title of Tuanku Rau, a person who had arrogantly taken possession of the title 'Yang Dipertuan'. By their joint forces, Mandeling was conquered. The news of the murder in Sosa reached them there. Across the mountains between Little Mandeling and Ulu Barumon, Tongku Tambuse marched to Sosa to take his revenge. Not prepared for this arrival, the population of Ulu Barumon had taken to flight, greatly alarmed, so that only Sosa could offer resistance. After a short fight, the population had to flee also. Only two strongly populated villages offered resistance. Only when they had been set on fire did the defendants surrender. A dreadful carnage is said to have been made, so that the chiefs of Sosa in future never had the courage to tear themselves away from the *padri*. On the contrary, later on they even became their most faithful allies. For a long time, Tongku Tambuse remained in Ulu Barumon, where he succeeded in gaining the confidence of the chiefs who had fled and the population, so that they returned to their dwelling-places. Islam was adopted and all the subdued chiefs of confederacies obtained the title of Kadli.

Whereas Tuanku Rau stretched his conquests as far as the Toba-lands and committed everywhere the most violent cruelties, most of the districts of Padang Lawas and Ulu Barumon fell without strife into the hands of Tongku Tambuse. Almost everywhere, the chiefs strove to obtain the title of Kadli. Those who would not become *padri*, sought refuge in Dolok. If the chiefs in the plain were prepared to join the army of the *padri* and cast in their lot with them, it was not so the case with those in the mountains. Repeatedly they undertook raids in the plains and robbed people, whom they ate in their mountains or made their slaves. Tongku Tambuse decided to put a stop to this and marched up against Si Minabun with his fanatic troops. Datu Bange, *raja* of Si Minabun, had left his village for fear of an attack of the *padri*, and built himself a fortress on the Dolok Si Minabun, a steep rock on the right bank of the Panei and, so to say, the key to the Dolok on that side. The rock was so impregnable that he could remain there for a year while the *padri* were encamped all around. He succeeded in causing them great losses from this favourable situation. The *padri* would perhaps never have got possession of the fortress, if treason had not delivered it into their hands. A brother of Datu Bange's showed them the way to climb the rock. When Datu Bange discovered the treason, he surrendered on condition that the lives of his people should be spared. But no sooner had the *padri* reached the rock than wholesale butchery was committed. Old people and children were pitilessly mutilated and murdered. Before the eyes of their wives and mothers, the men were slain and then thrown over the precipice, but not before they had witnessed how their wives and daughters were raped. The latter were bound afterwards and taken away as slaves and divided among the chiefs. Tongku Tambuse took possession of the maidens and made them his concubines in order to sell them later on for arms, powder, and lead. Every young maiden was worth a barrel of gunpowder. Datu Bange, his wife, his brother, and a few followers succeeded in escaping. Across the most impassable mountains, they sought a shelter in the dark forests of the Barisan Mountains and joined the population of the territory of the Sirumambe and Aek Hilung, who had gone to the almost unapproachable top of the Dolok Sordang. But as far as here they were pursued by the *padri*, who attempted in vain to reach the summit.

After this butchery, Tongku Tambuse marched against Huraba, a fortress near the Tabola. Various villages had fortified themselves there, who had put themselves under the command of Tulan di Gaja. He defended the fortress as long as he could. He could, however, not hold out against the joint army of the *padri* and Padang Lawasians and fled with his soldiers to the top of a steep sandstone rock which could only be reached on one side by a narrow mountain dam and elsewhere surrounded by deep ravines. There they were left alone by the *padri*, who marched as far as the right bank of the Bila River. This expedition was very successful, for the population, afraid of experiencing the same fate as Si Minabun's, had fled into the woods and to the tops of the mountains; only a few villages remained in the plain, but were soon subjugated.

Further, Tongku Tambuse dared not go. His forces had remarkably decreased. The great losses before Si Minabun, the tiring expeditions through the difficult mountainous country of Dolok, where many lost their lives or had to stay behind, the small increase through newly converted heathens, the small booty in prisoners-of-war, goods, and provisions, had caused the *padri* zeal to lessen. Many separated themselves from Tongku Tambuse, so that at Bandar, he could hardly dispose of 100 fighting men.

Therefore he went back to Ulu Barumon. He did not remain there very long. Tuanku Rau called him to Rau and Mandeling, where the population had rid themselves of the *padri* and offered their submission to the Netherlands Government. It was of great importance for Tongku Tambuse to prevent the Dutch from marching, and with a large army, he went to Rau. He arrived only, however, to see this district in the hands of the Dutch, who had built the Fort of Amerongen near Padang Matinggi and had ensconced themselves there. This happened in October 1832. The Dutch tried to get him on their side, but he asked such a high price that they could not deal with him. He did not leave Rau but remained in the village of Padang Matinggi, where he took an active part in the attacks on Fort Amerongen. In one of these attacks, in January 1833, he was wounded.

However faithful the Padang Lawasians had remained to him while he was amongst them, his long absence had weakened their zeal. As it happened, a certain Ja Buwaton, a native of Mandeling, had arrived at Aek Hayuara and had persuaded the chiefs and the population to drive the *padri* out of the plains. He had dreamt that he was the elected of heaven to protect the half-murdered village of Hayuara from the green banner. He looked upon this nocturnal vision as a sacred mission, left Mandeling, and arrived alone and unknown in Barumon. There he revealed his dream to the remaining population of Hayuara and Batang Moar and was accepted with confidence as leader in the battle. The youth succeeded so well in making himself worthy of this confidence, made the enemy shrink back so often covered with blood, and provided so efficiently for the defence of Hayuara, that both tribes did homage to him as to a person anointed by a deity and proclaimed him Sutan Hayuara.

A few hundred combatants descended the mountains of Aek Hayuara and fell into Hasahatan. Soon Ulu Barumon was rid of the *padri* and the whole of Padang Lawas rose against the chiefs appointed by Tongku Tambuse, who in part abjured Islam and adopted again their heathenish customs.

However, Tongku Tambuse, suffering from his wounds received at Rau, marched up to Padang Lawas. It was little trouble to him to subdue again the whole plain. They were so afraid of him that his appearance alone was enough to restore his authority. Many of the disloyal chiefs emigrated, however, to the territory downstream, for fear of revenge.

Only Aek Hayuara did not submit. Tongku Tambuse then marched thither with the chiefs of Ulu Barumon that had submitted again to him, but met with such a fierce reception that only a hurried flight saved him. This retreat crowned Ja Buwaton's work, who thereupon was elected principal chief. Tongku Tambuse tried once again to subdue Aek Hayuara, but when he did not succeed, he marched to Sosopan and Batang Onang, where the chiefs and population had turned heathens again. At the news of this arrival, however, they had fled to the forests and Angkola. The village of Tabat alone remained inhabited and offered resistance for a long time. But the village was burnt down and only the *raja* and a few of his followers escaped. Those who fell into the *padri*'s hands, were cruelly murdered; the women were taken and sold as slaves.

So, once again, the whole plain and the valley of Batang Onang were in the possession of Tongku Tambuse. He commanded the chiefs of Padang Lawas to try again to wage war against the mountain inhabitants. He himself went to Angkola and Mandeling. But the chiefs who had received this command, thought twice before assaulting the inhabitants in their own country. The most fanatic chiefs objected to begin a battle, where their lives would be at stake, against their customs. And they were certain that the mountain dwellers would not submit without offering a violent resistance. The defence of Si Minabun was still fresh in their minds and had made them sufficiently aware, that they were not powerful enough to take possession of fortresses so firmly built by nature.

However, the absence of Tongku Tambuse did not give peace back to these districts. The strife among the chiefs in the plain was the cause of it. From that moment, many wars waged until 1879 in this river-basin. They had got to know the value of money. With money, one could obtain power. People were sold and the money was used to make more slaves and to improve their status. The chiefs of Kota Pinang, Bila, and Panei were the buyers of the many people captured in the war, who, without discrimination, were made slaves, while the chiefs of the lower river-basin got rid of those slaves at a large profit to dealers in Pulau Pinang and Melaka. And when Tongku Tambuse, after a three-year absence, returned to these districts, he found very powerful chiefs, but large parts of the country quite without population.

His arrival seems to have restored rest to the country, so that the population returned to the villages. It seems that Tongku Tambuse had a presentiment that the end of the part he had to play had come, and that he, by leading a peaceful life, tried to make this end less fatal, or thought to avert his fate altogether. More and more he withdrew, surrendered his power, so to say, to the Padang Lawas chiefs and led the life of a priest. He had not foreseen, however, that the seed scattered by him would germinate so abundantly; that although he was no longer at the head of these bloodthristy fanatics, all these cruelties were committed in his name.

The Dutch troops that had forced him to leave Rau for good in 1835 and made it impossible to surprise the fortress at Kotanopan during the new year's celebration of that year, forced him also in the latter part of 1836 to leave his post at Mapat Tunggul, as that district, in fear, had offered its submission to the Government. His influenced there, which had been so great, was entirely broken. Yet he had tried, by an alliance with Tuwanku Imam of Bonjol, to maintain himself in a mountain pass between Mapat Tunggul and the Kampar-lands.

Indifference of the population, powerlessness of Tuwanku Imam, who was shut in his fortress of Bonjol, and want of provisions forced him to leave that place and return to Tambuse in August 1836. Pursued by the Dutch troops like a wild beast, the population of those districts, where shortly before he had ruled with unlimited power, chased him out of their districts, and so he was shot at in Rokan, where he had retired. With only a handful of adherents, he arrived at Tambuse.

He suspected that the Dutch troops would not leave him in peace, for immediately after his return, he fortified Daludalu still more and had many small *kubu* (fortified encampments) built round it. He did not meddle with it himself, but departed to Padang Lawas, the only district that had remained loyal to him.

For a long time already, Mandeling and Angkola had asked the Government of the Dutch Indies for protection. In 1837, they again repeated that request.

When Bonjol had fallen on 16 August of that same year, the Governor of Sumatra's Westcoast made up his mind to satisfy that request and to purse the *padri* further. He commanded Major van Beethoven to drive Tongku Tambuse back within the borders of his territory.

In November 1837, he marched up to Batang Onang, where the population joined his troops. Here a small garrison was left behind. The expedition went on to Portibi, where Tongku Tambuse had been in the past. The Dutch encamped on the edge of the plateau from which the valley, in which Portibi is situated, could be overlooked. Though living in discord, Hajoran and Si Minabun allied themselves with them.

The village was strongly fortified and was defended stubbornly. When the troops, however, had encamped on the other side of the Panei River, just opposite the open part of the village, resistance was no longer possible. The population fled and left the fortress in Dutch hands. Without defending themselves, many other villages submitted. Within a short time, the plain of Padang Lawas was subdued and Tongku Tambuse driven away. He went to Daludalu and fortified the village more and more. Near Mondang, he and the enemy met. After a short struggle, he had to flee in great haste. Repeatedly, however, he undertook raids and he even succeeded in surprising an outpost from which he was driven away soon.

From the beginning of 1835 until December of that year, the Dutch troops were occupied in taking the many entrenchments, put up round Daludalu. Every further march was contested by the enemy and consequently many skirmishes took place with many losses. After fresh troops had arrived, the attack was ventured, the fortress stormed and taken on 28 December 1838.

For Tongku Tambuse they looked in vain. It was said that at the last assault, he had fled in a proa. They never heard of him again, so that it is supposed he died during his escape. Others maintain that he fled to Melaka and died there. There is no reason for accepting this as the truth.

Tongku Tambuse is said to have had a kind nature, indulgent rather than severe. It cannot have been his intention to accept a general strife for the belief of Muhammad. Originally, it was his aim only to improve in his country that which weakened the true faith. In Mecca he had learnt to know improvements, and vanity as well as agreement with the dogma of the Wahabites made him wish that this religion should also be preached in his own country. That he did not choose the best means to reach his purpose, namely by calmly preaching as his father had done, and trying to increase the number of followers by leading a good life himself—how was this to be expected from a young man with a tropical temperament?

And yet if he had wanted to act differently, the time in which he lived would have made it impossible. Repeatedly, news came from the Padang Uplands. They heard how the *padri*-sect spread there; how the means used there were always successful. If Tongku Tambuse wanted to check the stream that he himself had set flowing, he could not have succeeded. Should his influence have been so great, he would have signed his own death sentence. He would have been accused of indifference and soon some fanatic would have murdered him.

In this way, he was dragged along to save his own life in that fierce war, which had begun in the west some years before. It must be ascribed to him, however, that the *padri* in the north, at the beginning of the war at least, did not commit such cruelties as they committed in the south. Not before Tongku Tambuse had allied himself with Tuanku Rau were atrocities done, which can only be equalled to those of the British India revolt in the middle of the last century. Old men were ruthlessly murdered; children slaughtered before their parents' eyes; old women had their breasts cut off and were then killed; young women fell into the hands of the commanders, who, after satisfying their sensual pleasure, sold them as slaves; young maidens were taken as concubines or sold to the highest bidders; men who were able to bear arms had to join those bloodthirsty hordes, after they had been converted. If they opposed anything, they were tortured, made slaves, or killed.

The ritual prayers had to be rigorously observed. Those who omitted to say them were treated as *kafir* and only by paying a high fine they could escape death. They were no longer allowed to eat *sirih*, and the teeth had to be filed. Cockfights were forbidden. All those who sinned against these rules had to pay a big fine or were made slaves.

Tongku Tambuse himself had never made himself guilty of those atrocities. It is true that he profited by them in the form of fines and slaves, but those also served to combat the heavy expenses of the war.

Tongku Tambuse should not have been a commander. He should never have led the operations of a siege or a campaign. Everything was left to the moment. But he possessed much personal courage. He was fine of stature, which showed all the better in his short doublet with brass knots. A turban of warp was his headgear. The natives, who in general attached much value to outward appearances, saw in him something divine.

If he had withdrawn in time, which would have been possible after the expedition in the Dolok had failed, he might have lived on in their memory as a holy man and they would have made offerings at his tomb. But seduced and misled on account of the great power which he had obtained, unbalanced by the respect they showed him, carried away by the homage offered him, and last but not least flattered in his vanity by the fear which they had for him, he took a pleasure in the part he played.

And yet, in spite of everything, there is something in the character of Tongku Tambuse that asks for our respect. He was the leader sent by God, the faithful one irradiated by celestial visions, who in his young soul was deeply convinced of a great and sacred ideal. Justice and law had to reign on earth and the happiness of men should be established for ever under the green banner of the Prophet. For this ideal he offered joy, rest, and safety. When it was written in the stars that his hour had come, he drew the sword without hesitating and let loose a war which ravaged the peaceful mountain districts of Sumatra like a tempest. Fortune and misfortune were his share in full measure, but they neither disturbed the simplicity of his character nor the purity of his soul. His mysterious disappearance is quite in harmony with his strange, adventurous life. Deep down in the lonely virginal forest lies the grave of the small, bold insurgent, who during his lifetime was perhaps more lonely than in death.

Padang Lawas

THE antiquities of Padang Lawas lie on the Upper Barumon River and its left tributary, the Panei, as well as on several branches of these two rivers, for the greater part in the hilly territory which, although wrongly, is said to belong to the Great Plain. They date principally from the twelfth and thirteenth centuries, although some older remains and others of a later period, too, may be discovered. The ruins comprise part of the great Panei Empire, which is mentioned for the first time in the sixth century in the Chinese annals under the name of Puni or Poli, which about the year 1000 ranked as the principal state amongst those of Sumatra; after this, it was conquered by the South Indian king, Rajendra-coladewa. In the following centuries, it procured for itself an eternized name on account of the establishment of splendid temples, and in the fourteenth century, it had to submit to the renowned East Javanese Empire of Majapahit, while on the arrival of the Dutch, it had already sunk into oblivion.

In the middle of the previous century, Padang Lawas came under the authority of the Netherlands. The Government of the Dutch Indies ordered Franz Junghun, the famous geologist, to explore this region. Junghun deserves the honour of being the first to have pointed out the Hindu antiquities to be found in these parts (1846). Although in remarking on these he confined himself to a few lines only, and the report by the explorer, Von Rosenberg, published ten years later, was very summary, nevertheless the work of these brave men, who entered this inhospitable region and observed there what would be appraised by future generations only, deserves respect. Thereafter, little notice of all this was taken until Dr P. V. van Stein Callenfels in 1920 travelled through Padang Lawas and immediately recognized the importance of it to science. His highly valued report was the prime cause of some excavations being undertaken by the Archaeological Service, which, however, in consequence of lack of funds, had to be discontinued.

Thus did the author of this book find matters, when, in June 1935, he entered Padang Lawas. He readily perceived, however, that good and proper work could only be achieved by a programme prepared with patience and care and then systematically

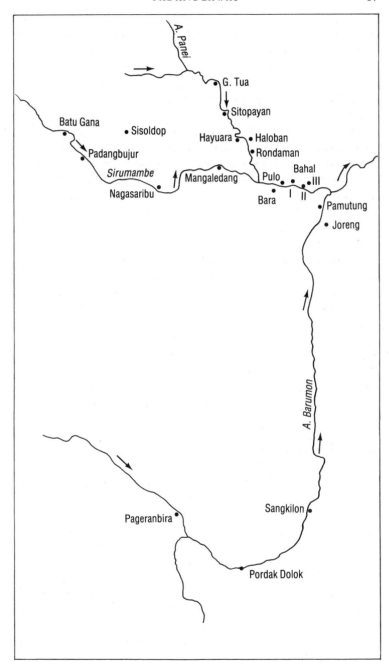

Antiquities of Padang Lawas.

executed. An exploration on such a scale demanded more time and larger funds than were at his disposal and he therefore decided to engage upon matters of primary importance to begin with. In other words: that the chambers of the temples had to be emptied of all rubbish, architectural drawings had to be made, and surveying and partial excavations had to be executed.

We are now in possession of comparative materials of all the ruins and we are able to form from these an idea of Panei architecture, which will undergo no change even if future findings are unearthed. It is, however, somewhat different with the plastic art. The temples are only sparsely decorated, provided with only a few reliefs and somewhat more with detached sculptures. The statues from the rooms are nearly all lost, and it is certain that many works of art are still to be found under the surface. It is therefore practically impossible to state a definitive and unchallengeable opinion with regard to the plastic art. Conclusions drawn from the specimens now available justify the statement that the Hindu Batak sculptors and bronze-casters were just such masters in their art as their contemporaries in the Island of Java. Truly beautiful works have been made by their hands.

The three most important Hindu Batak sanctuaries are Si Pamutung, Bahal I (to distinguish this from the two smaller temples at Bahal), and Sangkilon. They are situated on two terraces, the lower one or the first and the uppermost one or the second. Above these, on a separate base, rises the square main part of the temple with the roof. The roofs of Pamutung and Sangkilon are square and rise in amphitheatrical style; the roof of Bahal I is circular and decorated with wreaths.

On mounting the stairs, one arrives at a spacious landing surrounded by walls which leads to a footpath encircling the temple. The next flight of steps leads to a second, smaller terrace with a gallery. On ascending the third staircase, which is extremely narrow and small and which leads to the chamber, one perceives at Bahal I, to the left and to the right of the entrance, two life-size statues of men with penis erect, standing on the head of an ogre; at Bahal II, there are no statues of men but of prancing lions. At the other temples, there would have been similar figures, but, alas, they have been lost. Above the entrance is the grinning head of an ogre. Only at Sangkilon have we been able to excavate such a monumental piece of work; it had crashed and was covered with masonary from the great landing. Although a few pieces are missing, the form of the head has been wonderfully preserved. The rooms are almost cubical in shape and are not very large, their surface varying from 2.09 sq. m to 2.60 sq. m. Although the greater part of the rooms are now empty, they were formerly provided with altars and idols. As has previously been mentioned, the three largest temples are situated on two terraces, the others only on one. The entrance to the innermost sanctuary lies always in an easterly direction; in front is a terrace of brickwork and before that—all in a straight line—is the gate of the circular wall. Within the wall there is sufficient space for other buildings; either for terraces or small, massive monuments (stupas) or for decorated columns (*stambha*). The terraces were originally provided with a roof on wooden columns, and in consequence the Javanese name of *pendopo*-terraces may be applied to them. The temple staircase is usually lined on either side by demons holding clubs in their hands and who raise a threatening left forefinger. Elephants' heads with human figures in their mouths may also regularly be seen. Lions and other statues also occur frequently. Let us conclude this bare enumeration and occupy ourselves with the more active reality.

In June 1935 we set out to discover Sangkilon, a temple in the jungle, of which mention had been made in a few lines in a discoloured report. The guides were little acquainted with the position, so that we wandered about for a long time without much hope. Just when a quarrel threatened to break out, we suddenly saw a high, red tower protruding from among the foliage like an old castle on the banks of the Rhine. It was an astonishing sight and we were all very inquisitive and naturally extremely pleased at this discovery. The building was enveloped from top to bottom in enormous creeping-plants and trees, which, with their powerful branches, encircled the old walls in a grip of iron. The southern wall and the entrance had in the course of time crumbled away altogether and now only two of the walls and a part of the roof remained erect. On either side of the main stairs, partly submerged, but totally covered with moss, two sculptured elephants' heads with human forms in their mouths were visible. We also found the fragments of the sculptured bodies of lions. The *pendopo*-terrace was also found, whilst the circular wall could be clearly traced in the undergrowth and bush. Of primary importance to us was a high hill situated towards the north of the main temple, which, although covered with trees, showed with interruptions the remains of what once must have been walls. This hill was not mentioned in the literature, and was without doubt a sanctuary and it kept us guessing for a very long time to find out its origin. To the east, a small terrace was also situated.

In the afternoon, I commenced to clear away the rubbish from the room of the main temple. We had great expectations of finding the idol-statue amongst the debris; but we struck a square white stone, which we turned with the greatest care. Suddenly, one of the coolies pulled out of the rubbish a black object, a plate of gold with drawings and inscription. In great suspense, we continued to dig, and at first we found some scraps of bronze and then a small bronze urn. That night, alone in my tent, I cleaned the plate and perceived in the middle a square with *vajra* (flashes of lightning, which are of very great importance in the Buddhist sorcery). The first great secret (the religion) of Sangkilon, was thus disclosed; the second (the date), could be ascertained doubtless by deciphering the eight lines of the inscription. Later examinations revealed that the characters date from the twelfth century and that in Sangkilon, a Yamari idol was worshipped. The god Yamari is one of the most demoniac phenomena in Buddhism; he has three faces, 24 eyes, and wears a string of human skulls round his neck. Sangkilon was the centre of a horrible demonology. Later proofs were discovered at other places in Padang Lawas, too. A further exploration of the temple led us to ascend to the roof and to excavate the foundations where bands with beautiful spirals depicting leaves came to light.

We especially endeavoured to make a profile-drawing of the original building; it is essential for the study of architecture to possess profile-drawings of all these ruins.

The making of such a profile under the burning sun is a work that has to be executed with great patience. This naturally cannot be left to coolies, as very often parts of the cornice are missing, and on other parts of the temple, a thorough investigation is necessary in order to find out if the missing pieces are still in shape elsewhere. Some errors are therefore inevitable. The edges of the galleries are nearly all broken off or have slowly crumbled away; consequently, an accurate statement of width and height is impossible. It is also very difficult to find out if all the galleries were provided with balustrades. A point of uncertainty is often the transition of the body of the temple to the roof; this transition has very often crumbled or is covered with rubbish. The cleaning of the roof demands much valuable time and requires expensive scaffolding, so we were forced by necessity to abandon attempts.

The mysterious hill in the north at Sangkilon was excavated only on my second expedition (in September), and there I found a complete temple with a terrace and a room; an altar occupied the entire wall of this room but no traces of idols were found. On the occasion of the second visit, the forest had to a considerable extent been cleared and consequent investigations and explorations were more simplified than on the previous occasion. One hundred metres to the east of the temple site runs the River Sangkilon, a right tributary of the Barumon River.

Every day, when the sun stood at the zenith, we sprang from the high bank into the water and thus we drove away the wicked influences of magic, which without doubt still radiated from this Sanctuary of the Demons! From Sangkilon, we wended our way to the north to the confluence of the Panei and the Barumon Rivers, where Pamutung, the principal sanctuary of Tapanuli, is situated. With great expectancy we anticipated the outcome of this exploration, for the religion of this temple must have been the most influential in the country. We immediately fell under the mystic spell of this former group of buildings, where the *alang-alang* and numerous other plants have been allowed to grow profusely, undisturbed for centuries. Here and there ghostly faces gazed at us from among the foliage, the heads of elephants, of demons, and the grinning faces of lions. . . .

Full of hope, we set to work. Half-submerged in the soil, we remarked a hand-worked piece of stone, which immediately drew the attention. With great care, we excavated our find, which proved to be a beautiful top-piece with eight standing lions, each pair of bodies converging into one single head. It here deserves mention that in the plastic art of Sumatra, the forms of lions are often used as ornamental crown for the roof. Our interest was therefore now fixed on the roof of the temple. (See sketch on p. 72.)

A big ladder was put up and, armed with choppers, we climbed up. Aloft we chopped the trees and shrubs away and then made a remarkable discovery. The roof consisted of two square storeys, one above the other, which were surrounded by little stupas. As the stupa is an ornament of specific Buddhist origin, the religion of Pamutung, as well as of the greater part of Padang Lawas, had thus been elucidated. Probably, in times long past, a third storey would have been found upon the other two, a headstupa crowned with a parasol of stone. This heavy parasol had fallen somewhere in the rear of the temple. The headstupa had probably rested on

Reconstruction of the west side of the temple, Si Pamutung. Former-ly, the top was crowned by a large stupa.

the basis of lions already mentioned, and this again on a large lotus platform.

The author will not easily forget the survey of the roof; creeping cautiously along the huge cornice of approximately eleven metres, clinging sometimes to a single branch for support, taking measures and making notes with great pains, he was in a rather dangerous position. In the centre of the roof is a narrow aperture. For what purpose did this mysterious aperture serve in former days?

Apparently for a relic, a plate of gold with an inscription, or for something similar. From the roof, a beautiful view is afforded of the whole plain, which is surrounded by a rampart built of earth. Large herds of buffaloes graze in the brilliant sunshine of the afternoon, and even in the distance, their small wooden bells are audible.

To the north of the principal temple is a terrace made of natural stone. A peculiarity, because the temples in Padang Lawas are nearly without exception built of brick. The eastern staircase was excavated without delay and there two heads of large crocodiles, with human noses and lips with a hairgrowth bearing semblance of a moustache, were discovered. In the religion of the Bataks, the crocodile is an animal of eminent magic. It is purported to give the power to see into the past and into the present, to reveal the mysteries of the hereafter, and to govern the rain and the wind. It is therefore clear that the Hindus of Pamutung must have intentionally placed the crocodile along the sides of the stairs of their sanctuary. The faithful could, before climbing up to the terrace, first of all ask for aid from these magic images.

To the south of the main temple is a remarkable small building, the destination of which is not entirely clear; an octagonal top-building is visible which formerly was ornamented with a set of small turrets and decorated with a stonework of the heads of lions and snakes. The fragments excavated near this building may have belonged partly to the principal temple; no certainty is to be derived on this score. At this sanctuary, an important discovery was made. After one lotus-cushion, two pedestals of demons, one beautifully formed head, as well as other pieces had come to light, the spade suddenly revealed the finely moulded upper-torso of a woman with the hands folded in worship, surrounded by a border of flames and provided with a necklace, bracelets, large ear-drops, and a crown. The eyes are wide open, and from under the upper-lip two covered tusks protrude. No doubt we have here an image of the royal foundress of the sanctuary before us, the beautiful queen of Panei, who had her own image executed in a demonic form as a proof that she belonged to the sect of the Bhairawas.

The Bhairawas or Terrible Ones worshipped their gods under horrible solemnity, by preference during the night at cemeteries. At these orgies, they dedicated to the gods piles of human corpses, in high flaming fires; the stronger the smell of the burning corpses grew, the greater it pleased them, because this stench, which in the inscriptions is compared with the smell of ten thousand flowers, brought salvation from the sphere of generation. Usually the ceremony (which was a symbol of the destruction of the earthly bonds) commenced a few hours after nightfall. The living victims destined for sacrifice were laid down in a definitely determined attitude, which can well be seen in the drawings; resting on the back, the feet were folded under the body, the hands tied up and the head bent backwards, the chest thus being fully expanded. Then the priest would approach, and quickly inserting a large knife in the belly of the victim, he would pull it upwards with a jerk so that the whole body was ripped open up to the lower ribs. The victim would mostly die after a few minutes in violent pain. The priest would then place himself upon the convulsing body, cut away the heart, fill a skull with blood and empty it at a draught several times in succession. If by drinking this incomparable beverage, this superior wine, he gradually entered into a state of inebriation, then he would light the fire and would sink into deep meditation.

Towards midnight he would fall into an ecstasy, which is considered the highest purpose of the Bhairawas. Then he would jump up and start dancing wildly in circles in the light of the flames, swinging a rattle made from the bones of a dead man and ejaculating frantic laughter all the while. The more this hysterical laughter grew, the more pleasure it was thought to afford the gods.

Usually this horrible ceremony terminated in the company of women. It is not difficult to recognize in such rites the influence of Batak religion. Before the arrival of the Europeans, cannibalism was quite common among the Bataks. Anybody, who, like us, is intimately acquainted with the country and the people of North Sumatra, must necessarily know what an extraordinary importance sorcery, incantations, etc., still play in the lives of the population there.

Finding the demonic image of the woman at Pamutung is sufficient proof, too, that this greatest sanctuary of Padang Lawas was dedicated to a horrible Buddhist demon. This is, for the history of Sumatra, of vital importance and interest, because it pertains to the mighty and art-loving princes of Panei, who, for many centuries, occupied all the positions of importance in this region and suffered their influence to radiate over great parts of the archipelago and the surrounding countries. It may be taken for granted that the great demonolatry of Java in the thirteenth and fourteenth centuries and that of Minangkabau in about the same period were influenced and promoted by the prominent barbarian Buddhism of Tapanuli. It may even be assumed that indications testifying this are contained in the name of Si Pamutung (The Tempestuous, Sri Mada), clearly denoting the demonic character of this temple. In 1930, the fact was established that the Bhairawa-worship flourished in Padang Lawas,[1] but this was only supported

---

[1] Cf. the excellent article of Professor F. D. K. Bosch in Oudheidkundig Verslag 1930.

at that time by an image from a small temple, which cannot be regarded as sufficient proof that the principal sanctuaries of the country were exclusively consecrated to this form of worship. The above-mentioned image is remarkable enough to warrant a description of it.

The pedestal is formed by a rectangular plate on which is an oval double lotus cushion, and upon which then rests the corpse of a man on his back with the god dancing upon him. In his right hand, he holds a *vajra* (symbol of the lightning), and in the left hand, which is placed in front of the chest, he holds a skull-like bowl; with his left forearm he clutches a staff, pressing it against his body. The staff is broken at the top and has, for three-quarters of the length, a streamer hanging from it; flames emerge from his hairdress, around the neck he wears a string of human skulls. It depicts Heruka, whom the Sanskrit chapters described as follows:

One must imagine him standing on a corpse, covered in the skin stripped from a human being, besmirched with ashes, in his right hand a glittering flash of lightning and in his left hand the skull-staff provided with an [sic] dangling streamer and a skull-bowl filled with blood. His bandole is decorated with fifty human heads. Owing to tusks his jaws appear drawn, while a lewd leer shines from his blood-streaked eyes. His reddish hair stands on end, Aksobhya (the Buddha of the East) sits in the crown and rings are in the ears, he is attired with ornaments made from human bones and the head dressed with five skulls presenting the Buddaship and by virtue of his musing granting protection against the demons of the world.

If Heruka is mentioned in literature, it is usually as the god of the wizards, who is called upon by distressed priests to convert or to annihilate the unfaithful. What a violent power radiates from the diabolical god may be evidenced by an ancient narrative which is said to have originated in Tibet, which narrates of a king, who had been solemnly informed that should he break his promise and regard the veiled image of Heruka, he would vomit blood and this would result in his death. To sketch more clearly the sphere in which Heruka reigned, the following quotation from an ancient Javanese manuscript is certainly useful, as in it the terrors of a battlefield are described as the most fitting surroundings for the descent of the Lord of Buddhas:

This is the reason why a Buddhist bestirs himself to be virtuous in heart. He does not desire to indulge in human flesh, neither does he feel any inclination to satiate himself with food and pleasure. To procure insight is his aim, so that he may obtain power over death and life; this is the true purpose of his meditation. In such a state he becomes at one with the Lord of Buddhas, the summit of independence. His methods vary, e.g. he uses a dried leaf as a sun-shade during his unshaken devotion. Stinking blood pours over his head and trickles on to his chest, entrails twist themselves around his body, innumerable green flies sit on his face and creep into his eyes. But his heart is not allowed to stray in the efforts to make the god Heruka descend into him.

However, let us return to Si Pamutung. After further excavations carried on this site, we decided upon a visit to the sanctuary of Si Joreng Belangah, which is situated at a few hours' distance to the south, and which enjoyed only a cursory mention in the available literature. At that time we could not possibly surmise the important archaeological and artistical surprises that were in store for us there.

On a brilliant morning, we paddled in a cranky proa upon the Barumon River, along high, wildly overgrown banks, where the sunlight created enchanting yet whimsical shapes among bamboo, lians, and other climbing plants and ferns. The song of hundreds of birds escorted us on this fantastic journey. After we had disembarked and climbed the narrow path, which meandering took us upwards, we had still to walk a few minutes before we saw the small temple. The first sight, however, disappointed us much. Would there be any secrets to be unravelled in this small thing? It stood there desolate and barren in the *alang-alang* which almost reached man's height. First we cut away the undergrowth and the trees which stood on the stairs, and then proceeded to climb upwards. The room was empty; only in the northern and in the southern walls, two trapezium apertures had been hewn which had probably served for lamps or small bronze statues in former times.

To the south of the main temple, we then perceived a big lotus of stone. On being excavated, it became obvious that this had belonged to the crown of a stupa, a terrace with a superposed structure crowned with a sun-shade of stone. To say exactly what this crown looked like, is without a special study impossible; a still larger lotus-border followed then, the one which had been saved; alas, it had plunged down and now lay deeply covered with sand. Near by (in pieces and lumps) a high band of foliage was discovered, on which, on lotus-cushions, the Buddhas of the four principal points of the compass were seated, one of which had, however, disappeared. At the corners of the square, the usual lions completed the ornamentation.

A similar set of Buddhas was found on a beautiful column that we excavated in the north-west corner of the site. Rising from a double lotus-cushion, it is surrounded at the top by a pearl-string of foliage in stone, interchanged at eight places by lion-heads and medallions or shields; above the first, we observed small niches with statuettes of Buddhas and between them squat lions, two bodies having only one head. Similar lions are found on an Etruscian vase from the sixth century BC, as well as in Chinese, Indian, and Indonesian art.

No conclusive information is available regarding the purpose of such columns, so that we are at liberty to guess the purpose of the original use. Probably Buddha has been reverenced by it by childbirth, marriage, victory, or some other memorable occurrence; the erection of such a monument had a redeeming power and, generally speaking, averted magic dangers. On Java, little replicas of temples were therefore popular; if one had not the necessary money to build a complete sanctuary, then one erected such a column or miniature monument. At Joreng, we found no less than three of these columns.

The one mentioned above, however, has still a remarkable peculiarity, for it rests on a round pin and this pin fits again into a pedestal that we excavated in the north of the site. It is square-formed with projections, and on the upper plane of each projection is a large *vajra*, the magic symbol that we found on the plate of gold at Sangkilon, too. The sides of the small monument show four casements with dancing figures; one of these holds a drum in front of the body, whereon it beats with the hand. The small intersecting panels (at every turn there are four) are filled with foliage; the one is remarkable from the leaves of which looms the bust of a woman, who raises the left hand and holds the palm of the right in front of her breast. In the north-eastern corner of the site, we traced a sandstone foundation carrying the finest piece of the temple group.

It is a round, flat piece measuring 1.24 m in diameter and 0.44 m in height, the border decorated with large lotus-leaves, then smaller leaves above and an edge of alternate casements with rosettes, and over these there are unadorned squares. On the axis (not on the points of the compass) are four human figures representing lovely, half-demonic, half-celestial *yaksa*. All these figures have the hair puffed, wide-open eyes, and large ear-drops; two of them wear a chain over the chest, and one also the train of a garment over his left shoulder. Their demonic nature is tempered

to a lovely innocence and yields a deep survey in the state of the
soul of the Buddhist in those days.

We were, however, not to leave Joreng without getting a final
surprise. To the north of the main temple are two small hills,
evidently stupas. When we excavated the nearer one, we struck
upon a heavy piece of stone with a circular elevation in the
middle; on the east-side we found an inscription of two lines,
which stated the year AD 1179. This is the first date found on a
temple-court of Padang Lawas and mentions thus for the first
time, the date of erection of these interesting ruins.

From Joreng, we went to Bara on the southern bank of the
Panei River. As we were not very well acquainted with the local
situation, there was much trouble involved in getting a proper
place to stay. Finally we arrived in . . . , a place which was situated
about one hour's distance from the temple. It was nearly five
o'clock and the *raja* was absent; however, his relatives showed us
a small house in which we could cook and sleep. In about one
hour's time, he would come to pay us a visit.

Let it be understood that it had been a busy day and a bit of
hard work had already been accomplished in the heat of the
tropical sun. We were tired, hungry, and dirty, and longed for
one single thing: to undress quickly and to get to bed. However,
the visit promised by the *raja* prevented us from doing so. We
should therefore try to avail ourselves of this occasion to obtain
information regarding existing bronze and gold articles, if any.
Heavily did the claim of archaeology rest upon our weak shoulders!
Moreover, we had heard that the *raja* was a disagreeable and
exceedingly proud man. At seven o'clock sharp, he appeared in
our place of temporary dwelling, accompanied by some twenty
men; the whole room was filled with them, whereas still many
thronged outside who would not miss one word of the discourse.
Never before have I seen a man as stout as our *raja*; like a balloon,
he entered the room, took a seat on two chairs, and placed his
enormous, sausage-like fingers placidly on the table. We saluted
him with respect and told him the reason of our coming. Then I
produced a book on archaeology and showed him the numerous
beautiful pictures to be found in it. The *raja* put a pair of dirty
spectacles on his nose, took the book nearer to the light of the
smoking oil-wick, and looked inquisitively at the temples, the
statues, and the household-articles depicted in its pages. Especially
the articles made of gold drew his attention and he asked if it was
true that the Queen of the Netherlands, Sri Paduka Baginda

Maharaja Wilhelmina, always walked about with a crown of gold on her head and if eight pages were really necessary to pick up all the diamonds, which by each stride fell from Her Majesty's dress. I could fortunately assure him that this was perfectly true, and I asked him if sometimes small statues of gold were found in his territory! Statuettes of gold? Indeed, that had happened now and then in previous times; his grandfather had such things melted down and had a watch-chain made of the metal. Naturally we cursed this grandfather in our minds!

I was astonished by the sarcastic tone which the *raja* assumed in our company, as soon as archaeological matters were mentioned. Was it imagination or did he really want to make us ridiculous? Probably the weariness of the day had made us more sensitive than was customary. At all events, it incited us when the *raja* shrugged his shoulders and, with a sarcastic smile, glanced round as if to find out whether anybody believed in the words of the *blanda*, who asserted that a few weeks ago, he had found a plate of gold with an inscription in the temple chamber of Sangkilon. I was then so imprudent as to take the plate out of my pocket and to place it on the table; there was a mortal silence, the sausage-like fingers of the *raja* seized the precious article; he inspected very closely and all of a sudden doubled it over in the middle. . . . The blood congealed in my veins. As quick as lightning, I tore it out of his hands and let it drop into my pocket again. From that moment, we became enemies. I did not show it, but he must have felt it. Under an appearance of kindness, he opposed us, refused to lend coolies and declared not to be in possession of a proa to ferry us across the Panei. Fortunately we had the secret co-operation of some chiefs and of a great number of the population, so that the excavation met with no impediment. The first day was spent measuring the temple; the base was excavated only as deep as was necessary for making a definition of the profile; examination of the site was not undertaken. When we returned to Bara, the *raja* inquired ironically whether we had found any precious articles, and after a negative reply, he made a few comments bearing on unfortunate treasure hunters! The second day, I resolved to dig a trench across the whole temple-site. The coolies had not yet dug two minutes when their *pacol* produced a clicking sound by striking a hard article. Something of a green shade sparkled in the sunlight, and, kneeling down, I saw that it was made of bronze. Carefully, I loosened the surrounding earth with a large hunting-knife and lifted the mysterious article from the earth.

In front of us then lay one of the finest bronze ornaments that have ever been found in Sumatra, the nimbus a sitting statue. Out of the mouths of two elephants with tails like those of a fish arose a flaming border, which terminated at the apex in the grinning ogre-head of the Borobudur-type; beneath this head, two small elephants' heads *en profile* were visible. The centre of the shield consisted of an open lotus, set of inside with a borderwork of pearls. The whole work revealed an expressed South Indian influence. Naturally the spot where this treasure had laid hidden, was promptly inspected and we had the satisfaction to excavate a great number of bronze fragments of lamps, vessels, chains, etc. Moreover, we found a beautifully sculptured demon-head and sculptured lions. In short, the spoils were grand and not till late did we return homewards. A coolie carried on his back the grinning devil's-head, and the setting sun threw a strong red light on the dismal face. When the moon came up we reached the Panei, crossed the river and climbed up the high bank. When we arrived at the village and some children saw the head, a great tumult arose, windows and doors were thrown open, people stormed crying out of their huts, pointing to the head, dogs howled, children bellowed, and the *raja* (his shirt being his only attire) came out to find out the cause of all this commotion! His black, beady eyes opened wide in amazement when he beheld the head, the sausage-like fingers ascended perplexed in the moonlight, the baggy cheeks swelled, and a soft moaning sound escaped from his throat. Was it true after all? Had the *doktor batu*, notwithstanding his predictions, been favoured by fortune? How was it possible! For a moment the world stood still on its axis; just for one second, the *raja* was flabbergasted. Then, suddenly, he declared, with great decisiveness: 'That head belongs to me, you cannot take it!' Now it was my turn to smile; I gave the order to take all the ornaments to our house and, for a little while, I went into the village. When I returned, the beautiful plate of bronze had vanished. . . .

We were almost at our wit's end. Shut off from the inhabited world, in the jungle where only the word of the malignant *raja* was law, it seemed to be impossible to get the precious ornament back. Certainly I might send a courier to the controller in Gunung Tua, and even then, at best, I could only expect to obtain a reply within a few days, and our provisions were not sufficient for such a long stay and our plans, too, prevented me from doing so. Indeed, the longer we waited, the more opportunity the *raja* had of allowing the plate to disappear. I felt my heart tightening within me. In my mind's eye I saw the reproaching look that Dr Bosch, the head of the Archaeological Service, would give me and I could hear him say: 'So inconsiderately do you handle the things I entrust to your care.' Late that night, an inspiration came to me. Secretly, I sent a trustworthy boy to the *raja*'s spouse, who, by the way, was expecting a child, and who had asked me the day before to let her have some medicine. I had, so ran my errand to her, compassion on her and would gladly help her; she longed though for a nice little boy, I surmised. Well, then, she should not look too much at the small elephants on the plate of bronze, as she, too, would run the risk of bearing a small elephant if this advice were neglected! The good and honest woman had sufficient confidence in my wisdom, for the plate returned home! When her husband heard of it the next day, he flew into a rage, came to our house with six men, and sought high and low ... but in vain. During the night, I had ordered a servant to carry the plate to the opposite bank of the Panei River and to bury the treasure there under a heap of leaves. Invisible hands saw to it that in the course of the day, our find reached Gunung Tua safely. Today it may be admired in all its glory amongst the collection of bronzes in the Museum at Batavia.

About Bara something else remains to be related. The chamber of the temple was filled with rubbish and we were more than inquisitive to know whether anything was to be found there. We had already a number of hard days behind us and the clearing of the room in the red-hot heat of the sun in clouds of dust had acted detrimentally upon our frayed nerves and we could hardly stand. I decided therefore to discontinue the work; we were not far from the bottom now, but it was very improbable that under the thin layer of rubbish an article of any importance could come to light. Later on, in Palembang, I had my doubts about this. Had we employed our best efforts in our investigations? Was it not possible that, under the last layer of stones, there rested still fragments of an idol? In September, I arrived in Padang Lawas for the second time and I then decided to try my luck again at Bara's ancient sanctuary.

This was not so easy, as the Panei River had risen very high, and carried in its swift current so many branches and trees that to cross this river was not void of danger. The opposite bank appeared moreover to be transformed into a mudpool through which one had to wade knee-deep. But when we saw the walls of the sanctuary fresh and red in the morning-sun, bordered by low trees and shrubs, all our troubles and cares were soon forgotten and we immediately set to work, full of renewed hope. And behold, half an hour later, we had excavated an altar and in front of this was (prone) the beautiful pedestal of a statue, decorated with lotus-rosettes and spirals and provided with a robust snake's-head, through which the sacrificial water flowed away by means of the mouth. Although the artistical value of it was not trifling, still greater was its historical worth. Pedestals with snakes belong only to Sivaitic temples; Bara was also a Sivaitic sanctuary, the only one of the preponderant Buddhist Padang Lawas.

To the east of Bara, we made an equally pleasant discovery, although of quite another kind. In the literature pertaining to the antiquities of Tapanuli, the following is to be found: Pulo, remnants of a temple with fragments of statues. Naturally, we inquired time and time again after this Pulo, but nobody seemed to be able to tell us where it was situated. One day, however, a native casually mentioned that on a small hill, some stones might be found. We immediately set out to the spot indicated and, indeed, among the high grass, we came across pieces of stones, but the appearance of these did not look encouraging. What prevented us from setting fire to shrubs and bushes? Nothing whatever. And suiting the action to the word, a joyful crackle of flames soon sprang up all around us and presently, after the elapse of half an hour, revealed the outlines of a heap of stones. The clearing away of debris followed quickly; a few replicas of sunshades in stone which we found, were proof that the sanctuary was Buddhist. In the rubbish, we found decorated pieces and mouldings; the excavation did the rest.

Pulo is built on a mound supported with stones; there is no room for an enclosing wall, only on the north is a little space left. On this side are then (in departure to the rule) the stairs. In the north-west corner of the temple stands a small building of natural stone. The temple proper was formerly a threefold stupa, in the centre and on each side of which stood a tower. The excavations yielded more than 15 parasols. The decoration of these towers consisted of strings of pearls which poured forth from the mouths of ogre-heads; between these were bells, whilst now and then, soaring celestial bodies with fly-fans were discernible. In addition, around the stupas were numerous small towers.

The base was formerly decorated with eleven reliefs, of which I found five more or less complete, of one only the head and the arm, of the five others only remnants of arms and legs, which had lost all value for science. They depict the dancing figures of an elephant, a bull, a monk with skulls as ear-ornaments, a demon, and a man with raised leg. Although Buddhist in nature, they originated from Sivaitic theology, which creates the world in divine dance. If one knows how very scarce the reliefs of Padang Lawas are, one will understand how glad we were with this find.

We determined to take these panels to the Museum at Batavia, so that other people, too, could enjoy the sight of them. The great question was how we should transport the very fragile and brittle stone-ornaments. Wrapped up in clothes and in bedding, they were carried with great tenderness and care, and we transported the reliefs safely through the bush. Once we arrived in the inhabited world, they were packed in cases and forwarded by steamer to Batavia.

Every archaeologist feels a certain satisfaction when his finds have been placed in the care of a museum, but, alas, some disappointment, too, with regard to the surroundings in which they are found to have been placed.

A museum, however tastefully it may be arranged, is much like a charnel-house. The brilliancy and the romance of the original surroundings are gone; nobody knows how much fear or joy the explorer felt when he discovered his treasures. In our mind's eye arises the hill of Pulo again in the white, quivering sunlight; we again witness the great emotion of the first relief that a boy all of a sudden laid at our feet, we see again the large herd of buffaloes running with thundering hoofs along the bank of the Panei River, the heads erected and sniffing in a mysterious odour....

The Batak Magic Wand

THE stick, cut from a special kind of wood (*kayu tunggalan*), has a length of about 1.70 m. In hard wood, figures of human beings and animals are often artistically carved in a row above each other. The wand ends in an iron point, with which it is driven into the ground during ceremonies. In some places and in the priests' language, the iron is said to be made 'by people from all points of the compass of Linggapayung and coming from the four princes, 7 times forged and 7 times melted and made into a deadly iron'.

The topmost figure bears as a rule a helmet; in a little cavity of the head, the atrocious magic broth called *pupuk* was deposited, and round the head, red, white, and black threads were wound diagonally. On this tricoloured turban is stuck a plume of human hair, horse hair, or cock's feathers.

On most wands, seven figures of human beings are seen, also the figures of a snake and of a bull or ox. As one knows, the number 'seven' plays an important part in Batak religion. According to the Toba Batak, every human being possesses seven souls. The Toba origin of the *tunggal panaluan* is generally recognized by the Bataks. But although the country near the legendary mountain Pusuk Buhit is accepted as the place where the first sacred sticks came from, the magic wand is found in all the Batak provinces.

Of its origin, the following legend is told:

At Si Dogordogor Pangururan on the island of Samosir, the division between land and water had already taken place, when a certain man lived there, called Guru Hatiabulan. He was a heathen priest and was named Datu Arak di Pane. His wife was called Nan Sindak Panaluan. They had been married for a long time before this woman became pregnant.

When she was expecting at last, it took abnormally long before the child was born. Everyone in the village thought it a mysterious case. At the time, there was a famine in the country. The weather was unbearably hot and hard crusts covered pools and swamps. In consequence of this continuous drought, the Raja Bius (head of the communion of sacrifice) became very uneasy. He went to Guru Hatiabulan and said to him, 'It is advisable that we should find out and ask the just deity why drought and famine have continued for such a long time. Such a thing has never occurred.'

Guru Hatiabulan replied, 'Everything is possible.' Then said the Raja Bius, 'Everyone is astonished at your wife's long pregnancy. The midwives declare that this pregnancy has lasted too long.'

A quarrel arose about these words, but no one was wounded or killed.

Meanwhile, the wife gave birth to twins, a boy and a girl. Immediately after the children's birth, the rain came down in torrents. All the plants in the field and in the wood lived and the world looked fresh and green again.

Guru Hatiabulan had an ox killed to reconcile the evil powers. He called together all the old people and the chiefs to a feast, on which the names of the children should be made known. The boy was called Si Aji Donda Hatahutan, the girl Si Boru Tapi na Uasan.

After the festive repast, the guests advised that these children should not be brought up together. One should be taken to the West, the other to the East, for the birth of twins, especially of a different sex, is a very unfavourable thing according to old conceptions.

Guru Hatiabulan, however, did not take any notice of the wise councils of the old ones and chiefs. In the long run, however, it was proved that the wise men had been right. Guru Hatiabulan built a little hut on the sacred mountain Pusuk Buhit, where he took his children. A dog had to take care of them and every day Guru Hatiabulan brought them food.

When the children had grown up, it happened that the girl, during a walk, saw a tree called *piu piu tanggulon* or *hau tadatada*, the trunk of which was full of long thorns. This tree bore ripe, juicy fruits.

Si Boru Tapi na Uasan wished to eat the fruits and therefore climbed up the tree. She picked some of the fruit and ate them. But at the same time, she was swallowed up by the trunk and became one with it. Only her head remained visible. Her brother waited until the evening for her return and then went to the woods to investigate, where he called her name in a loud voice. In the neighbourhood of the tree, his call was answered by the girl, and when he had drawn near, she told him how she had been, as it were, swallowed up by the tree.

Si Aji Donda climbed up the tree, but he also was absorbed by the trunk and grew one with it. Both cried for help, but their pitiful voices were lost in the profound darkness.

The next morning, their dog came running along. The animal

jumped against the trunk and the dog, too, was swallowed up by the wood and only the head remained visible.

Guru Hatiabulan came as usual to bring food for his children. When he did not see them, he followed his son's footprints and at last reached the tree, where he saw only his children's heads and the head of the dog. He was overcome with grief. Guru Hatiabulan then went out to look for a wizard and found one called Datu Pormanuk Koling. The *datu* came to the tree accompanied by many people from far and near, for the event had become known everywhere. Musical instruments were fetched and the *datu* commenced his work. He mumbled prayers to dispose the spirits favourably and did whatever he could to break the charm. After having done the necessary ceremonies, he climbed into the tree. But he was also swallowed up.

Dumbfounded, Guru Hatiabulan and the spectators returned home. They did not give up hoping, however, and looked for another *datu*. A great wizard was found named Marangin Bosi, or Datu Mallantang Malliting. This person went to the tree but was absorbed, too.

Now Datu Boru Si Baso Bolon came under the tree. He also was swallowed up. The same thing happened to the *datu* Horbo Marpaung and Si Aji Bahir or Jolma So Begu, who was partly human, partly devil. A snake was also swallowed up.

Guru Hatiabulan was at his wits' end. He had spent a great deal of money on the *datu* for music and sacrifices to the spirits. Whatever was asked of him, was eagerly paid by him, but now he had lost heart.

Some days later, a *datu*, Parpansa Dinjang, announced himself. He declared with certainty that he could set the people at liberty. Guru Hatiabulan believed in the *datu* and provided him with everything he asked for. The *datu* declared that they should sacrifice to all the spirits: the spirits of the land, the spirits of water, the spirits of the wood, and all the others. After that, the people would be set at liberty.

Guru Hatiabulan prepared the sacrifices according to the *datu*'s indications. They then went to the tree with all the village people, and after the *datu* had made use of his witchcraft, he cut down the tree. When the tree fell, all the heads had suddenly disappeared, also the heads of the dog and the serpent. Everyone was dumbfounded, but the *datu* told Guru Hatiabulan to cut the tree to pieces and to carve in wood the images of the people who had disappeared. Thus it was done. He cut the trunk into pieces and carved in a stick the images of five men, two children, a dog, and a serpent.

After these nine images had thus been obtained, everyone returned to the village. When they had arrived there, the gong was struck, while an ox was killed in honour of those that were represented by the images. The stick was placed against the front of a rice-shed, after which Guru Hatiabulan danced. After that, *datu* Parpansa Dinjang executed an ecstatic dance; in this way, he made the spirits of those swallowed up, enter into him. After these spirits had taken possession of him, they began to speak. They were the spirits of:

1 Si Aji Donda Hatahutan;
2 Si Boru Tapi na Uasan;
3 Datu Pulo Punjung na Uli, Si Parjambulan Si Melbuselbus;
4 Guru Manggantar Porang;
5 Si Sanggar Maolaol;
6 Dari Mangambat, Si Upar Mangelele;
7 Barita Songkar Pangururan.

They said, 'Say, Father Sculptor, Thou hast carved our images and we have eyes, but cannot see, we have mouths, but cannot speak, we have ears, but cannot hear, we have hands, but cannot grasp. We curse Thee, Sculptor.'

The *datu* answered (from the same mouth), 'Don't curse me, but this knife, for without it I could not have cut your image.'

The knife replied, 'Do not curse me but the smith, for if he had not forged me, I should never have become a knife.'

The smith said, 'Do not curse me, but the bellows, for without their blowing, I could not have forged anything.'

The bellows said, 'Do not curse us, but Guru Hatiabulan, for if he had not commanded us to act as we did, we should never have done this work.'

When it concerned Guru Hatiabulan, the spirit spoke again from the wizard's mouth, 'I curse thee, Father, and also thee, Mother, who has given birth to me.'

When Guru Hatiabulan heard this, he replied, 'Do not curse me but curse yourselves. You that have fallen into the pit, you, killed by a lance, and you not possessing any descendants.'

Thereupon the spirit said, 'When it must be thus, Father, use me henceforth as:

1 Rain-conjurer in the wet season;
2 Rain-maker in the dry season;
3 Counsellor in the governing of the country;

4 Fellow combatant in the war;

5 Causer of corruption in sickness and death and, at the same time, the power to track down a thief or robber.'

After this, the ceremony was over and everyone went on his way.

Here follows another legend:

Long ago, there lived a *raja*, and one afternoon, after a night in the full of the moon (*tula*), twins were born to him—a son and a daughter, who grew up together.

When the royal children were about six years old, it was observed that their relation was much too intimate, but though everyone disapproved, the *raja*'s son paid not the slightest attention to public opinion and continued to treat his sister in a way not allowed according to the *adat*, i.e. as a lover.

The son was called Si Tapi Raja Na Uasan (one suffering from thirst, from *uas*—thirst) and the daughter, Si Tapi Donda Hatahutan (the silent, timid); *donda*, a Sanskrit word meaning 'staff' is considered by the Bataks to mean 'silent', at the same time 'compelling respect'. *Tahut*—fear, anxiety.

Both children were very beautiful in face and body.

When they were ten years old, Si Tapi Raja Na Uasan raped his sister out in the fields (*ladang*). Si Tapi Donda Hatahutan complained to her parents of her brother's behaviour, but as the parents loved their children very much, they did not punish them according to the *adat* decree, i.e. hanging both sinners until death followed.

Quietly, the lovers were separated, by absenting the brother for a short time and bringing Si Tapi Donda Hasautan to a kampong situated about two days' journey east from her own village, where a maternal uncle (*tulang*) was to take charge of her. (Note that the name is now Si Tapi Donda Hasautan, *saut* meaning 'accomplished, happened', i.e. the carnal union had taken place.)

When Si Tapi Raja Na Uasan failed to find his sister upon his return, he was inconsolable. The parents declared that she was dead and buried. In reality, they had buried a banana trunk, representing a human body, a substitute image or *porsili*, and they showed him the grave.

Si Tapi Raja Na Uasan, mad with grief, went to the grave in the full of the moon, to exhume his sister. Great was his astonishment when he dug up the *porsili* (Malay *silih*—recompense, reparation, substitution; Sim. Bat. *parsilihi*) and his surprise turned into joy when he realized that his beloved sister must be alive. To find out where she was, he secretly made inquiries among the *raja*'s courtiers, and thus he learned that his sister was kept hidden somewhere in a kampong east of his father's domain.

At once, he journeyed eastward, and in a certain village, he saw his sister pounding rice. He embraced her ardently and at once eloped with her, with the intention of bringing her back to his own kampong. The rice which she had been pounding, they took along as provisions.

When the absence of Si Tapi Raja Na Uasan and Si Tapi Donda Hasautan was noticed, a search party was sent out from both kampongs to look for the royal children.

In the meantime, after walking for a day and a half, the small supply of rice was exhausted and the two began to look for a fruit tree, so that they might appease their hunger with its fruit. At last they found a *tanggulon* tree and Si Tapi Raja Na Uasan climbed into it in order to pluck its sweet fruit. He threw some fruit to his sister and then told her to climb into the tree so that they might eat their meal together.

But when brother and sister tried to descend from the tree, they found they could not move. Unconsciously, they had become petrified and now remained, as it were, glued to the tree trunk.

A monkey, which came to eat of the *tanggulon* fruit, also stiffened and could not get away. A snake, Mihim-Mihim(an) (i.e. the enemy, the hypocritical betrayer), which crept into the tree, also remained there and changed into wood.

After a month's search, the uncle and his attendants found the lost children in the *tanggulon* tree and ordered them to come down, but they were unable to obey him. The uncle, thinking this was the work of evil spirits, summoned experienced *datu* or *guru* (magicians, necromancers) to free his niece and nephew from the enchantment. All in vain—it seemed as if they had grown into the tree for ever. But as various magicians had used their supernatural powers to free the *raja*'s son and daughter and the most powerful spells were in vain, they finally decided to build a simple inn near the *tanggulon* tree so they could spend the night near the two whom fate had treated so cruelly. They also decided to do everything in their power to free the unhappy victims, even if they had to summon the most powerful necromancers from foreign countries.

A certain Si Baso Bolon (wise woman or midwife) climbed into the tree, above the place where Si Tapi Raja Na Uasan was petrified. She shook the tree in order to free brother and sister, but to no purpose; Si Baso Bolon also grew into the trunk.

Then they brought the famous *guru*, Pangpang Abuanna (the crippled or chilly; *pangpang*—paralysed), a wise man, whose right leg was crooked. He was carried to the 'Harangan Rimbu Raja' or jungle, where Si Tapi Raja Na Uasan and his sister had been changed into wooden images in the *tanggulon* tree. This *guru*, Pangpang Abuanna, assured the family that his powerful magic could free the royal children and all the rest from the tree.

But in order to cast his spell, he, too, was compelled to climb into the tree, and since his crippled leg made this impossible, he was assisted. He encircled the tree with his arms and tried to ascend, but lo and behold, even the great magician turned cold and stiff and remained stuck in the tree.

As a last resort, a great buffalo was tied to the tree in order to pull it down. The name of the animal was Horbo Payung (the Guardian Buffalo). But even this was in vain; the buffalo turned at once into wood and became a part of the tree trunk.

Then it was decided to fell the tree with a sort of axe (*tangkei*), but though hundreds of axes were used, one after the other broke into pieces as soon as it came into contact with the trunk.

Then a great fire was kindled at the foot of the tree, to burn it down, but the wood refused to catch flame.

From Nagori Mandailing they summoned Guru So Halompoan Datu So Haginjangan (the unsurpassable, invincible magician) to use his power in order to free those who were imprisoned in the tree. This *guru* was a Muslim, who arrived after about two weeks. As a reward for his efforts, he demanded seven buffaloes, seven cows, and a *tumba* (2 L.) of gold. All this was promised to him; the famous magician did his utmost to cast a spell over the tree, but all his wisdom and all his supernatural powers were in vain. Guru So Halompoan Datu So Haginjangan wept bitterly in shame and humiliation. At last he began to implore Allah, and as he prayed, he received the heavenly message not to attack the tree with an axe but to cut it down with a *sambilu* (sharp sliver of bamboo, used to sever the navel string of a newborn child). The *guru* did as he was told, with the result that, at last, the tree was felled.

For two and a half months, the *raja*'s people had been mourning the loss of the royal children, so now it was decided to bring the tree trunk to their parents' house. For two days, they carried the trunk with the people and animals shrivelled into wood. Through the forest they went, until one morning, they arrived at the kampong, just as the cocks were beginning to crow.

They crowed at the top of their voices that Si Tapi Raja na Uasan and Si Tapi Donda Hasautan were arriving. The *raja*'s wife (*puang bolon*), who had heard the commotion, promised that if the report were true, all the poultry would be killed for a great feast.

'Bu-uh,' mooed the cow, and so affirmed what the cock had just told. When the *ranee* heard this, she hastened to the *raja*'s apartments and told him the glad tidings. In his joy, he announced that if the news were true, all the cattle should be slaughtered and a magnificent feast given.

About eight o'clock in the morning, the tree trunk arrived at the village, where all the inhabitants and all the animals were in a fever of excitement.

When the tree trunk, with its burden of wooden images, was carried into the village, the people wept, and the parents covered their children's faces with kisses, for strangely enough, the faces had not become stiff. But since no power in the world could free the royal children from the wood nor restore them to normal life, the *raja* decided to promote the tree to the rank of staff (*tungkot*) and to keep it as a sacred relic (*pusaka*).

The staff with the living heads was kept in an alcove above the roof of the *rumah bolon*, *pantangan* (pronounced *pattangan*) and was given the name *tunggal panaluan* (*tunggal*—masculine; *panaluan* derived from *talu*—defeated).

A year after these dramatic events had taken place, a fire broke out in the *raja*'s kampong, but the *rumah bolon*, where the *tunggal panaluan* was kept, was spared. The village was rebuilt around the house of the village chief.

Still a year later, war broke out with a neighbouring kingdom. Two days before this event, the *tunggal panaluan* announced the enemy's coming, and in consequence, the villagers were on their guard and able to take necessary measures for defence. Nevertheless, the battle was lost and only the *rumah bolon* was found to be impregnable.

A courtier by the name Si Barowei kept watch in front of the *rumah bolon*. When the enemy was about to attack the house, the *raja*, the *puang bolon*, and all the inhabitants were filled with fear. Si Barowei alone was filled with courage and took his stand in front of the *rumah bolon*. The *tunggal panaluan* whispered to Si Barowei that he must grasp the magic staff and so attack the enemy without fear.

With the staff in his hand, Si Barowei performed a war-dance in front of the *rumah bolon*, singing a war-song all the while. A band of warriors in multicoloured panoply advanced to attack him, but he held the staff before them, whereupon they retreated and so Si Barowei defeated the entire force of the enemy.

When the country was threatened by an epidemic, the *tunggal panaluan* warned the people in advance and prescribed what measures must be taken. The *guru huta* (village priest or necromancer) performed a dance with the staff in his hand, and the sickness was averted.

Gradually, the staff's protective power became known far and wide, so that henceforth all manner of people came to seek the *guru huta*, named Rambang Sihala, and to beg his help and advice. Even *guru* from distant countries were instructed by him. Guru Rambang Sihala sold copies of the *tunggal panaluan* for the sum of *f* 24.—and that is why the Batak Lands have such a large number of magic staffs today.

Before performing a dance with the *tunggal panaluan*, it is customary to bring sacrifices to the magic staff, and all the various images are fed with the special food designated for them.

In some places, the *tunggal panaluan* is kept in a special house, 3 × 3 m, situated next to or in front of the *rumah bolon*. This house also bears the name 'pantangan'.

Long ago there lived a *raja*, and one afternoon, following a night in the full moon (*tula*), his wife brought forth twins. The children were a son and a daughter (*marporhas tubu*). As afterbirth she produced a lifeless lump of flesh, in the form of a cucumber, with only two apertures, the mouth and the anus. It also had the male organ.

The dead child was buried under the *pamispisan* (the stroke of ground where the rain drips from the roof), a custom observed by the pagan Bataks even to the present day. And, as the third child must have been a boy, it was called Si Tunggal Panaluan (*tunggal*—masculine, little man; *panaluan*—the third, thirdly).

The two royal children grew up together. They ate and slept together and wore the same clothing. At every meal they demanded enormous quantities of meat, and if their wish was not gratified, they became enraged and could not be pacified. Both were very beautiful and always they romped and played together. The son was called Si Tapi Raja Na Uasan (this name seems to signify 'lustful' and 'insatiable') and the daughter, Si Tapi Donda Hatahutan (the timid).

This playful intercourse between two almost full-grown children was strongly censured by the people, as being in conflict with their *adat* (customs). Intimate relations between brother and sister are called in Batak '*mardaon begu*'. The parents, too, disapproved of their children's conduct, as it diminished their own prestige.

As the children always demanded quantities of meat with their meals, they were a great expense to their parents. The latter therefore decided to have the son, Si Tapi Raja Na Uasan, brought to his maternal uncle (*tulang*), so that the children might be separated, in the hope that in the course of time they might forget each other. The uncle lived on the opposite shore of the sea.

Separated by the deep water, the royal children wept night and day and pined away. The parents therefore allowed Si Tapi Raja Na Uasan to return home, and day by day the relation between brother and sister became more intimate, so that all the people were filled with loathing for them.

One beautiful moonlight night, the two royal children fled from their parents' home and ran into the woods.

When the *raja* saw that they were gone, he searched everywhere but could not find them. Various *guru* of the land were consulted and these declared that brother and sister must remain in the forest. The *guru* were then sent out to look for the children, promising to return within seven days, whether their search was successful or not.

And so the following *guru* were sent forth, one after the other, to look for the royal children, but they failed to return within the specified time:

1 Guru Datu So (ha) Ginjangon (the unsurpassable, incomparable magician. '*Guru datu*' is a pleonasm);
2 Guru Pangpang Abuanna (the crippled, chilly);
3 Si Baso Bolon (the great midwife);
4 Jolma So Begu (half human, half evil spirit);
5 Datu Salah Maruhum (the unrighteous, the bribed, he who does not obey the *adat*, the wilful, perhaps this name means 'the destroyer').

The buffalo, Horbo Payung, and the snake, Ulok Mihim-Mihim, who spoke the human language, were also persuaded to look for Si Tapi Raja Na Uasan and his sister, but these, too, failed to return.

Then envoys were sent to look for mighty magicians from other countries and they were found in Nagori Langgam Sisi

(*sisi*—edge; thus at the end of the world, Ultima Thule, hence very far away). They were Guru Tantan Debata (*tantan Debata*—descending god) and Guru Aji Musa (*aji*—secret magic, producing fear). After the envoys had told these two *guru* what had happened, the latter solemnly promised that they would find the royal children and restore them to their parents. *Setangan baju* of money (enough to fill a coat sleeve—*f* 120.) was to be the reward.

The *guru* arrived in the land of the raja and at once set out on their search. Before long, they returned with the tiding that Si Tapi Raja Na Uasan, Si Tapi Donda Hasautan and the various *guru* were imprisoned in the *tanggulon* tree in the forest and unable to free themselves. The royal children did not wish to return to life because they had sinned so terribly against the *adat*. The various *guru* who had been turned into wood, declared that they, too, did not wish to be freed but chose rather to remain with the children. However, they consented to be brought back to the village, on condition that they might be regarded as a sacred relic (*kramat*) and named after the third, stillborn child, Si Tunggal Panaluan.

This message was at once brought to the *raja*, who accepted the conditions, since he wanted the children again at any price. In the wooden figures, the souls were still alive.

Guru Tantan Debata and Guru Aji Musa then accompanied the *raja* and all his people to the forest to bring Si Tapi Raja Na Uasan and his companions.

In the presence of the whole assembly, Guru Tantan Debata asked exactly what foods must be given to each separate individual, upon which the following list was specified:

I Si Tapi Raja Na Uasan;

    1 *daroh matah* (fresh blood),
    2 *bagod* (palm wine).

II Si Tapi Donda Hasautan;

    1 *boras pinahpah* (young rice, pounded),
    2 *bagod.*

III Guru Datu So (ha) Ginjangon;

    1 *daging sipitu dai* (meat prepared in seven ways),
     a) na malum,
     b) nilabar,

  c) niangu—angurhon,
  d) sinalenggam,
  e) tasak tiga,
  f) pinanggang,
  g) nilompah,
 2 *bagod.*

IV Guru Pangpang Abuanna;

 1 *ihan tinutung* (roast fish),
 2 *garam* (salt),
 3 *pege* (ginger),
 4 *bunga-bunga santungkul* (*kembang sepatu* or *bunga raja*,
  Hibiscus rosa sinensis),
 5 *bagod.*

V Si Baso Bolon;

 1 *bogar-bogar*, consisting of:
  a) gaol na masak (boiled bananas),
  b) dali na masak (boiled corn),
  c) suhat na masak (boiled *keladi*),
  d) tobu (sugar-cane),
 2 *bagod.*

VI Jolma So Begu;

 1 a portion of what the others received,
 2 *bagod.*

VII Si Horbo Payung;

 1 *saput ni pangulubalang;*
  a) bulung ni birah (leaves of a *keladi* variety),
  b) bulung ni langge (a sort of *keladi*),
  c) bulung ni suhat (a sort of *keladi*),
  d) bulung ni latong (a sort of nettle),
  e) bulung ni ampuspus (a creeper resembling *keladi*),
 2 *bagod.*

VIII Ulok Mihim-Mihim(an);

 1 *tohuk* (a sort of frog),
 2 *bagod.*

IX Datu Salah Maruhum;

1 *tinaruh manuk na masak* (a boiled chicken egg),
2 *garam* (salt),
3 *bunga-bunga* (hibiscus),
4 *bagod*.

A raw chicken egg serves to anoint the whole staff. The horn of the Horbo Sinanggalatu (triumphant buffalo) is used as a beaker (wonder horn—*sahan*). Besides this horn, a bag or sack is the usual attribute of the *datu*.

Now Guru Tantan Debata cut down the tree with his knife, *piso solam dibata, iumpat dimejer hilap, itombomhon dumugur tano*, i.e. 'when the knife is drawn from its sheath the lightning flashes, and when it is stuck into the ground the earth trembles'.

Before the tree was felled, Guru Tantan Debata held a long speech, asking the figures how they wished to be treated. During this talk, he strewed yellow rice (*boras binorna*) and manipulated a bunch of three kinds of flowers (*rudang ragi-ragian*). The ceremony is repeated even at the present time by every *datu* who carries the *Tunggal Panaluan*.

The trunk and its collection of images was carried to the *raja*'s house and left in the eaves of the *rumah bolon*.

We will say something about the use of the magic wand (*tunggal panaluan*).

The conjuration of rain. Sometimes it is necessary that the rain shall be conjured, e.g. on the occasion of a feast, during the cultivation of the soil, for a journey, and such-like events. If rain has to be conjured by means of the magic wand, the *tunggal* should be wrapped up in a white cloth. Round the top of the stick, a sweet smelling plant (*banebane*) should be wound, the figures of the staff should be rubbed with the yolk and white of a fowl's egg and certain biscuits (*itak sigurguron*) should be offered to eat. While biscuit is offered to the wand, the *tunggal* is addressed as 'Si Boru Tapi na Uasan'.

Rain shall not fall before the feast is over, the agricultural work shall be finished, the journey made, etc. During this action, no formulae need be said. At the end, the wand must be held upside down, 'the legs against the rain', by which the rain will take to flight.

Rainmaking. The *tunggal* gets a bush of red flowers. The staff is wrapped from top to bottom in strips of red material. Salt, ginger, and fish are given to the wand and it is addressed as 'Si Aji Donda Hatahutan'. Then it is plunged into water from the sacred spring, dwelling place of honoured spirits and in which a special kind of cut stone is laid, which is used for causing disease and is called Sanggapati na Bolon. When the *tunggal* is moistened in this way, it is going to rain.

Consultation in matters of governing. When a *raja* wants to talk over matters of great importance and things of great weight relating to the governing of the country, he must sacrifice first to the magic wand. The sacrifice shall consist of a special kind of *pisang*, the bunches of fruit grown upside down (*pisang sungsang duri* and *nangka*). The staff is addressed as 'Sangkar Pangururan'. The *raja* goes to his meeting, leaning on the wand. The meeting will then be a peaceful one.

In the same way, the *tunggal* is used as support when a proposal of marriage to a girl is made. A sacrifice of *sirih* is made. The staff is decorated with a string of beads and wrapped in a special kind of texture (*abit ragidup*) while on the eyes of the images, the fiery-red pips of the *pandia* shrub are stuck. In this case, the staff is called 'Si Sanggar Meoleol' (waving reed).

Ceremony on waging war. Before going to battle, sacrifices are made to the wand consisting of fresh palm wine, fish, salt, ginger, and roasted meat. The staff is afterwards entirely wrapped in red, white, and black strips of material and it is addressed as Guru Mangantar Porang. During the battle, the commander holds the *tunggal*, leans on it, and holds it in front of the attacking enemy to cause fright.

The causing of diseases and death. For this ceremony, the wand can only be used together with the Si Biaksa. The Si Biaksa is obtained in the following way.

An enemy taken prisoner in war is killed, cut to pieces, roasted in iron pots, adding several herbs. The substance obtained in this way, is kept in bottles, pots and stone barrels (*guriguri*) and a great magical effect is ascribed to it.

Sacrifices are regularly made to the Si Biaksa, and in bringing sickness and destruction, the causing of bad luck in general, the assistance of the Si Biaksa cannot be done without. However, the Si Biaksa, which is supposed to contain the soul of the dead, also brings good luck to its owner and wards off ominous powers, being bound to the owner's will, submitted to his power and altogether subservient to him.

The following sacrifice is made: a dog with spots like a tiger, a red cock whose spurs have just come, seven roasted little fishes, seven little red flowers, seven biscuits, a fish pasty, a roasted fowl, a bottle of palm wine, a calabash, a cucumber, a stalk of sugar-cane, and a ripe *pisang*. All these things are sacrificed, that is to say offered as food to the *tunggal* and the Si Biaksa.

While this sacrifice is brought, the ill-omened wishes are uttered. If, for example, one wishes an enemy's sickness or death, the *tunggal* is addressed as 'Si Dari Mangambat, Si Upar Mangalele', the little poisonous serpent that averts, the poisonous serpent that pursues. These words are spoken: 'Say, my Father in Heaven, Si Dari Mangambat, Si Upar Mangalele, cause . . . to be destroyed.'

To cause a thief to be ill or to make him die in connection with a track he has left behind. It is not necessary to sacrifice for this; the possession of the wand is sufficient, but the co-operation of the Si Biaksa is necessary. When the track of a thief has been dis-covered, some earth of the track is taken which is wrapped in the leaf of the *lanting* plant. This packet is brought home and put in the Si Biaksa pot, uttering the wish that the thief may fall ill or die.

Bindu matoga.

Mandudu. The word '*mandudu*' means the warding off of bad omen and the obtaining of happiness and bliss, everything according to the wizard's regulations.

If anyone wants to raise these secret powers, several preparations will have to be made. First, the magic figure is drawn on the ground in yellow, white, and black flour close to the entrance of the house, where the *mandudu* is to be held by the wizard. This magic figure is shown in the equilateral drawing on p. 98 called *Bindu matoga*.[1] The sides are in this case 1 m long.

In the centre of the drawing is put an axe and a fowl's egg. Point 5 is directed to the East (Habinsaran). The line joining the points 5, 6, and 7 must be parallel to the front of the dwelling of the man, where the *mandudu* is to take place. An elevation or altar (*langgatan*) is erected near to point 1. To the altar is tied a red dog, a cock, a spade, a rake, a plough, a yoke, a comb, and weaving tools. On a *pisang* leaf on the altar, the following dishes are arranged by the *datu*: rice; fowl's eggs; sugar-cane; roasted padi; kneaded biscuits; cakes; cucumber; roasted fish; boiled fish; fresh palm wine; two cocks; a red one and a white one, boiled in blood and cut into small pieces; *jeruk* juice; and a basket of *padi* on which a fragrant plant (*banebane*) is scattered.

When all these ingredients have been exhibited, they begin to play the musical instruments. The *datu* rubs the staff with a raw egg and pushes it before point 1 into the ground. Beforehand, the white, black, and yellow flour with which the *bindu matoga* was made, is kept in readiness.

---

[1] In my opinion, the *bindu matoga* is derived from the Hindu *mandala*, a very old figure, which in turn originated from religious tokens in sand like those to be found in Australia and among the Pueblo Indians in North America.

The Batak magic wand may be akin to the Bengal vrsakastha, the bull-shaft, a wand for departed souls, carved with human faces, animals, flowers, etc. This wand is implanted at a consecrated place; there are some reasons to suppose that formerly this custom existed among the Bataks, too, and that their magic wands stood for the houses of the chiefs like the totem-poles of the Indians in North-west America.

I believe that the *tunggal panaluan* was originally a symbol of the demon of initiation, who swallowed up the initiates; at the same time, it was the mystic body of the totemistic forefather, with whom his descendants must remain in touch.

In the Ethnographical Museum in Hamburg is a *tunggal* with the head of a hornbill; such wands are already depicted on the bronze drums of Dongson.

The *tunggal panaluan* is the pendant of the Australian *nurtunja* and *waninga*, totemistic poles with feathers and human hair; at the initiation, the young men must embrace them.—F. M. S.

This black, white, and yellow flour is put in a basket and holding this basket, the *datu* begins to perform a dance, using the so-called *pangaraksaon* or giant's tongue or secret language.

He invokes the highest deity, the tutelary spirit of the soil and the crops (*boraspati ni tano*), the serpents of the holy places (*naganaga sombaon*), the female waterspirit *Saniang Naga*; then he calls upon the lightning of the eight points of the compass and slowly walks around the *bindu matoga*.

Then the *datu* takes the magic wand and takes his stand on the seventh point. He begins to hum and to sing. He pretends to give birth to the wand, to feed it with rice finely chewed by himself, he carries it on his back and in his lap, and he caresses it as a mother her baby. The chants sung on these occasions by the *datu*'s differ. Everyone improvises chants, as well as he is able to, with the intention that happiness should be obtained, bad luck warded off.

Then the *datu* shoves a piece of reed (*arung*) across his fingers. Thereupon he cuts off the head of the dog at one stroke, after which he bites an ear from its head and offers it to all the figures of the *tunggal*. Then he kills the red cock, the head of which he likewise offers to the wand: He pretends to feed the *tunggal* with all the dishes on the altar.

After the sacrifice, the *datu* drags the dog and the cock over the lines on the ground, until the *bindu matoga* is quite wiped off. Then the dog and the cock are given to the host.

Finally the *datu* drags the scaffolding with all the things on it to the entrance of the village.

The host may take back from there everything he wishes for himself.

The same *bindu matoga* figure may be used for causing ill luck to an adversary.

This black magic is only used at night, towards midnight. All sorts of similar rites take place, stated invocations are made likewise and mysterious formulae pronounced. These magic actions are called *manurungi*.

Samosir

THE Island of Samosir lies in the Toba Lake, in North Sumatra. The west and south ascend gradually into a hill district, then changes suddenly into a high plateau, which rises on the east side to a height of 1 600 m, sloping abruptly into the Toba Lake. In the centre is a wide, barren highland. The region is strangely fantastic—pierced by straight-walled, narrow gorges. Here flow numerous rivers, of which the largest springs from the western cliff. There are no actual mountain peaks. The island has no forest, with the result that in the rainy season, the little rivers change within a few hours into mighty floods, which are very destructive.

In the dark ages, volcanoes belched forth their molten lava over Samosir. On all sides are colossal masses of cliff and boulders, scattered over hills and dales as by a giant's hand. From this material the inhabitants of the island have wrought beautiful things—high stone ramparts with round and square corner towers and bastions, planted with dense thickets of thorn bamboo, so that no enemy might venture to force their way into the little villages. Only two sides have small gates, which are closed at night by a complicated sort of gate. Then the 'huta' sleeps in solitude, like some ancient town in Medieval Europe. Everywhere are scattered the picturesque, forlorn ruins of these old forts, often high and inaccessible on the cliffs, darkly outlined against the clear, starry sky. Forsaken eagles' nests, deeply tragic, consisting sometimes merely of a high, round tower.

These artistic, beautifully constructed walls are the first objects to attract the attention of the scientific explorer, whose wanderings begin on this remarkable island. Nowhere in the East Indian Archipelago have structures in stone been wrought with so much artistic beauty and architectural skill.

The village green is divided into two halves; on one side are the houses, on the other the rice granaries, both constructed on separate stone terraces. In front of the houses are rice troughs of stone, neatly hewn, sometimes beautifully ornamented, so that they are veritable works of art.

It is worthy of note that these rice-blocks are set on a base of four or five other stones and thus form a sort of dolmen. Sometimes, next to the rice-block, a flat stone lies on a number of boulders, forming a real dolmen. Similar slabs are found at Limbong, on the south slope of the volcano Pusuk Buhit. They are placed in a circle and serve as seats for the heathen village chiefs (*parbaringin*). It is of course impossible to determine whether these seats are the remains of a prehistoric culture, but even if this is not the case, they are none the less remarkable. For they reveal the fact that those who made these monuments were inspired by an age-old thought. Indeed, the entire Batak art of plastic stone is permeated with an ancient tradition.

Interesting is a dolmen in Limbong, which serves as receptacle for the head and hoofs of a buffalo, slaughtered every year at the beginning of the rice planting. The blood of this sacrifice is supposed to encourage the growth of the crop. We see here the same relation between buffalo, megalith and rice as in all the stone cults of South-East Asia.

The people of Limbong no longer know how old these monuments are. Since Bataks usually know precisely how many generations ago a monument was founded (at least ten generations or about 500 years), there can be no doubt that these memorials are the most ancient in the Batak Lands. I estimate them to be about 1,000 years old, but it is quite possible that they are even older, going back to the beginning of our era. Perhaps they were even constructed by the Batak's ancestors who, according to a generally accepted tradition, were settled in Limbong.

Samosir lies in the midst of the Batak country. The principal Batak tribes live around the lake—on the south shore the Tobas, on the east the Timurs, on the north the Karos, and on the west the Pakpaks. All these regard Samosir as their homeland, and it may therefore be surmised that this island contains all sorts of ancient relics, of the greatest interest to the study of the Bataks.

The climate is agreeable, probably due to the vast expanse of water which slowly absorbs and then radiates the heat. The humidity is slight. No wonder the oldest Batak tribes settled in this region.

Their chief means of subsistence are agriculture, cattle raising, and fishing. The chief farming product is rice, which is planted on dry as well as on irrigated fields. During recent years, large crops of onions and other vegetables have been planted, which thrive very well, forming an important source of income.

Most of the cattle belong to the native chiefs, since the common people cannot pay for them.

Many of the natives earn their living by fishing. Everywhere in the village near the lake, nets are made, both for own use and for sale. Weaving is also an important industry and is a favourite occupation for women and girls. Formerly the people spun their own yarn. Woven stuffs are traded in all the markets. The making of pottery is also important.

The chief districts (*marga*) are Sumba and Lontung, respectively in the north and in the south. The *marga* is a geneaological unit and owns the ground. Formerly there were three castes—the *raja*, consisting of the village founder and his descendants in the male line; the *ripe*, consisting of free and prominent citizens (*boru na bolon*), the latter of whom were married to the *raja*'s daughters and could in turn become *raja*, in case they founded a new village, while this was not possible for the ordinary *ripe*; and the *hatoban* or slave caste.

Very interesting, also, was the information collected concerning a jointed doll, which is made to dance at the feast of the dead. At Samosir and on the south shore of the Toba Lake, the name '*si galegale*' is used for an almost life-size wooden doll with jointed limbs. It is mounted on a long chest with wheels. In front of her is a little doll, with folded hands, which are raised in salute when the large doll dances. The construction of this figure takes about four months.

When a child dies or some important *raja* dies childless, a headless doll is made, on which is placed the skull of the deceased. The face is stained yellow with the yolk of an egg and in the eye sockets are placed scarlet fruits or eyes of metal. In case the skull is broken, a wooden head is made. The dead man's soul now descends into the doll, who is led by an explicator, his head wound in a turban. The bystanders now also begin to dance and to present the doll with money, *sirih* and cigarettes, all of which the '*tukang mejan*' puts into his pocket.

The dancing is intended to placate the spirit of the departed. An old woman sings of his virtues. The doll rides about on the chest, embracing friends and relatives. The eyelids are movable, and since there is a moist sponge in the head, the image can even weep. The dancing of this doll in the moonlight is an imposing spectacle, making an indelible impression on all observers. The figure is dressed in costly garments and wears a horsehair wig, also a beautiful head kerchief and brass ear-rings. The skull of either a man or a woman may be set on the body, on which may be vaguely discerned the curves of a woman's breasts.

Formerly there were even dolls with heads on which was nailed a human skin; these dolls could move their eye-balls and put out their tongue.

Here is the legend of Si Galegale's origin:

Once upon a time, there was a man named Datu Panggana (Sculptor), who went into the forest. There he saw a tree, tall as a man and without leaves or branches. 'If one made an image of that tree it would be something precious,' he thought. And so it happened that he carved the tree into the form of a woman.

Now it chanced that Bao Partiga-tiga, a dealer in garments, beads and golden ornaments, also came that way. He saw the image and it occurred to him that he might dress and adorn it. He therefore put some garments on it, put rings in its ears and then saw that it was very beautiful; so fair, indeed, that he could hardly tear himself away.

When evening came and he wished to return to the village, he tried to remove the garments and the jewels, but he could not; they were attached to the image. He wept over his loss, but was finally compelled to leave his property behind.

Next there came Datu Partaoar (the Healer), who had a medicine which would prolong life, raise the dead, and even recall the spirits of bodies which had already gone into dissolution. When he saw the image, he was much amazed at its beauty, and he therefore conceived the idea of using his magic potion on it. He did so; the image came to life and became a human being, whom he brought back to the village.

The wife of Datu Partaoar received her with joy and adopted her as her own daughter. She called her Nai Manggale.

When market day came, they brought Nai Manggale in solemn procession to the market-place, playing the drums meanwhile to announce to one and all that they had adopted her as their daughter. Nai Manggale danced in the market-place and all who saw her swayed in rhythm with her beautiful cadence.

When the market people had returned home, the news of what had happened reached the Sculptor and the Trader. They went to the Healer and each of them laid claim to Nai Manggale.

'She is my daughter, for I carved her image,' said the Sculptor.

'She is my daughter, for I clothed her and gave her jewels,' said the trader.

'She is my daughter, for I called her to life,' said the Healer.

As they could not come to any agreement, they began to shout at each other. The Healer fought against the other two. But as each had a just claim, no one was victorious and no one lost. Even the *raja* could see no way of settling the dispute.

At last the problem was submitted to a man named Si Aji Bahir-Bahir, the Half Man. He was asked to solve it and proposed the following: The Healer should be considered as her father and should have the right to give her hand in marriage. The trader should be her brother and as such would receive a share of the dowry. The Sculptor should be her maternal uncle and would receive an uncle's share. The *raja* and all the parties concerned agreed to this agreement.

A certain Datu Partiktik, who lived to the south-west, asked for the hand of Nai Manggale, but she would have nothing to do with him because he was not as fair as she. Then he put a magic spell upon her, so that she finally consented to marry him.

But though they were married for a long time, they had no children, and at last Nai Manggale became ill and died.

During her illness she had told her husband that he must have Datu Panggana make a life-size image of her, to call it Si Galegale, and to have a dirge played before it. If this were not done, the spirit of Nai Manggale would not be admitted to the abode of the dead. She would find no rest and would therefore be compelled to curse Datu Partiktik, so that he would have no sons and daughters. Datu Partiktik did as his wife told him.

For this reason, a *si galegale* is always made for one who has died childless, so that the spirit of the dead may have no harmful influence. This dancing ceremony is called *papurpur sepata*, the dispersing of a curse.

It is difficult to form a clear and complete idea of the position occupied by the *si galegale* in the Batak community. It was probably brought to Samosir by megalith builders. It is known that formerly it danced by the great stone sarcophagus; indeed that several dolls with the skulls of ancestors were made to perform around the coffin. We are concerned here with a scientific problem of unusual interest.

In an aesthetic sense, also, Si Galegale has a place of honour. No one who has seen her dancing and weeping in the green mists of Samosir, in a night filled with stars and silence, will ever forget her. Thoughts of love and immortality surrounded her. The spirits of the dead are safe in her keeping, raised above every delusion.

I have previously mentioned the stone sarcophagus. The existence of these monuments has been known for many years, but no one has ever taken the trouble to study them. The task of our expedition was to carefully study and photograph all stone coffins. In this way, we were able to bring to light a megalith cult hitherto almost entirely unknown, with numerous interesting ceremonies and feasts.

On the fore side, these coffins have a great monster head. They all lie on the coast, their faces turned landward. As a rule, the figure of a man crouches under the monster head, on the opposite side is the figure of a woman; occasionally these figures change places. The woman's head is nearly always made of a stone differing from that of the coffin. Sometimes she carries a small bowl for holy water. In her hands she holds a mortar. The monster head has large, round eyes and three horns curved backwards. On the neck is a row of pointed, upstanding bristles. The middle horn frequently had a long, oblique, curved point with an ornament. In two cases this consisted of a buffalo's head. This was an ancient head-dress of the Batak chiefs and is still found quite often in a different form in the images of Nias.

The coffins stand either in the village or outside, sometimes on a foundation of stones, sometimes merely resting on the earth. In the latter case, the greater part of the coffin is sunk into the ground. They are painted with floral motifs; the usual colours being red, white, and blackish-blue.

These coffins serve as a resting place for the skulls of the dead. The heads are first buried in the ground. A year later, they are dug up and, with festive ceremonies, are placed in the coffin. The cover consists of several pieces, which can be lifted without difficulty.

Whenever a *raja* wishes to have a coffin made, he summons a sculptor. The latter needs at least ten helpers and delivers the coffin in about two months. When the work is begun, a buffalo is slaughtered and the sculptor offers a prayer. His tools are a hammer and chisel, a crowbar and an axe. Far away in the mountains, a suitable stone is chosen. It is hacked roughly into shape and placed on a wooden sledge with rollers. Then hundreds of natives drag it down to the plains, a task which often takes months. Everyone is glad to help, for the *raja* gives them food and has a buffalo slaughtered every day.

At the back of the coffin sits a '*hasandaran*', an old man or woman, in whom the spirit of the dead has descended. It is thought that the '*hasandaran*' makes the stone light by sitting upon it.[1] She cries continually, 'Pull!', while now and then she performs a magic dance.

Arrived in the village, the coffin is completed. The sculptor obtains as reward ten buffaloes, two golden ear-rings and twenty Spanish doubloons. Generally, the coffin has only one hollow, but at Huta Ginjang, on the west shore of the Toba Lake, there is a coffin with two chambers. In the foremost are kept the skulls of the *raja*, in the rear those of the family.

At Sipira, in the mountains of South Samosir, we found a costly Chinese plate of green porcelain. On this lay the skulls of a man and a woman, covered by a plate of the same material, with a floral decoration. Formerly the skulls were dyed red with *sirih*. From time to time, they were removed from the grave and dances were performed with them in the light of the moon. Meat and palm wine were put into the mouths, the living spoke to the dead and wept over them. These impressive ceremonies served as a memorial to the dead.

The skulls were also kept in tremendous urns, of which thirteen were found. One is hewn from the cliff and remains attached to it. Occasionally there is a seated human figure on the top with a sunshade over its head, or a human figure is carved on the side wall.

These urns differ especially in their covers, of which we distinguished two types, concave and convex. The concave line may be short or long. In the latter case, a pointed cover is formed, sometimes crowned with a receptacle for holy water.

We found coffins at Lumban Raja, Naibaho, Hapotan, Simbolon (2), Naingolan, Si Pingan, Huta Rihit (2), Pangaloan-Banjerpasir, Gorat (2), Huta Raja (5), Si Duldul Huta Hotang, Sipira (4), Huta Gurgur, Tomok (8), Simanindo, Simarmata, Binanga Borta, and Lumban Suhisuhi. Urns were discovered at Pangururan, Pancu (2), Huta Bolon, Lumban Julu (2), Gorat, Tolping (3), and Simanindo. The coffin at Lumban Raja has a remarkable feature; under the monster head is the figure of a *standing* man.

The coffins of Pancu are the largest on the island.

In the coffin at Siriaon, we found eight skulls. The one at

---

[1]Dr P. Voorhoeve kindly supplied me the following note: In Simalungun, the dragging of a rice-block or large beams for a chief's house occurs under the supervision of a medium (*turahan*), a young girl from a good family, who incites the drawers and sometimes springs on the mortar or the beams and makes them 'light'.

Pangaloan-Banjerpasir is badly mutilated. The urn at Gorat is not sculptured in one piece, but built up with rings of stone. It contains not only skulls but also bones.

As we have already said, we found at Sipira a coffin with skulls and Chinese plates. It is a remarkable fact in itself to find a coffin of this kind not on the coast, but in the interior. It was surrounded by a stone house. The coffin has a volute at both ends, instead of a monster head. Under the rubbish of the room lay a wooden cover with a triangular section. The skulls between the two plates had belonged to a certain Panaharan and his wife. Why the other five skulls did not lie on plates, no one could explain. Probably because they had belonged to people of lesser rank. These plates are called *pasu* and are very valuable. Not far from here is a low hill, from which protrude the fragments of at least three coffins.

Sipira lies high in the mountains. A few kilometres beyond, on the coast, stand a number of pillars in a rectangle 4 × 12 m. The two on the west side have a sculptured ox head. Formerly there was a roof over these pillars and the boat of a prominent *raja* was kept there. In the neighbourhood are other pillars, too.

Farther north, near Tomok, lies a group of no less than eight coffins on a low hill. They lie NE–SW. The largest coffin contains the skeletons of a man and a woman, thus not the skulls of an entire family. Next to this coffin lies a smaller one, almost entirely sunk into the ground. Immediately behind the monster head sits a human figure, with the right hand held over the breast. All these coffins have a cover with a triangular section. They are shaded by mighty trees.

Simanindo has many remarkable sights, among others a shrine facing to the west, with a stone image on its roof. Close by are a sarcophagus and an urn, both hewn from the natural rock. By the lake shore stands an oval stone chest, in which is kept indigo to dye the yarns used in weaving. The village has houses with magnificent carvings, beautifully coloured. The gables terminate in a high peak and are adorned with buffalo heads. In one of the houses is kept a very beautiful wooden image of a woman, with hands folded over the breast and a round pillar on the head. It represents a certain Si Boru Saragi.

At Simarmata, on the north coast, stands a rough coffin on the shore. Cover and contents have disappeared. The large stone is simply hollowed out to serve as a coffin.

It is remarkable that besides at Samosir antiquities are also found on the shore of the Toba Lake. Our explorations in this field brought to light the following.

On the south-west shore, at Parsingguran, stands a magnificent stone sarcophagus. At the rear end sits the figure of a woman with a bowl on her head. The great monster head has a gentle, inquisitive smile and an expression of deep resignation. This image is one of the greatest and noblest works of art ever produced in Sumatra. Under the image sits the figure of a man with knees drawn up and a filet of flowers on the head. Nose and upper lip have apparently been restored at a later date. Traces of red and blue paint are still plainly visible. The stone has been brought from a place lying 3 km to the north, the transport taking three days. In the vicinity stands the largest and most beautiful urn in the Batak country, crowned by a seated human figure.

A few kilometres farther east, at Huta Pulopulo, lies a second coffin. At the back sits, not a woman, but a man with armlets and a hat on his head. Inside the head and at the top of the hat is a deep hollow, probably used for a magic potion, which was poured into the image to give it a soul.

A highly unique and remarkable sarcophagus is found at Aek Godang. It is not only ornamented with the head and tail of a monster animal, but even has feet. Besides the figures at both ends, there is a third in the middle of the coffin. Formerly the monument stood under a roof, on the pillars were hung the jaw-bones of pigs, which had been slaughtered when the shrine was built.

Far to the south, at Tangga na Godang (Tarutung), lies a sarcophagus of an entirely different type. On the fore side is a large human face and a very small body with arms. It is the sarcophagus farthest south in the Batak country and I owe its discovery to Dr J. H. Maasland.

Let us, however, return to the west shore of the Toba Lake. Lumban Pangaloan is a lovely village, surrounded by high walls and bastions, covered with bamboo. On the village green stands a remarkably beautiful coffin, on a foundation of great stones. Here, also, are some artistic rice troughs.

At Silalahi lie an unfinished coffin and an urn. Strangely enough, the coffin still contains skulls.

Farther south, at Huta Ginjang, we found a coffin with two chambers; in the foremost were kept the skulls of prominent chiefs, in the rear those of their families. The monster head is pointed and adorned with an ox head.

On the south-eastern shore of the lake, there are also various antiquities, for instance, at Lumban Rang (Porsea). Here are decorated pillars on the top of the coffin. To the left and right of the fore side are small ledges, which formerly contained images. By the coffin stands a square urn with pyramid-shaped cover also a short broad pillar, which formerly served as the base of an image. In the urn lie the skulls of a certain Ompu Boliton and his son Parihuluan, in the coffin lie the bones of the five sons of Parihuluan. In the coffin also lie gongs, drums, and oboes, so that the dead may make music in the hereafter. As we know, the Dayaks of Borneo also give musical instruments to their dead.

At Lumban na Bolon lies a coffin with a cover in one piece. At Huta Bagasan lie two, of which one has a head on which is a bamboo with horsehair. Under the head is a large face. The last four coffins differ from those at Samosir, in that the monster head is not broad but pointed. At Balige, in front of a house, stands a beautifully decorated coffin, which has not yet been hollowed out.

Farther to the east are found coffins and urns of a different kind, which have been described this year by Dr P. Voorhoeve and G. L. Tichelman.

We also made a study of the proas in the Toba Lake. Some have a figure-head in the form of a bird, a buffalo, or a horse. In many houses the dead are buried in a proa, with the head of a hornbill. Similar boats are represented on bronze drums in Tonkin, in the fifth century BC. On these drums are also depicted houses in the Batak style of architecture.

Nias

Nias is almost entirely covered with hills and mountains. Especially through the central part, there are numerous mountain ranges. Here, also, is the highest peak, the Bawo Lolomacuwa (886 m). In the south are coral formations. In the Eocene period there was a land age, with rich vegetation which formed a layer of brown coal. Then the country began to sink, this process being caused by eruptions which occurred from the Oligocene to the Miocene Age. The soil is andesite and basalt incorporated in lava. Most of the land was covered by a shallow sea. About the Quartiary Age, Nias arose above the surface of the water and sediments were deposited in the reef caverns. Fossils and sedimentary stones enable us to determine the Eocene, Oligocene, and Miocene Ages.

To the south-east, the sea is magnificent. In front of the coast lie numerous red-brown coral reefs, sharp as swords, over which thunder the breakers. A vast green mass of water is seen approaching; it mounts high in the air and then in a wide curve crashes down on the reef, with a sound as of subterranean drums. Just before the breaker reaches its zenith, all the water from the cliff streams in a thousand little rapids back into the sea.

All sorts of remarkable shells and little horns are washed ashore by the waves, and it is amusing to see dozens of crustaceans scrambling through the sand with their houses on their backs. There are also lovely birds. One lies down in the sand and looks into the tops of the coconut trees, like great, symmetrical wind-roses. The sun sinks into a blue sky full of little white clouds and from the vast deeps of the Indian Ocean great waves roll into the bay.

Deep in the jungles of south-east Nias lie the mysterious remains of villages long deserted—great terraces and altars, on which stand round tables with great monster heads, double rows of pillars, crowned with figures of deer and rhinoceros-birds, mushroom-shaped stones on which graceful dancers once bent and swayed.... And among these relics, lost among reeds and bamboos, are small, beautifully decorated coffins, the covers adorned with the figures of birds and lizards. In these coffins lie half-rotted skulls, staring sombrely from hollow, black eye sockets at the stranger who has come to profane their rest.

At twilight a strange atmosphere pervades the place. Silent and ghostly, the columns arise in the scarlet sunset glow, the animals stare with stony eyes into the western sky, where lies the land of the dead. Over the dusky mountains, evening approaches and suddenly it is night, the silent blue night of Nias, night in an isle of dreams, filled with waving ferns and the crests of royal palms. . . . A gentle whispering is heard; in the pale starlight the animals seem to be calling each other in muted tones. . . .

What is the significance of these monuments? They were erected as memorials to certain feasts, given by a native chief in order to increase his own prestige. They also served to propitiate magic powers, so as to obtain a higher rank in the hereafter. Such feasts may also be given for the dead, in order to elevate them to a more important sphere in the spirit world. Feasts of this kind are given by many of the peoples of Further India and are closely related to the megalithic cult. The English call them 'feasts of merit', the Germans 'Verdienstfeste'.

The close relation between these feasts of rank and the megaliths in Nias and their resemblance with those of Further India is truly remarkable. Megalith feasts are the very core of Nias religion and society, so that one has the fullest right to speak of a megalith culture.

The elevation of a Nias chief into a higher rank was not only a family question, but also served to bless the entire tribe. The ceremony may take place only after the fashioning of golden ornaments and the slaughter of a slave. When enough gold and a sufficient number of pigs have been collected, a variety of jewels are made, first those belonging to a woman. These ornaments are a filet, an ear-ring, a necklace, and a covering for the head. The first three are made simultaneously. If there is enough gold, the fourth ornament may also be made; otherwise, this is done later with a separate feast, during which a gold-embroidered jacket is made for the man. He also has made for him a kris and an ear-ring. The feast for the making of golden ornaments is called *fanao o gana a* and costs from six to twelve pigs. The man and the woman are then carried around in a wooden sedan chair (*osaosa*), adorned with the head of an animal.

For the making of jewels, a slave is necessary. Whoever wears new jewels is doomed to die, because of the powerful magic which they radiate. Now a slave must divert this evil magic by first wearing the gold himself. When the gold-embroidered coat is ready, a large stone is hacked into the form of a clothes-rack. The slave is then compelled to hang the coat on this rack, immediately after which he is beheaded. Only then may the feast of gold take place, whereby the man gives money to his father-in-law and to the latter's maternal uncle, to his own maternal uncle, and to his mother's maternal uncle.

The next stage is the making of a golden dress and jacket for the woman, in which ceremony a stone *osa* with three heads is made, but no slave killed. The reward for making an *osa* is four hams. For the carving of eyes, ears, and jaws of the *osa*, ½ *pao* is paid. This ½ *pao* is laid in a plate of water, with which the *osa* is then sprinkled and sanctified.

After this feast, the man may have made a golden umbrella, a head kerchief, and a neck chain. For these a pillar is erected, an *osa* with a head is made, and a slave killed. The priest receives 3 *pao*, as pay for making the wooden image of a god, also 1 *pao* for thrusting the image through a hole in the roof, so that all the sins of the family may leave the house in this way. For a feast of this kind, no less than a hundred pigs are slaughtered.

When the last jewel, a bracelet, is made for the woman, a stone bench (*harefa*) may be erected for her on the village green. Hereby a woman slave is killed and her head buried under the *harefa*. Twenty or thirty pigs are slaughtered and 1 *pao* is given to the woman's parents or to her brother. The woman's father or brother then leads her to the *harefa* on which she performs a dance, wearing all her golden jewels. When she comes to die, a woman slave must be slain, to serve as a 'cushion'. But first she must clean the woman's skull, oil it, and place it in a stone pyramid. The slave's head is boiled, cleaned, and then hung in front of the house.

The next feast for the man includes the setting of a bench upon a hill, at some distance from the village. Near the bench is planted an *ewo* tree and fifty or a hundred pigs are slaughtered. During these ceremonies, the man gives his parents 1 *pao* and declares to all present that he has completed all the feasts, which implies that the very highest honours must be paid to him after his death.

The man may then give still another feast, if he so desires, during which a stone bench is placed within the house. For this service, one pig is paid. The priest then makes an image and slaughters a pig and a chicken. The founder of the monument then has tied about his throat a silken band, by which he is led to the bench, where he sits down. Finally, twenty or thirty pigs are slaughtered.

When the man dies, a living slave is laid in the grave. In his mouth is placed a bamboo tube, connected with an opening in the coffin, through which flows the moisture of the corpse. Another slave or his head is laid to the right of the coffin, to serve as a 'staff' for the deceased.

If a man wishes to marry, he must first provide a mushroom-shaped stone for the girl. When he begins to look for this and while it is being cut into shape, his father kills a pig. In about four days, the girl's father is informed of the state of affairs and his help is sought to 'turn the stone'. He also slaughters a pig by the stone. The stonecutters receive a ham as reward. When the stone is completed, the girl's father and the people of his village bring it to the village of the young man. Sometimes, the girl sits on the stone.

The marriage feast lasts for two days. On the first day, the stone is brought; on the second, the girl is led by a silken neck kerchief from the place beneath the ancestral images in her house to the stone, where she is given a special name. She then sings the praise of her father and of the guests-of-honour and expresses wishes for their welfare. After this, she is led back to her home, where a number of women perform a sacred dance and the guests are given a great feast. A piece of meat is cooked for the girl's father, who says he cannot eat because of his grief at parting with his child. Then 1 *pao* of gold is laid upon his plate and the young man's father says, 'Eat now, soon you shall have 6 *pao* and the other members of the family shall also have something (at the most, 3 *pao*).' The girl's father is then persuaded to eat, after which he goes home. In the meantime, the pigs have been slaughtered and divided. After three or four days, the promised sum is brought to the girl's father, while the girl returns.

We have told about these customs in detail, in order to make plain what an important part is played by these stone monuments in the life of the natives of Nias. The number of pigs slaughtered and the number of *pao* paid is a matter of considerable thought. There is perhaps no place in the world where the rôle of the megaliths in a primitive society is so plainly to be seen as in Nias.

Similar megalith customs among the Nagas of Assam are also deserving of careful study, because they are of extraordinary interest to ethnology. In some years, Western civilization will destroy these customs and the megaliths of South-East Asia will perhaps be as great a mystery as those of Europe.

We will now give a brief description of the antiquities themselves. For a few weeks we camped at Lahusa Idano Tai, in the south-eastern part of Nias, whence we made trips to various monuments in the vicinity. These consist of long rows of megaliths, which formerly stood in front of the houses. The villages, however, have long been deserted, the houses have disappeared and only these stone monuments are left in the desolate wilderness. There are still a few villages with monuments, but these are much smaller and cruder than the ones I have already mentioned.

Pure megaliths of magnificent design and execution are found in the south of Nias. These monuments, however, differ from those at Lahusa. It must also be mentioned that nearly all the villages of Nias lie high and isolated on the hills, this being an urgent necessity, because war is being waged continually. For the scientific explorer, these hills are a source of grief, especially when they have to be climbed in the heat of a burning midday sun!

The monuments of Lahusa give a good impression of the plan of an old Nias village green. It consists of a rectangle, 16.50 × 40 m, the axis running NW–SE. The two extremities terminate in a stone terrace. On the north-west side stands a great, square column (*behu*), crowned with the figure of a bird. On the terrace there is also a round, mushroom-shaped stone (*niogaji*), a smaller stone of the same form, upstanding pillars, plain or decorated, and benches with animal heads (*osaosa*).

A *behu* serves to make the name of a native chief immortal and may only be erected after a head has been cut off. The severed head is laid on the figure of the bird. For a woman's marriage, a *niogaji* is made and she dances upon it. An *osa* with one head commemorates a man, with three heads a woman. All these monuments serve as the final resting place for the founder's soul. They are found by the hundreds on the village square and the people of Nias know exactly to whom each belongs.

In order to avoid repetition, we must pause for a moment on the subject of *behu*, *niogaji*, and *osaosa*.

Behu are square pillars or huge, rough, unhewn slabs of stone, placed in rows along the village green or at both extremities. Sometimes they are ornamented with figures of rosettes, breasts, a necklace, or other jewel. Often they have a flight of steps on three sides. In Tetegewo is a *behu* with a large knife. On top there is usually a bird which, however, cannot always be plainly distinguished. Sometimes one recognizes a chicken and again a rhinoceros-bird. The latter is sometimes portrayed without a horn but may be identified by its long, downturned bill. Other specimens have a short, snub-nosed bill with a horn. We saw a large, unusually well-formed head of a rhinoceros-bird (40 cm long), with horns on the head and large ornaments in the ears. The portrayal is, of course, not true to life. For instance, the beak is too long in proportion to the horn. The sides of the beak are convex instead of concave, the ears are on top of the head instead of at the sides.

At Cudrubaho is still another specimen with horns on the beak. Four-footed birds are also not uncommon. Sometimes the wings are spread and the back has a flat surface to hold a severed head. But often, too, the wings are folded. On rare occasions, the *behu* has not one, but three birds.

The rhinoceros-bird is called in Nias *gogowaya* or *lailuwo*. He is sacred to the creators of the earth and to all who create anything at the present time, especially goldsmiths. The main reason for placing him on the *behu* is to guard the dead, but he is also supposed to attract the soul or the shadow of gold in some magic way, so as to enrich his master. For the same purpose, the natives of Nias place massive stone money chests in front of their houses. The *behu*, indeed, may be erected only after the village chief has had his golden ornaments melted and fashioned into new forms.

As the pillar (*behu*) is the typical monument for a man, so the round, mushroom-shaped stone (*niogaji*) is dedicated to a woman. Very often, the *behu* and the *niogaji* stand side by side. As a rule, the *niogaji* has a height of about one metre, but there are of course larger or smaller specimens. The smallest I saw has a diameter of 63 cm, the largest a diameter of 207 cm (Sisarahili). The base consists of a short pillar, which changes into an ogive-shaped section with a flat upper surface. The ogive is often beautifully decorated. The simplest form of decoration consists of grooves, sometimes edged by a band of rosettes, squares or loops. Two specimens at Tetegewo have triangles and rosettes, another, spear-

Ornament of a *niogaji* at Tetegewo.

shaped ornaments. The most remarkable, however, is a *niogaji*
with alternate triangles and spirals, among which two lizards are
portrayed. *Niogaji* with triangles on the upper border are found at
Cudrubaho and with circles at Tuhegewo.

One naturally wonders what the real purpose of these ogive
decorations is, for, unless one bends down, they are practically
invisible. It is possible that they were not made to please the eye
but in order to attract some magic power.

These stones nearly always stand on the ground or on a foundation, occasionally on a pillar about 80 cm high. Quite often
they are surrounded by stones of an equal height, or built into a
terrace (Cudrubaho), an inexplicable fact.

As we have said before, the wives of prominent village chiefs
perform dances on these stones. In this connection it may be
mentioned that most of the *niogaji* produce a musical sound when
struck with the flat of the hand. It is quite possible that formerly
the dancer produced this sound with her feet or that she was
accompanied by the clapping of hands on the stone. During our
explorations, whenever there were children in the vicinity, they
always began to strike the stones and to accompany each other.
The effect is very pleasing, since every stone has a different tone.

Osaosa indicates an oval wooden disc with the head and tail of
some fantastic animal. At certain feasts, the tribal chief and his
wife have the right to be carried in it. In the region of Lahusa,
stone *osas* are erected in commemoration of a feast of this kind,
for which human heads are required. They are made, thus, not for
the dead but for the living. We may classify them as one-headed
specimens for men (*si sara bagi*) and three-headed specimens for
women (*si tolu bagi*). The large ones are usually round or rectangular, the small ones oval. The large specimens have three
heads and the small, only one. They rest on four feet or low
pillars, or on two broad supports, sometimes merely on a round
shaft. Sometimes there are no feet whatever. The large stones in
honour of women have breasts carved on the undersurface or on
the front edge; the smaller are plain. The one-headed stones
sometimes have male genitals, but also occasionally female breasts.
Sometimes they stand on a high, round shaft or small specimens
are placed on a high pillar. The latter occasionally cover a font.

The heads are supposed to represent deer, although no outsider
can recognize them. With their curling lips and broad, protruding
tongue, they remind one of exotic orchids and belong to the very
best decorative art which Nias has produced. In the jaws, great

incisors are visible, sometimes even tusks. The nose resembles
that of the rhinoceros-bird. On the head are two small horns, the
eyes are window-shaped, the ears wear ornaments. Around the
throat is a necklace. Very peculiar is a specimen with a human
head at Cudrubaho. There are also small monuments without a
head, having only a volute and a tail. A one-headed specimen
with grooves on ogive and shaft stands at Barujir (the south-east
wall), one with triangles on the edge is at Cudrubaho.

Let us, however, return to Lahusa. One of the most beautiful
monuments there is near a square terrace on the south-eastern side
of the green. It is a pillar 3.60 m high, crowned by the figure of a
deer. Over the back of the animal (which looks more like a dog
than a deer) is a ridge of upright scales. The tail is decorated with
four volutes. On the head are two horns. Straight through the
body is a hole. The base has volutes and tails, on the fore side of
the column is a small altar. North-west of this monument stand in
a row two more pillars with three-headed *osa* on top and a pillar
with a beautiful rhinoceros-bird. By this last monument is an
artistically decorated *niogaji*. Here, also, we found the head of a
crocodile and three human heads of stone, as a substitute for real
skulls.

Back of the little terrace just mentioned, stands the image of a
woman with upraised hands; the top of the head is flat and on it
sits a bird. Near her stand two pillars with rhinoceros-birds; the
one farthest to the right has female breasts and four feet. Around
the throat is a necklace. Both pillars have projections on the fore
side and are thus probably clothes racks.

The terrace on the south-east side has several benches, behind
which are five smooth, convex, decorated discs. Two have a bowl
at the top, the purpose of which is unknown. In the centre pillar,
a lizard is engraved. On the terrace is also a headless animal with
widespread feet.

We shall make no mention of the numerous other monuments
on this square, as we do not wish to make this chapter a mere dry
summary. For the same reason, we will take merely a bird's eye
view of the other groups of megaliths, recounting only their most
remarkable features.

Not far from here lies Cudrubaho, from which place there is a
magnificent view over the south-western part of the country and
the Susuwa River. The town lies on a steep plateau and differs
from Lahusa by being spread out over a long stretch of country.
Here, also, the chief monuments are five enormous pillars, sur-

mounted by birds. To the north-west is a terrace, on which is the seated figure of a man. Near by is a pillar with a lizard, on the top is a bowl closed by a three-headed *osa*. Behind this terrace are three other long, narrow terraces and *niogaji* with pillars. The north-eastern side of the field is enclosed by a wall, behind which lies higher ground. The wall, therefore, has several steps. Near by stands a pillar with a hole in one side, in which was kept the head of the departed. This reminds one of the custom of placing skulls in tree trunks or wooden pillars as observed by various tribes (for instance in Borneo). On the south-western edge of the field is a column with capital and grooves, resembling the Egyptian style.

An unusually beautiful group of megaliths lies at Tetegewo. After traversing two long rows of monuments, one sees two large terraces, one above the other, with pillars and figures of animals. On the upper terrace, we found two skull coffins in the form of birds and another with a trapezium-formed cover. In one of these coffins lay two broken porcelain plates. These plates are always broken on purpose. The front of another coffin has a relief of a human being with arms and legs outspread. Tetegewo has the most beautiful *niogaji* in all Nias.

Tuhegewo, in the immediate vicinity, also has numerous re-markable antiquities. We found no less than nine skull coffins, of which two have a lizard on the cover. Two coffins had a skull on a plate, another was ornamented with rosettes over the entire surface. We found here, also, a large *osa* with the head of a hornbill, a pillar with volutes and a knife, as well as a pillar with a necklace, ears, and a head ornament. The small terrace has curved upturned points, so-called *ewe*, resembling the wooden ornaments so often found on the houses of native chiefs in Nias.

The *ewe* is added either to an oval or to a square house and may be made only after a certain feast has been given. Usually there are two, sometimes four, either plain or decorated with rosettes. Each *ewe* is supported by an arm-shaped ornament, under which are sometimes a necklace and breasts. The chief's house at Cudrubaho has even a pillar, decorated in the same way and with *two* upraised arms. The stone *ewe* on the terrace at Tuhegewo are the oldest specimens in Nias and have thus a special historical value.

In the village of Sisarahili is a three-headed *osa*, in which the outer heads represent rhinoceros-birds—a rare specimen, therefore. There is also in this village a skull coffin in the form of a mythical animal. Downstream, on the steep bank of the Susuwa River, lies an interesting group, enclosed fore and aft by terraces. The north terrace is of most importance. Here stand five pillars. The centre pillar has a three-headed *osa*, the outer heads belonging to birds with upturned beaks. To the right stands a skull coffin in the form of a monster with breasts, to the right and left of these breasts are upturned arms, ending in volutes. The coffin is supported by a human figure with raised arms. On the left corner of the terrace stands the largest *niogaji* in Nias; at the centre a two-headed *osa*, slightly concave on the upper surface. We do not know the purpose of this rare monument.

Among other antiquities, we should like to mention two skull coffins and a large cover with a lizard. Also the figure of a woman with upraised arms. In the right hand she holds a sword, on the head stands a bird with outspread wings. Next to this image stands a pillar with breasts. Conspicuous is a pillar with raised arms and a hornbill on the top, also a pillar with a human face and prominent ears.

At Orahili, much as destroyed by an earthquake a few years ago. Here we found a number of round bowls, some with covers. One specimen was beautifully decorated. It is said that a few years ago, these bowls were made out of *niogaji* and now merely serve for household purposes. An old man, however, remembered that formerly skulls were kept in them and that formerly *wooden* skull coffins were kept in the houses. Conspicuous is a small *osa* without a nose but with a beak-shaped upper jaw. In the neighbouring village of Safaroasi, I found a similar specimen.

The most beautiful thing in Orahili, however, is the chief's house with its high, pointed roof and lovely woodcarvings. The motifs are a woman's breasts and two-tailed lizards. To the right of the steps is the figure of a woman, mated with a lizard. On the roof is a serpent-shaped boat, in which stand seven wooden images. Similar boats are found in Toba and on the house-shaped mausoleums of the Jarais in Indo-China.

Barujir is remarkable for the high wall on the south-eastern side. To the right and left ascend flights of steps. At the foot of the right stairs, we found nine skull chests; at the top, five more. One has a cover, on which is a bird with outspread wings. On the wall is also a round pillar with a circle of pegs at the top, apparently a sort of clothes-rack. At the south-west corner of the square lies a small terrace with raised curves (*ewes*) and near by, a human image. In the middle of the square stands a large *niogaji*. A kilometre to the south-east lies another small group, of which the principal monument is a small terrace with two volutes.

Hiligombo may be reached by a steep flight of steps, from the north or from the south side. Here we found seven skull chests and a large round skull pot. By this pot stands a strange, bird-like image on a pillar, not separate but carved out of the same stone. North of this group lie two terraces, to the south another small group.

Tomöri is 15 m long and 50 m broad and has three terraces. On the highest of these stand two pillars with birds and two skull chests, also a human head of stone.

The second terrace is empty, but the third again has bird pillars and two stone heads in human form. At the very bottom and to the left is a chest with a lizard on the lid, and near by a chest in the form of a rhinoceros-bird with a square lid on the back. On the other side stands a similar bird chest. South-east of this group lie three more little terraces with stone protuberances.

We will now leave these regions and make our way to the south, where the culture of Nias has had its most beautiful development. Here is a people imbued with the spirit of music and art, a people of simple sculptors, singers and poets, dreamy, meditative and full of mysticism. As they have lived, so they die, quite simply and soon forgotten. The souls of the dead are like a sigh heard in the rustle of the evening breeze.... Over the deserted graves glows dimly the Milky Way, the Celestial River, the surge of whose waves can be heard when the weather is clear....

One twilight evening, we came to the village of Hilisimaitano. We mounted a flight of steps with artistic carvings and lovely volutes. And suddenly there lay before us a large village with rows of houses on both sides of a broad, paved street. The blue twilight dimmed the outlines of the high roofs, from which curled faint clouds of smoke. Men with broad, round straw hats on their heads and a spear over the shoulder were returning from the fields. Children brought water in hollow bamboos. A lone dog barked, then all was still. The evening wrapped Hilisimaitano in an atmosphere of deep rest, like a miracle from ages primeval....

We stepped into the broad, central road. To the right and left, stone monuments are placed in long rows before the houses— simple benches and ornamented obelisks, round tables with a motif of leaves, a chair with a crocodile on the back. These stones serve to commemorate the dead and are often made during the lifetime of the person concerned.

Under the house of the aristocrat Samago, we noticed a coffin, three metres long, with the head of a deer. Horns and beard were made of gilded tin and fastened to the head with iron wire. The sculpturing was not yet completed, as the founder had just had the stone brought a month before from Botohilitano, 18 km away. Hundreds of people had dragged it over the hills, and Samago had been compelled to give great feasts and to pay dearly. But he did both with pleasure, for now his name would be immortal, the heartfelt wish of every man in Nias.

On the south-east coast, at Hiliganowo, stands a similar coffin, with a tiger head. It is richly painted and was erected only last year. It contains the remains of a certain Sihuwa. The dead man can no longer enjoy the lovely view over sea and waving palms but perhaps in his sleep he hears the sound of the breakers and the deep voices of the evening wind. . . .

These stone coffins in animal form were a tremendous surprise, especially because of their relation to the sarcophagi of Samosir. Their construction is entirely modern; the idea behind it, however, is very old. The prototypes must be sought in similar *wooden* coffins, found to this day on the Batu Islands, and which were also found twenty-five years ago in the Hinako Islands. The stone coffins of Samosir must also have been preceded by wooden chests, such as are still found here and there in the Pakpak Lands.

The second surprise was the village of Bawomataluwo, which lies high and inaccessible on a hill. After climbing hundreds of steps, one turns around to look over miles and miles of mountains, valleys, and gardens of Nias. Far in the distance, Lagudri Bay lies gleaming in the morning sun.

The chief's house in this village is one of the finest bits of architecture ever made by a primitive people. In front stand the round, stone tables and obelisks of the forefathers. The roof ascends steep and high. The gable is adorned with three dragon heads.

We mount a short flight of steps and walk through a forest of pillars, so large that a man cannot span them. Like immense pylons of an Egyptian dream temple they rise, row on row, dark and deeply impressive. We mount a dark flight of stairs, enter a door, and stand then in a large, dusky chamber, in the heart of a gigantic castle. In the warm ashes of the hearth, dogs lie sleeping. . . . From the ceiling hang drums, one of which is cannon-shaped and 3 m in length. Whole rows of pigs' jaws, cunning hooks in the shape of birds, flat baskets with plates, etc., adorn the wall. In the centre arises a pillar which unfolds into a flower, cleverly carved and of wondrous beauty. The walls are of dark-stained wood, in which have been made all sorts of figures, even an entire ship with its crew and a shoal of fish. And if we look carefully, we even see doorknob ornaments of a grace and delicacy almost unbelievable.

At the rear of the room hangs the figure of a pendant ape, with a bronze ring in its mouth. On festive occasions, it is the custom to hang a whole pig on this ring.

Against the walls sit people with magnificent Mongolian features. The pale brown of their skin harmonizes wonderfully with the dark brown of the wall. They are the silent witnesses of a world of beauty which is doomed to vanish, of a people and its culture whose dying fills us Westerlings with pity and reverent silence. . . .

We open a door and look down a flight of steps, where children are playing. They turn around and look up. . . . Through a crack in the ceiling, a beam of golden light falls on their upturned brown faces. The impression is of something primeval, a picture by Rembrandt. . . .

In this district, a very remarkable feast was formerly given, concerning which I gathered information only with the greatest difficulty. Whenever a chief had no children or when he had attained to great power, he gave a so-called tiger feast. All the villages subject to him were then compelled to bring a huge wooden tiger image, which stood on a platform and was carried by as many as forty men. The chief himself also made a tiger image and a more than life-size image of a woman in a dancing pose, to represent his wife. When all the images were assembled in the village square, dances were performed and the noble deeds of the chief were praised in song. On the back of his tiger image was laid the head of a slave and another at the feet of the woman image. After this, all the images were carried in procession around the village and over the entire country, where they were everywhere received with offerings of rice and palm wine. It was believed that this processional gave the chief and his wife more bodily vigour and strengthened their souls. The ground would also be more fertile and the crops more bountiful. During this journey all strife must cease. Men and women were completely free and abandoned themselves to their lusts in the most shameful manner. After twenty-eight days, the images were hurled into the Gomo River.

Some of the old people declared that the tiger was sometimes replaced by a rhinoceros-bird and that the woman represented the mother of a number of ancestors. In ancient times she had become pregnant because the feather of a bird had fallen on her lap, and for this reason the descendants were not allowed to kill the rhinoceros-bird. At the feast in honour of these images, the men danced with great masks, which were provided with a hornbill's head.

One could easily write much more concerning the culture of Nias, but for the present I shall restrict myself to the mentioning of a few new points of view, revealed by these recent explorations. First, however, I wish to express my gratitude to M. A. Bouman, Deputy Commissioner of Nias, who procured for me much valuable information and always helped me in the most generous fashion.

Even the most superficial consideration teaches us that the culture of Nias is related to that of the Nagas in Assam. In both countries, social life is largely dominated by the megalith institution and the necessary feasts and ceremonies involved by them. In Nias this is more the case than in Assam, for among the Nagas there are only a few tribes (such as the Angamis), who possess a highly evolved megalithic culture. Among the Aos, Semas, Sangtams, Changs, and Yimsungr, the stone memorials are replaced by forked, wooden, Y-shaped posts. In Nias, also, wooden monuments are often used in place of stone. Among the Nagas as well as in Nias, the accompanying assignment of rank assumes a prominent place.

Among the Bataks, megaliths do not play such an important rôle that one can speak of a megalith culture. Their feasts are not given to honour the living but to glorify the dead. Whenever a village chief has died and his tribe has increased after a number of years, they decide to elevate his spirit into a higher rank and to declare him a *sumangot*. For this purpose a great feast is given, and the bones are exhumed and placed in a stone memorial. If the tribe continues to increase, the *sumangot* may be elevated to the rank of *persombaan*, for which ceremony numerous buffaloes are slaughtered.

Among the Nagas and the natives of Nias (also in lesser degree among the Bataks), the form and decoration of the house are closely related to the owner's rank. In Nias, the *ewe* (outstanding points) may be added to the house only after certain feasts have been given and a stone pillar erected. The figures of a woman's breasts may be added only after golden breast ornaments have been made, whereby a woman slave is killed. The number of steps is in accordance with the rank which the house owner has attained.

In spite of the differences which exist between the Nagas and the people of Nias, the similarities between their megalith cultures are so striking and so numerous that there can be no doubt of their relation. *They must at one time have had a common land of origin and this can have been nowhere but in the valley of the Irrawaddy.*

Not only ethnologically but also anthropologically, the two peoples appear to be related. A charming anecdote will serve to illustrate this much better than a tiresome discussion. During my explorations in Nias, I allowed the inhabitants to see numerous photos of strange peoples and asked them to point out those which portrayed their own countrymen. After a few moments, an old man pointed to a couple of photos and said, 'These are of our people, but they have dressed themselves a bit queerly.' They were photos which Dr C. von Fürer Haimendorf had made of the Konyak and the Kalyo Kengyu Nagas!

Since my explorations in Sumatra (1935 and 1936) and in Nias (1938), I am inclined to include Nagas, Niassers, Dayaks, Filipinos, and Formosans in one large group. The anthropological characteristics are a short, vigorous, conspicuously beautiful body. The hair is straight, the Mongolian features numerous. Among all these people, megaliths in wood or stone, promotion feasts, and head-hunting play a prominent part.

The Bataks and the Lampongs (in South Sumatra) came at a later period and still later the Malays penetrated as a wedge between them. At least four megalithic cults have penetrated Sumatra—in Palembang, Jambi, Kampar, and the Batak Lands. These probably came from Tonkin. The megalith culture of Nias, however, came from Burma.

Further investigation must prove how far right these hypotheses are. Only the co-operation of various scholars can solve the problem.

Prehistoric Monuments

Kampar

DEEP in the mountain regions of the equator, on a tributary of the Kampar Kanan, lies the village Aur Duri. Tremendous, jagged peaks on all sides isolate it from the inhabited world; it is reached after a long journey over mountains entirely covered with dense forests and nearly always shrouded in thin veils of mist. But now and then the mist is dispersed by a gentle breeze, massive peaks and gorges are revealed, and between them, deep valleys with tender green *sawah* and toy houses. Sunbeams play in silver streams and the gentle murmur of waterfalls mingles with the chirping of rice birds.

In this idyllic seclusion of the vast jungle, in this bit of forgotten Paradise, lies Aur Duri and here, to our surprise, we found the remains of a mysterious culture, columns with curved capitals, beautifully chiselled and decorated with flowers. One might say enormous kris hilts, with leaf motifs, volutes, and human faces. Sometimes they stand in a row, sometimes in the neighbourhood of a stone platform. Often, a small column stands next to a large one, presumably the grave stones of a child and his parents. Occasionally, a flat stone lies in front of the column.

Similar monuments are found in the vicinity of Suliki and Payakumbuh, though less numerous. The profile is usually rectangular, the sharp corners are smoothed. The curved finial points south or south-east and under it sometimes appears a simple decoration. Around the base, there is occasionally a band with a buckle. There can be no doubt that some of these columns represent human beings. The decorations differ from the usual Malay motifs, proving that these columns were made by a people older than the Malay race. Who they were and when they lived, we do not know. About 2,000 years ago, however, South Sumatra was inhabited by a race of megalith builders. It is therefore quite possible that a similar people lived at the same time in Central Sumatra, in the land of Puar Datar, at the source of the Mahat, a tributary of the Kampar Kanan. We cannot thus be far wrong if we estimate the beginning of our era as the time when these monuments were built.

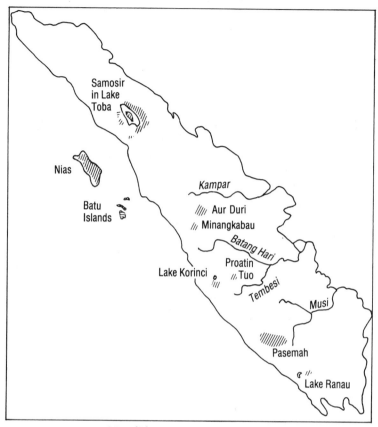

Megalithic Remains In Sumatra.

Their founders were also presumably the makers of the mono-
lithic tools found in several places along the Kampar Kanan (Sibiruang,
Muara Mahat, and Kuok). These tools show a remarkable resemblance to those used for a similar purpose in the Malay Peninsula
and we will therefore turn our attention first to this region.

Now we find also in Melaka menhirs having a curved finial and
a conspicuous likeness to the columns of Puar Datar, the only
difference being that the former are rough and unfinished while
the latter are carefully finished and decorated. The former may be
compared with the rows of stones in South Sumatra, although the
latter are generally smaller and rounder. The great, rough stone
fragments of Melaka really bear the greatest similarity to the
monuments of south-east Nias (Tetegewo, Tuhegewo).

At Pangkalan Kempas, in Negeri Sembilan, stand a few columns of which one, strangely enough, is called *pedang* (sword or kris). Like the pillars of Sumatra, they are adorned with volutes, also with conventional figures of animals, such as a bird, a horse, and a dragon. Certainly it is no accident that a pillar at Guguk (Puar Datar) also has the conventional figure of an animal, bearing a strong resemblance to a fish with a bird's head.

Now it is well known that the people of Melaka and Negeri Sembilan originally came from Minangkabau, and it is certainly not by chance that in this latter country we also find large, unfinished fragments of stone. Naturally we cannot determine whether these monuments originated in the Malay Peninsula or in Sumatra, but there can be no doubt as to their relation.

When we seek to explain their meaning, however, we encounter serious difficulties. The present inhabitants of these regions give an account of them, it is true, but it is extremely doubtful if their assertions have any value. How often does it not happen that ancient monuments are surrounded by legends which have no relation to their original purpose? Only when these accounts agree with observations on living megalith cults they have value.

The inhabitants of Puar Datar say that these columns are partly grave monuments to their ancestors, partly memorials to the founding of a federation (*tanda negri*), and partly the boundary of assembling places where folk games were formerly played. The chiefs sat on the flat stones and leaned against the pillars. Formerly these monuments stood near the council hall (*balei*). Near the pillars, buried gold is sometimes found, and at their dedication there was a sacrifice of buffaloes.

This information tallies so exactly with our observations in Nias that there can be no doubt as to its accuracy. Probably the pillars also have some relation to the feasts of merit. It is even possible that their form may have some historic and religious connection with many Malay and Javanese kris-handles. Originally the form of the knife-haft must also have indicated the owner's rank. In both instances, an attempt has been made to portray the founder of the tribe.

At the same time, one must not lose sight of the fact that menhirs with curved summits are also found in other parts of the archipelago, i.e. in Nias and Flores. The Was, on the border of Burma and Yunnan, erect rows of great wooden pillars, the tops of which are often curved. Every pillar has a hollow, in which is kept a severed human head to encourage the growth of the crops.

Ornaments on Megaliths in Middle Sumatra.
1–11. Aur Duri
    6. Transverse section of a pillar
12–13. Koto Tinggi
14. Guguk (Suliki)

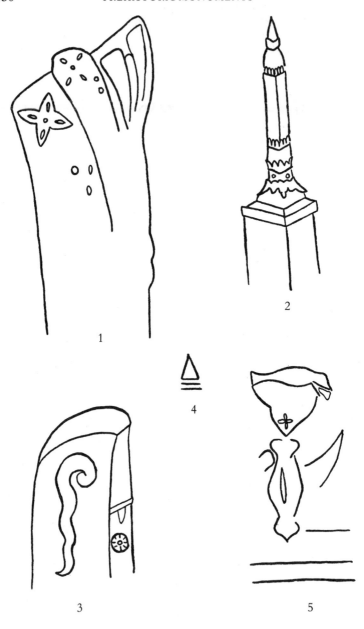

Megaliths in Middle Sumatra.
1. Koto Tengah   2. Pinnacle of a pillar at Guguk
3. Balubus   4–5. Ornaments on a pillar at Guguk

In Puar Datar, menhirs are always moved near mosques and council houses, proving that the people are still conscious of the relation between house and monument. In Pasemah, we find a relation between menhirs and spirit houses (*rumah poyang*). In Aur Duri there is a terrace 1 m high and measuring 5 × 5 m, apparently an ancient place of worship. The present inhabitants, however, assert that it was formerly the meeting place of four mighty chiefs (*tanem batu nini berampe*), i.e. the *datu* Raja di Balei of Muara Takui, the Bendaro of Mahe, the Mungkal of Sirih, and the Ketalowe of Mojoindo.

The prehistoric monuments of Central Sumatra have always been held in some reverence and there has even been an attempt to adapt them to the new religions. For instance, at Guguk (Payakumbuh) stands a beautifully sculptured pillar, 4.50 m high, with a Hindu summit. King Adityavarman (fourteenth century) often made use of sacred, prehistoric pillars for his inscriptions. At Kubu Raja are three 'leaning stones' (*sandaran*) or sunray stones (*batu pancar matahari*), where formerly the *raja* held council with his *patih* and *tumenggung*, while all faced to the south. In front of the central stone lies a flat slab. In Minangkabau, the *rajo nan tigo selo* or 'lords on the three stone seats' are very well known. The *batu palimauan* is also known, the stone on which the *rajo ibadat* is purified with lemon (*balimau*) before attaining his new dignity. In addition there are several crude images and rice-blocks with inscriptions.

On the graves of the *raja alam* at Gudam are even found two pillars with beautiful decorative Muhammadan motifs. On a grave at Pagarruyung we found a monolith with a faint resemblance to a human form, wearing a girdle and two krises. At Guguk (Payakumbuh) also stands a stone bowl said to have been used for the drinking water of fighting-cocks.

Finally, attention must be called to something very remarkable. At Sintuo in Minangkabau is found a stone terrace with several seats. On the west side is an altar of rough stones, on which lies a stone broken in two and therefore called *batu bertikam*. The legend relates that the famous law-giver, Pepatih Sebatang, pierced the stone with his kris during a quarrel with his equally famous adversary, Kyai Katumenggungan. This certainly is a modern interpretation, and it may be assumed that the place was sacred long before the birth of these two law-givers. Pierced stones are worshipped in many parts of the archipelago as a symbol of femininity.

A curious instance of this is found in the Malay Archipelago. A remarkable square pillar in Pangkalan Kempas has four inscriptions—two in clear-cut Arabic from 1467 or 1468, and two in fainter letters in old Javanese. Below these inscriptions, a circular hole is cut straight through the pillar and just large enough to allow the passage of a man's arm. A second pierced stone lies on a hill near the town of Melaka.

Korinci

The people who live south-east of Lake Korinci were formerly head-hunters. It is said that more tiger people live here than in any other part of Sumatra.

They build remarkable houses with beautiful woodcarvings. In the attic are often kept miniature houses, adorned with coloured cotton. In these little houses lie many old relics (*pusaka*), such as inscribed buffalo horns, tree bark and bamboo, articles of clothing, weapons, gongs, stones, etc. They belong to the chiefs' wives, who came at certain times to burn incense and strew rice before them. These ceremonies are accompanied by the singing of sacred songs in a strange language.

The people hold these *pusaka* in great honour. They offer sacrifices and take oaths before them. The *pusaka* may only be touched by women, and are brought down on important occasions, such as war, epidemics, the reception of illustrious guests, the installation of chiefs, etc. A buffalo is slaughtered, then the sacred relics are carried around the village, while the people sing and rejoice, burn incense, scatter burnt rice, shoot off guns, and beat on gongs and drums.

On this occasion, slaves, called *dayang-dayang*, perform a dance. The *dayang-dayang* are the property of the *pusaka*. Formerly they were public women who, while dancing, made themselves tipsy by drinking great quantities of palm wine. Some of them became possessed by spirits and uttered confused cries, which were supposed to be a message from the gods. In addition to women slaves, the *pusaka* also have men slaves, called *buda andah*, and even special fields (*sawah rapat*), of which the harvests belong to the chiefs. It appears that formerly the *dayang-dayang* and the *buda andah* were entrusted with the care of the *pusaka*. The chief gave them a part of his income, but they had to collect it themselves. They formed a special caste and were held in bad repute. Now this condition has ceased to exist.

At several places south-east of the lake, cannon-shaped stones are found. At Lumpur Mudik lies a specimen 3.25 m long and pointing north. The rear surface has a diameter of 1 m and has in the centre a vague hump, surrounded by five shallow, concentric grooves, alternating with low ridges. It is said that this cannon was fired at the Gunung Korinci, the highest mountain in Sumatra, and that on this occasion, part of the summit of Gunung Pepat flew off.

A little farther, at Lulo Kecil, lies a second specimen, which is 4 m long, undecorated, and pointing south. The largest stone is at Muak, is 4.50 m long, and points to the north-west. A fourth is said to lie on the north slope of Gunung Risi. It is octagonal and points to Gunung Mesurai.

The first question which arises concerning these mysterious stones is, how old are they? It may be conjectured that they are imitations of ordinary cannon and so were made, at the most, about four centuries ago. It is, however, not plain what purpose was served by these imitations. They were useless for war and for religious purposes real cannon could better have been used.

Now in Jambi, farther east, are found stones bearing a remarkable resemblance to the above, and most certainly made during the neolithic age. Moreover, at Jujun, on the south shore of Lake Korinci, were found a bronze cuff, the fragment of a kettle-drum, a bronze vase and decorated fragments from the neolithic age. It therefore seems likely, though the statement cannot be proved, that the cannon also date from this period.

Apparently, they are memorials to illustrious chiefs and lie in the vicinity of graves. They were cut into phallic form to endow the people and their fields with increased fertility. Certainly women formerly made votive offerings to these stones and prayed for the blessing of children, just as they still do near real cannon.

To this day in Korinci, great stone stairways are built, leading to the villages on the hills, exactly as in Nias.

Jambi

South-east of Korinci, in the district Proatin Tuo (Jambi), lie twelve cannon-shaped stones, which are from 3 to 4 m long and flattened on the underside. The narrow fore part points to the east, the rear part is flat and decorated. The largest stone lies at Tanjung Putih; it is broken in two and portrays a primitive, crouching figure with upraised arms. In the right hand, he holds a sword bent over his head, in the left hand, an indeterminate object. At Dusun Tua lies a stone with the figure of a human head; at Gedang, a stone with a woman (head mutilated) and a man (?). In most of these stones the upper surface and the sides are ornamented. The specimen at Dusun Tua has a meander on the upper surface and five gongs on each side.

This last monument justifies the theory that these monuments must have been built by people who were in contact with a land where the meander was indigenous, and without a doubt this must have been China. The sculptors thus probably came from Tonkin, whence so many people migrated to the Indonesian Archipelago. Perhaps they were in Jambi already at the beginning of our era, in which case we have here the earliest records concerning gongs.

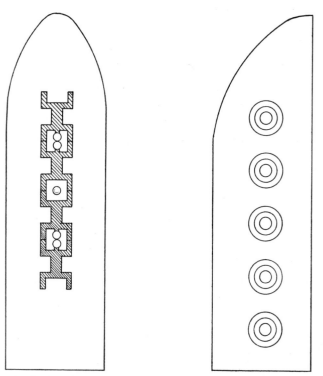

Rough drafts of a megalith at Dusun Tuo, Jambi, 3.40 m long, 0.90 m wide. On the upper side are four human figures; in the middle, a square gap (28 × 28 cm, 8 cm deep); in this gap, a round gap, 6 cm wide and deep, probably for sacrifices. On the side are five gongs. On the front side (not reproduced here) is a human head.

It is reasonable to suppose that these pillars are monuments to the dead. In the immediate vicinity were found red, blue, and yellow beads, also bits of gold and a bronze spear point. The custom of hanging gongs on a tombstone is found among the Dayaks, while in Toba we saw a sarcophagus in which gongs lay.

North of this region, on the farther bank of the Merangin, in Tanah Rena, grottos have been found, showing traces of a neolithic flake cult (Ulu Cangko).

Upstream, on the Batang Hari, were found Chinese ceramics from the Han period, i.e. red, porous earthenware with a green glaze. This indicates that Chinese were buried here at about the beginning of our era and is the oldest evidence we have of the relation between China and Jambi.

Pasemah

Concerning the origin of the inhabitants of Pasemah (Besemah), the following legend is told. During the Golden Age of the Javanese kingdom (fourteenth century), a brother and sister, Atong Bungsu and Putri Sendang Biduk, came with a number of followers from Java. The sister settled at Palembang, where she soon became a mighty princess. Her brother went into the interior and arrived at the place where the Pasemah River flows into the Lematang. Here the water was swarming with *besemah* fish and therefore Atong Bungsu settled here and founded Benua Kling. He had four sons, who became the founders of four families. The most remarkable of these sons was Serunting Sakti.

According to another legend, Serunting was the son of the giant, Poyang Panjang, who needed nine servants to support his genital organs[1] and so was called Sembilan Gelas (nine basket loads). Some say that Serunting himself needed the carriers and that he was born of the sun. Poyang Panjang was married to the princess Tenggang, a daughter of the Ratu die Gunung Ledang, near Pagarruyung. No children were born to them, however, so one fine day they went to Padang Langgar to dance and pray and to act as if they were rocking a child.[2] Suddenly a child ran to

---

[1]Probably a play upon words, since *gelat* means 'penis'. Cf. Mills, The Rengma Nagas, p. 165: 'Now Ndü had a penis so enormously long that he could wrap it nine times around his waist.'

[2]A similar custom in order to get children is also to be found in Samosir. The man and the woman bear a wooden doll, representing a child, on their back and dance with it.

meet them and they called him Serunting. He grew up, became *sakti* (a magician) and married a beautiful girl, with a brother named Ria Tebing.

The brothers-in-law planted their fields side by side in the forest, separated only by a felled tree trunk. The bark facing the field of Ria Tebing turned into gold while on Serunting's side grew nothing but toadstools. Sometimes, at night, Serunting turned the trunk around, but in vain—the gold was always for his brother-in-law and the toadstools for him. This spoiled their friendship; hard words were spoken, and they even came to blows. But since both were magicians with equal power, neither was victorious.

Ria Tebing, however, noticed that when he called to his brother-in-law during the fight, the latter's voice came from different directions, and so he persuaded his sister to coax this secret from her husband. Next day, she told her brother that Serunting had the power of hiding his soul in an *alang-alang* leaf and that he could be wounded only by piercing the *alang* with the stem of a *bamban* leaf.

Immediately Ria Tebing resumed the fight, pierced a trembling *alang-alang*, and Serunting fell with a terrible wound in his leg. From the broken reed flowed a drop of blood, out of which was born the Crippled Tiger. His descendants live on the Dempu volcano and are hostile to all people except to the descendants of Serunting.

Serunting was so depressed by this treachery that he decided to seek death by drowning himself in the sea. He baked a great pot of clay and in this floated down the river. The pot landed near Mount Seguntang, where lived an old man from Majapahit. He spat into the mouth of Serunting, thus endowing him with the magic power of changing people into stone by a mere word. Henceforth, he was called Si Pahit Lidah, Bitter Tongue, because his saliva was fatal.

Serunting now returned to his village, where he found that his wife had died of remorse. Ria Tebing fled west with his followers, to the woods of the Bukit Barisan. Near the Broken Mountains (Gunung Patah), their spirits live to this day in the form of little green birds, hostile to the descendants of Serunting.

For years the latter lived without a wife, until one day, he saw his reflection in a well and suddenly felt lonesome. Soon after, seven nymphs hung their veils on the branches of a tree and began to dance by the well. Serunting succeeded in seizing one of these veils and so obtained the nymph Sanggul Bagulung as his wife. She bore him a son, who became the founder of the Semidang tribe.

On this occasion, Serunting suddenly remembered that he had not yet given a wedding feast and decided to do so at once. From far and near, the people streamed to attend the cock-fights. Among the guests were three youths who came to a tragic end. Before returning home, they asked Sanggul Bagulung if she would dance for them. The nymph now asked Serunting for her veil and began to dance. To Serunting, it seemed that her feet did not touch the ground, and, fearing that he might lose her, he cried, 'She is vanishing!' At these words, the nymph began to weep and lament, for now she was compelled to disappear in reality. Her husband was inconsolable and, in his fury, he cursed the three youths and changed them into stone.

Filled with thoughts of vengeance, he now wandered all over the country, damming the rivers and flooding the fields. But his end was approaching. At the outlet of the Komering, it was observed that the river was running dry. Now there was a giant named Matempat, who had no magic power but two extra eyes, hidden under the hair at the back of his head. He journeyed to the source of the Komering, found Serunting near Lake Ranau, under the Great Sugar Palm (Enau Risi or Enau Rebo) and challenged him to fight. One of them had to lie face down under the tree, while the other hurled a spear at him. Serunting climbed into a tree and hurled his spear at Matempat. The latter, however, saw the spear with the eyes at the back of his head and managed to evade it. But when Serunting's turn came, he was fatally wounded.

Matempat climbed down from the tree and was curious to find out if the tongue of his famous adversary actually was bitter. He kneeled down by the corpse, opened the mouth, and carefully licked at the tongue. At the same moment, he was turned into stone.

The petrified bodies were later divided by the people. Every man took a piece and laid it in his field or in his village, to assure a rich harvest and many children.

A grandson of Serunting, named Sangga Rujungan, one day was changed into a tiger and devoured his own daughter. Often he appeared in the villages when a feast was being celebrated, but harmed no one. By offering a *sanggal*, a sacrifice of rice and four eggs, the people could always summon him and ask his advice.

The figure of Serunting Sakti (Si Pahit Lidah) has something tragic, something which touches the heart of every Malay. This young man, with his strong and noble character, seemed destined for a life of happiness and good fortune. The gods, however, had decreed otherwise. They gave him a treacherous wife and aroused his righteous indignation by the tree with gold and toadstools. A fight with his brother-in-law and a humiliating defeat were the result. The proud heart of the Malay was so humiliated that he no longer wished to live, but sought death. This favour was not granted to him. He was compelled to live, endowed with supernatural power. But with this power, he also got a feeling of intense loneliness. He made a second marriage and this, too, ended in tragedy.

With a heart full of bitterness, Bitter Tongue wandered through the pleasant land of Sumatra. Near the lovely blue Lake Ranau, death at last freed him from his sombre existence.

Between Serunting and Si Singamangaraja, the mysterious royal Batak priest, there are several remarkable points of similarity. Neither was a true ruler, but both exercised more than regal power over their countrymen. Both were endowed with magic power; their curse brought death to all adversaries. Serunting could cover bare mountains with verdure; Singamangaraja could make rain. Both were able to grant the blessing of children, both controlled the secret laws of nature.

Naturally there are differences between the two, chiefly psychological. Singamangaraja personifies the hard, merciless Batak; Serunting the emotional, tenderhearted Malay.

It is interesting to note that the people of Pasemah also have a form of *shamanism*, one expression of which is known as 'tilol'. As a rule, this takes place in the case of sickness or when someone has been accursed by the spirits. A *tilol* seance usually begins about 8 o'clock in the evening and often lasts until dawn. On this occasion, use is made of the village square, which is covered with mats. On the mats must be placed the following objects: two pieces of white cotton cloth; a short sword; a small basket (*petrah tali nyawe*), in which are a scrap of linen cloth, a loop of white thread to which is tied a silver ring or a needle, a white cup filled with rice, an incense burner, water in a white cup, a saucer of rice porridge and steamed gluten rice, and a plate with the following contents—a pile of *sirih* leaves, on which is laid a leaf of *gambir*. On top stands a miniature rice-block with three hollows. The central hollow contains water, the other two, rice powder and a bit of cotton. On one side of the block is placed a twig of *selasih* or *cendane*, on the other a straw cigarette. The plate also contains five bits of *pinang*, a *gambir* leaf pasted with *sirih*, and a leaf of *sirih* folded into the shape of a pepper pod.

For a seance of *titol*, two people are required—the medium (*ayam tilol*) and his leader (*dukun tilol*). Only men are allowed to act as mediums, and the only requirement is that they soon become unconscious. As a rule, every village has someone available who has already served in this capacity.

At the beginning of the seance, the medium must be entirely covered, especially his eyes, nose, and ears. Also, incense is burned. Before beginning his journey to the spirit world, however, he is struck on the forehead with the twig of *selasih*, while the *dukun* says that he must now be on his way. Now the *ayam tilol* begins his journey, and in muffled tones he tells of his experiences. Generally he first meets some wild animal, after which he ceases moving about.

As soon as the *dukun* observes this, he urges the medium not to be afraid but to go on. Sometimes the medium stops before a bridge which is being built, so that there is no connection between the two banks of a river, and it is amusing to see how he makes a leap from the ground as if he were indeed taking a jump. Farther on, he encounters an iron pot full of a red-hot liquid, then a huge caterpillar and the spirits of those who have met an unnatural death, as, for instance, in childbirth. At every encounter the same thing is observed—the medium is afraid and hesitates for a moment, while the *dukun* tells him to have no fear and urges him to go on.

At length he arrives in the land where the spirits abide and now he can begin to ask their council. Often it is Poyang Ketunggalan, also called Poyang Pagar, to whom they turn for information. The Poyang takes possession of the medium and speaks through his mouth. He calls the name of one of the bystanders, who replies, 'The *ayam* has come to you, o Poyang, beseeching you to turn aside the disaster which has been visited upon us. Tell us what evil we have done.' Usually this entreaty must be repeated several times before the Poyang replies. The evil deed is usually murder, perjury, or adultery. Those present are now in a high state of tension, especially the sick man's relatives being seized with fright. It is very rare, therefore, for the charge to be denied.

Now they must give the Poyang a sacrificial meal, confess their guilt, and beg his forgiveness. The *ayam tilol* is given a copious meal, two pieces of cotton cloth, and ten rice cakes. The *dukun*, also, is invited to a feast and given a present of money.

Another form of shamanism is *mutos gentong*, in which, however, no *dukun* is necessary while women, also, may act as medium. Those who are adapted for this rôle are regarded as belonging to a higher order than the *ayam tilol*. Here, too, the medium must take a journey to the spirit world, thereby losing her own name and being given the name of a soul.

A third form of shamanism is *tenong*, a form of augury. According to whether use is made of rice grains, a pickaxe, a fish trap, etc., it is known as *tenong padi*, *tenong beliyong*, etc. The *dukun* invokes various gods, until suddenly the grains of rice begin to move, which is a sign that one has reached the god who has caused the sickness. The *dukun* asks what crime the sick man has committed and what remedies he must use. Now he names all the various medicines, until the grain again begins to move.

The *perubatan* occupies a prominent place in the folklore of Pasemah. It is a shield of woven bamboo, the front of which is ornamented with small beads and shells. It hangs on a band wound with cloth, while on the underside all sorts of strange things are fastened—dried pods, locks of goat hair and goat's horns, bits of fish jaws, shells, etc. The *perubatan* is an abiding place for the soul and is made whenever a woman expects a child. As soon as the child is born and has been washed, the *perubatan* is held before it and these words spoken, 'I call you, o soul, and beseech you for a long life,' the idea being that the child's soul is united with the *perubatan*.

The shield is now kept at the back of the house and produced again when the child's navel string has severed and he is brought down to the river for the first time. As a rule, this ceremony is performed by some woman chosen for her skill in reciting magic formulas. She takes the child in her arms and hangs the *perubatan* over her shoulder. At the moment that she descends from the house and sets foot on the ground, she prays for the child. Arrived at the river bank, she repeats her formulas, begging that the child may have a long life and that he may be spared from all misfortune. The water is conceived as the abode of good and evil spirits, the *perubatan* serving as protection from the latter.

When the child is brought for the first time to the village of his mother's family, the *perubatan* is again worn over the shoulder. It is also used if a child happens to eat his own excreta. This is considered an evil omen which may even result in the soul leaving the body. And now a strange ceremony is used in order to recall the soul. The child is placed in one of the village houses, while the mother (with the *perubatan* over her shoulder) knocks at the door of various houses, asking if anyone has seen her child. After she has knocked at six houses, she approaches the seventh, where she has previously left her child, and repeats the question, which is then answered in the affirmative.

Now she enters the house and while she walks seven times around her child she says, 'I call you back, O soul. Throw away all that is foul and unclean and when you are purified return to me.' In this way, evil is averted.

Finally, the *perubatan* is used when the child has had some accident, which has not terminated fatally. The child, however, has been so frightened that the soul has left the body, and now it is recalled with the aid of the *perubatan*. If a child falls so hard that it cannot utter a sound, it may not be picked up at once, but only after someone has walked around it seven times with a *perubatan*.

If the *perubatan* is lost—for instance, when a house burns down—it is believed that the child is doomed to become ill. In all haste a new *perubatan* must be made, to which the soul may be fastened.

Perubatan.

When the child is five years old, the shield is no longer considered necessary, as the soul is then sufficiently united with the body. One *perubatan* may be used for several children, so that it is not necessary to make a separate shield for each child.

The *petrah tali nyawe* is a small basket, in which are found a skein of white thread, a cup of rice, and a silver object. The meaning of these things is as follows: the cup of rice, which has been cleansed from all impurities, is the symbol of a pure conscience; the skein of thread serves to tie the soul; while the silver object indicates that one has a 'white heart', a calm mind. The silver is usually a ring or a coin.

The *petrah tali nyawe* is the assembling place of all the souls in the family, so that they may not fly away. It is carefully put away in the house and must be present at every sacrificial feast. Then the soul basket is placed at the head of the mat on which the various dishes are served. A sacrificial meal is supposed to placate the gods and the ancestral spirits who, though invisible, always take part in the feast. The object of setting out the *petrah tali nyawe* is to commend the souls of those present to the good spirits and as a symbol of pious humility.

In Pasemah, small-pox is the most dreaded of all diseases, and when there is an epidemic of this sickness, it is said that heaven and earth have been disturbed. In order to prevent other villages from being infected, the people assemble by night in the spirit house, bringing the *petrah tali nyawe*.

Besides the thread, the cup and the ring, there is also a string of shells, the number of shells indicating the number of souls in each house. The baskets are then entrusted to the guardian of the spirit house, where they are kept for seven days and seven nights. The guardian himself lies down to sleep, in the hope that the gods may send him a dream, revealing how the collected souls of his fellow villagers may be protected from the dread desease.

For the descendants of Semidang, one of the six tribes of Pasemah Lebar, this ceremonial must be repeated every year, immediately after the harvest. Apparently it is hoped that this will have a prophylactic effect. On this occasion, the baskets are kept only for three days and three nights in the *rumah poyang*.

To bind the soul, an iron object may also be used, preferably a knife of some particular make. This is done only after a revelation.

To make holes in a field, use is made of a stick, the point of which is carved in the form of a penis, for the natives of Pasemah believe that the rice has a soul and is a woman.

Ngawal is a secret magic, the object of which is to bring the soul of the rice from a neighbour's field to one's own, so that the harvest may increase. When the harvest is almost ripe, a fire is made in the immediate vicinity of the field which is to be blighted. Into the fire is thrown all kinds of filth, so that the stench may frighten the rice soul and cause it to flee. The next day the field is again visited and on the trident (*tunggul penjulung*)[1] are laid an egg and some rice porridge, in order to placate the seven river gods, meanwhile complaining and begging them to increase the rice harvest. After this, seven rice stems are cut off and the owner of the field is supposed to give some trifle, for instance, a straw cigarette.

In the meantime an assistant remains in the field, going through the motions of winnowing the rice and heaping it into a basket. In a secluded corner is placed a cage, in which it is hoped that a bird may be caught. This bird is related to the rice soul, and when it has been caught, it is brought to the owner's field and given the best of care. When all this has been done, the soul of the field will migrate to the other, insuring a rich harvest.

Prehistoric Monuments

The natives of Pasemah came originally from Pasemah Lebar, a plateau in the Barisan Mountains, with an average height of from 500 to 1 000 m. To the north, it is bounded by the Gumai Mountains, to the west by the Dempo volcano, to the south by Gunung Patah, while on the east there is no definite boundary.

---

[1] The *tunggul penjulung* is a bamboo stake, which is set up in the middle of the field. The top is divided into three points and is sometimes crowned with a bird. The points are held together with a cross lath. At the foot often lies a great stone, on which is laid rice, cakes, *sirih*, etc. On the trident is laid a skein of thread, while on top are laid bits of iron and coins. Often, green twigs are fastened to it. Apparently, we have here a symbol of the tree of life, which in some magical way encourages the growth of the crops. From this point, the seed is sowed and here a sacrificial meal is offered after the harvest.

The *tunggul penjulung* is the abode of the rice soul. On one stake I saw a tiger tail. No doubt we have to do here with a very ancient relation between tigers and rice. One recalls the tiger images of Pageralam (*marga* Pagergunung).

In the Deccan and Konkan, the figure of a tiger made of dry leaves of sugar-cane is posted at a conspicuous place in the fields for protecting the crops of sugar-cane. Then, one man is held to represent the tiger, and is asked to run, beating his mouth with the palm of his hand as he runs. The rest of the party pursue him and beat him with pieces of the cane. Cf. R. E. Enthoven, The Folklore of Bombay, p. 308.

From Pasemah Lebar these people migrated during the course of the ages, chiefly because of the scarcity of good fields suitable for agriculture. The oldest migration was probably to Semendo, a plateau south-east of Pasemah and began from the village Perdipe, on the right shore of the Lematang.

The inhabitants of this village were from early times followers of Islam, a fact mentioned by Presgrave in 1818. They read the Koran, took ritual baths, observed the *puasa*, etc. They had a leader of their own, who bore the title of *nabi penghulu*. Concerning this tribe, named Semendo, tradition relates that their *adat* is of Javanese origin. A religious teacher (*santri*) from Mataram first revealed these precepts to their forefathers, when they were still a wild tribe, wandering about in the forest.

At Kebanagung, near Pageralam, there is still an old Muhammadan grave, where a *nabi penghulu* lies buried, perhaps this very *santri*. At any rate, various figures in relief wear a typical Javanese kris.

In Pasemah and environs, we find a great number of prehistoric megaliths—upright stones, troughs, rice-blocks, dolmens, chests, images, and terraces.

The upright stones are in groups of four as well as in rows. At Tinggi Hari is an interesting pillar with the relief of a man and a crocodile, reminiscent of the pillars which the Dayaks erect for their dead (*hampatong*).

The troughs are used partly to hold skulls, partly for holy water (*anggir*). This water averted the influence of bad magic and was used for ablutions during the marriage ceremony, after funerals, in times of war, etc.

The rice-blocks sometimes have six hollows. This number is in connection with the rank and standing of the owner, as in the Batak Lands. One of them is adorned with a serpent.

The chests are painted inside with pictures of men and buffaloes, apparently portraying the soul on its journey to the underworld. There are also pictures of monkeys, with three fingers on each hand (religious mutilation?). Professor Heine-Geldern has compared these paintings with Chinese grave frescoes from the Han period. The colours used are yellow, red, and brown. This peculiar combination reminds one of the Lampong cloths, on which ships are portrayed, and also of certain shields in Borneo. Undoubtedly these colours and motifs have come down from a very ancient art of painting, which has existed at one time in large parts of South-East Asia.

The stone terraces are reminiscent of the earthen terraced pyramids of Toba, still built above the graves of illustrious Batak chiefs.

The images naturally surpass all the other monuments in interest. In the main they represent human beings on elephants or buffaloes, but there are also other figures. Often the images of men wear a short tunic, helmet, chain, and sword. We will not attempt to describe them all, but will linger only with a few.

A few kilometres north of Pageralam was found a magnificent stone in the form of an elephant. At the left side of the animal kneels a warrior with a pointed helmet[1] on his head. With both hands, he clings to the elephant's ear and looks back. Around his neck is a bronze ring, in his girdle a great sword, and on his back a bronze drum. His legs are encased in bronze rings, predecessors of our modern puttees.

On the other side appears a warrior with the same equipment. He wears a twofold girdle, from which in front and behind hangs a slip of cloth. Around the right wrist is a broad band; compare the bronze cuff of Jujun (Korinci). The man has just arisen and is placing his right foot on the bent foot of the elephant. In a moment the animal will raise his foot and set the man on his back.

An exploration of this place in 1936 brought to light a number of great stones. Ten metres west of the *batu gajah* were stones arranged in a square. There can be no doubt that this is a cemetery. It lies in the immediate vicinity of a place where a small lake flows into a tiny stream. Probably the churchyard was made here for a special reason and the lake formerly had some religious significance. In fact, most of the antiquities of Pasemah lie along the rivers.

The *batu gajah* was evidently erected by two chiefs, whose particular merits gave them the right to have themselves immortalized with an elephant. It served as their grave monument, their soul stone, in which their spirits might find a last resting place after death. Possibly they had the stone made during their lifetime.

Something similar is found among the Sea Dayaks of Borneo, where occasionally the Feast of Elephants (*Gawai Gajah*) is celebrated. The feast may be given only by a warrior who has been especially lucky in war and has severed a great number of heads.

---

[1]Professor J. H. Hutton draws my attention to similar-shaped cane hats of the Daflas in North Assam.

A long pole is erected with a wooden elephant at the top, and near this pole a sacrifice is made.[1] Similar images are found among the Kenyah Dayaks.[2]

The elephant is still found on the remarkable weavings with ships, which are made in this district, as well as in Kroë and the Lampongs.

Urns in elephant form are found in the eastern part of the Batak Lands (Simalungun), also images of warriors on elephants.

The elephant as grave monument in primitive form, made of cloth and filled with straw, is also found among the Lhota Nagas of Assam.[3]

In a more perfected form, they are found in China, for instance, on the avenue leading to the Ming graves, which is flanked by pairs of elephants. This motif occurs already in the Sung and Tang periods and traces of elephants have even been found in Chang graves, i.e. at a much earlier period than the images of Pasemah.

The elephant images of South Sumatra thus have no relation to the Hindus, as has often been asserted, but were inspired by Far Indian and Chinese models. A striking proof of this is found in our *batu gajah* itself. On the back is chiselled the head of a fabulous animal with tusks, and similar heads are found already in the older Chinese art.[4]

The elephant also appears on the prehistoric bronze drums of Bima and Saleier.

Let us now consider the tiger images. At Pageralam (*marga* Pagergunung) is a group representing two tigers in the act of mating. Between the paws of the tigress stands a human figure. On the hill of Palakkunduran, where the Air Mulak flows into the Lematang, lie the fragments of a huge image group, representing a tiger which has sprung upon a buffalo in such a way that the hind feet have a strangle grip on the victim's head. The great tiger head was broken into two pieces, which were found buried in two different places. Some portions are so pulverized that reconstruction is impossible.

What is the meaning of these mysterious images? In order to answer this question we must remember the attendant tiger, the

---

[1] E. H. Gomes, 17 Years among the Sea of Borneo, p. 215.

[2] Elshout, Geneeskunde der Kenja Dajaks, p. 22 (plate).

[3] J. P. Mills, The Lhota Nagas, p. 159.

[4] C. Hentze, Objets rituels, croyances et dieux de la Chine antique et de l'Amerique, fig. 49.

belief in which is prevalent throughout Sumatra. Many people are supposed to have an animal of this kind, whose woe and weal are inevitably bound up with those of his master. In many Malay villages one hears stories of people who make friends with tigers, ride through the forest on the animal's back, and learn the art of fencing from them. Often this friendship takes the form of a certain degree of relationship, the one being identified with the other. Here the tiger is considered as a sort of double and the fate of the two is closely intertwined. Ethnologists call this phenomenon 'nagualism'.

The Batak tribe (*marga*) Baliyat is not allowed to eat tiger meat and the Minangkabau tribe (*luhak*) Agam declares that they all descend from the tiger.

The image at Palakkunduran may have been erected by some prominent person as tribute to his attendant tiger, to glorify the might and power of this animal double. No doubt it was purposely set up at the confluence of two rivers because such places are believed to have an evil magic. After the founder's death, his soul found a resting place in this image and was united forever with the great attendant tiger.

The erection of an image of this kind was probably only granted to those who had first given a tiger feast (as in Nias) or who had won the name of 'tiger' by their prowess in head-hunting. This title is still held in great honour among some Malay and Batak tribes. Hairy people can go without fear to the village of Talang Pisang on the Dempo volcano, where only tigers live. It is not so very long ago that prominent chiefs in Kroë had a wooden tiger image placed in the gable of their house.

A remarkable parallel is seen in the *hampatong* or soul pillars of Borneo, carved with all sorts of human and animal figures and usually erected after the last death feast. A special group is formed by the tiger images which carry a human being on their back or sit on a man's head. Sometimes tiger images were made for a *raja*'s funeral and the animal was supposed to accompany the dead in the next world. Sometimes these images were set up in the death house.

Now the tiger is not found in Borneo. By *harimau* the Dayak means the *macan dahan* or wild cat. The tiger poles are therefore not inspired by an indigenous culture but must at some time have been brought from another country. But from which country?

This we may learn from the pillars which show a tiger fighting with a serpent. This motif is also found in China, whence it proceeded to Siberia in the form of wolf and serpent.[1]

The image at Pageralam, with the human figure between the paws, reminds one of a similar bronze image from the Chinese Chou period,[2] and also of two wooden figures from Borneo. One, on a death house at Lakum on the Lower Mahakam,[3] represents a tiger with an old village chief in his jaws; the other, at Kasungan in the South-east Division, portrays a tiger-cat, with its forefeet on a human head.[4]

The motif of an animal or monster holding a human being in its paws is also found in Siberia and North-west America (totem poles). As to the original idea new research must be made in each particular case. It is usually impossible to find the exact solution to the problem, because the original significance has long been forgotten. The all-devouring demon of initiation, the destructive waning moon and the primeval man probably form the foundation of this motif. In the image of Pageralam, however, we are reminded most of a human being and his attendant tiger.

The image at Palakkunduran turns our gaze on several bronze objects from Ordos (North China) and Luristan (Persia), on which are portrayed deer and horses being attacked by tigers. However great may be the distance which separates these images, still a certain relation is apparent.

An image from Tebing Tinggi (Pasemah) also bears some relation to Ordos. It represents three wrestlers and probably has reference to a ritual contest, the purpose of which was to increase the fertility of the fields or the chief's magic power.

At the sacrificial feast of the Batak ancestor, a bull is sacrificed, after which there is a wrestling match between the butcher and the leader of the feast. In the Nikobaren, the men wrestle in front of the village spirit pole; while among the Lakher in British India (with their important megalith cult), wrestling matches take place during certain religious ceremonies.[5]

The Lusheis of British India believe that the kingdom of the dead is guarded by a man who shoots at the souls of the departed. However, he spares those who during their lifetime have killed some animal, for instance a tiger. These tiger souls follow the

---

[1]Hentze, figs. 67 and 68.
[2]Hentze, Mythes et symboles lunaires, p. 167.
[3]Verslag Midden Borneo Expeditie 1925, p. 143.
[4]Lumholtz, Through Central Borneo 2, p. 351 (plate).
[5]Parry, The Lakhers.

hunter in the hereafter and sometimes he rides on them.[1]

Finally, there is the custom of the Lotha Nagas (Assam) of placing bamboo tigers on their graves.[2]

Very interesting, also, is a stone with relief at Air Puar. Two men with pointed helmets each hold a buffalo by a rope, while together they hold a drum. Under the drum appears a dog; a crocodile bites him in the leg.[3]

It is difficult to give an explanation of this representation. Involuntarily one thinks of the story of how shamanism originated among the Kubus. A dead dog was made alive by beating drums, saying prayers, and slaughtering buffaloes.

But it is also possible that the great chiefs are simply portrayed with their heraldic symbols of wealth (buffaloes) and dignity (drum) and with their heraldic animals.

The drum is an attribute which stands in close relation to the rank of the tribal chief. Various information seems to indicate that a man had the right to place a drum in his house only after the sacrifice of a slave or a certain animal (buffalo, dog, rabbit) or after a certain feast has been celebrated. The spirit of the victim then lived in the drum and when it was struck, his voice was heard. No doubt the figures of men and animals pictured on prehistoric and modern bronze drums bear some relation to this phenomenon. For instance, in Dongson (Tonkin) has been found a drum with the figure of a dog.

In South Nias, it is related that formerly, once a year a drum feast was celebrated, during which the villagers sang and danced around a great, cylindrical drum; they burned incense, laid down bits of raw meat on it, and struck it with severed heads. When the feast was over, the tribal chief sat on the drum and was given a new title, 'Great Sun', 'Tiger', or some similar name. Perhaps these titles have some connection with the sun which appears on prehistoric bronze drums or with the tiger head pictured on modern Javanese drums (*tong-tong*). In later times wooden images of people, birds, and lizards were laid on the drum. The significance of this is no longer known, but an old man said he supposed they were meant to guard the drum.

As for the dog and the crocodile, the Batak tribe of the Sembiring relates that their tribal father was once saved by a dog.

---

[1]Shakespear, The Lushei Kuki Clans.
[2]Mills, The Lhota Nagas, pp. 158–9.
[3]See my Oudheidkundige Vondsten in Palembang, Bijlage C, pp. 9–10.

Members of the *marga* Tompul are not allowed to eat dog meat. The Minangkabau tribe (*luhak*) 13 Kota descends from a dog. The Bukit Besar, near Air Puar, is supposed to be a woman mating with a dog. The spirit of a dog seems formerly to have been a mighty warrior (*pangulubalang*). A great dog tomb, built of heavy blocks of sandstone, is on the right bank of the Barumon, south of Unte Rudang, while a smaller one lies south of Gunung Tua. In Simalungun are found urns with the bones of dogs. The figure of a dog is also carved on the Batak magician's wand.

The close relation between human beings and crocodiles is known throughout Sumatra. At Nias, the crocodile was formerly the emblem of the mightiest tribal chiefs.

We will now let the stone images rest for a moment. In connection with what we have seen elsewhere in Sumatra and Nias, we may say with considerable certainty that feasts of merit were given at the time when they were founded. Soon we shall find an entirely unexpected corroboration of this fact.

Now a few brief remarks regarding the bronze culture. The images prove that the founders were already acquainted with bronze. They made drums, helmets, swords, neck bands, armlets and anklets, etc. In the Pasemah, indeed, bronze rings with spirals have been found, also pendants and ear-rings with a human face, a bowl with an animal face, etc. In Korinci was found a vase with spiral ornaments, a cuff, and the fragment of a drum; a meagre harvest, to be sure.

The discovery of a bronze spear point near one of the cannon-shaped stones in Jambi proves that the builders of these monuments also knew bronze.

The megalith builders of Central Sumatra may also have used bronze tools for making their pillars, but, alas, we have no tangible evidence of this fact.

And the Bataks? Their wonderful objects of brass were probably inspired by some prehistoric bronze art. During my wanderings I saw some bronze objects, which differed very much from the decorative art of the present time. It is simply unthinkable that Batak megalith builders were not acquainted with bronze, and it may be that at some future time prehistoric objects in this metal will be brought to light.

It cannot be proved that Nias also knew bronze during the neolithic period, but it is quite probable. Not long ago, artistic bronze lamps were cast, with figures of a dog, a dragon, a hornbill, etc.

Pepadon. In the Lampongs there is a peculiar custom which allows the chiefs to buy a title and a *pepadon* for money. A *pepadon* is a wooden seat with the head of a bird, a dragon, an elephant, or a horse. Formerly payment was made in buffaloes, rice, etc. The possession of a *pepadon* confers all sorts of privileges—one is allowed to wear certain jewels, to be carried in a sedan chair with the figure of an animal's head, to erect a gate in front of the house, to demand a certain dowry for one's daughter, etc.

There are a great number of *pepadon,* the one more important than the other. It is even possible to be promoted from one *pepadon* to another, while in every district these seats and the privileges attached to them are different.

Now, it is not my intention to give a lengthy review of the *pepadon* system. I simply wish to call attention to a few particulars.

Formerly a *pepadon* might only be erected after a man had cut off four heads. These heads were struck against the bench and later kept in a chest under the seat. The jaws of the wooden animal's head were smeared with blood. In Kroë the seat was called *krosi bulampok*; it was placed on a great stone, around which was hung a drapery with the picture of a ship.

The tribal chief and his wife were brought to the festal grounds in a wooden ship on wheels.[1] The prow had an animal head, usually that of a rhinoceros-bird, an elephant, or a buffalo. In the middle of the ship was a baldakin, on which was placed a rhinoceros-bird or a serpent made of cloth. To right and left were poles, decorated like trees—on the branches hung beads, shells, little pots, pieces of cloth, coins, delicacies, etc. The number of objects depended on the rank of the owner. The articles which hung on the tree were later pulled off by the young folks.

Formerly the dead bodies of tribal chiefs, in full regalia, were set down in these wagons. Around them were placed wooden dolls and animals made of cloth. The trees were also replaced by long poles with feathers, and crowned with birds. Rice was scattered in the ship, after which it was hurled into a deep ravine.

Living people thus had the right to be carried in a *perahu andak* or *perahu garuda.* In some districts, the woman was allowed to rest her feet on a slave, who was killed after arrival at the festive grounds. Beside the ship walked men, who dragged over the

---

[1]Similar ships on wheels are also in China and in medieval Europe, where they were accompanied by buffoons. Animals on wheels are at the court of Kota Waringin in South Borneo. They are called *tunggangan* and are the seats of important people.

ground brass plates tied with long strings of cotton cloth. In front of the procession walked four women, holding a great banner in the form of a crescent moon, with the picture of a ship. The dancing girls were allowed to wear twelve brass bracelets on each arm, and on their heads they wore a boat-shaped metal crown.

Across the road was stretched a rope, which was severed by two masked clowns. One was a man and had to walk as if he were lame; the other was a woman, usually the chief's sister-in-law. When the rope was cut, they had to pay a certain sum of money or to give some rice; also, they had to submit to being beaten by the guardian of the rope. In some districts, he gave them a slight prick with a knife, upon which they were supposed to give a loud yell.

The task of these clowns, indeed, was to make trouble continuously. Now and then they even hindered the progress of the ship, pulling it alternately from one to the other. Clumsy jokes were the order of the day and they were allowed to say anything that happened to come into their heads. They swore that black was white, that high was low, that great was small. They also turned upside-down everything on which they could lay their hands and the coarser their actions, the better the festival.

In the procession was also carried a cake, in the form of a crocodile or a rhinoceros-bird. Around it lay numerous coins. This money was later divided among the family and the cake was cut into pieces, of which everyone received a certain portion. The most precious bit was the lower jaw, which was given to the tribal chief. The eating of this cake was supposed to encourage the growth of the crops.

The owner of a *pepadon* was also allowed to have a back to his chair. For this, also, a human head or a buffalo's head was necessary. This back was decorated with figures of breasts and rosettes; in rare specimen, a great penis was carved. The back of the chair was therefore intended to represent a human being.

European writers have always declared that the *pepadon* system originated in Bantam (Java). It is surprising how long this mistaken notion has been maintained, since it is quite plain that all these ceremonies have the character of the megalithic feast—promotion in rank, feast of merit, great extravagance, titles, privileges, head-hunting, and finally the erection of a memorial. And along with these ceremonies appears also what ethnology calls the '*potlach*'.

Now there is very little difference between the feast of merit and the *potlach*. The megalith feasts in Nias and in lesser degree those in the Batak Lands bear a striking resemblance to the *potlach*. The Javanese element in the Lampong feast of rank is therefore purely circumstantial, and appears only in few irrelevant details.

The owner of a *pepadon* may allow his wife to dance on a brazen salver, reminiscent of the round dancing-stones of Nias. And what is a *pepadon* except an *osa-osa*? The *pepadon* owner may also erect a gate in front of his house. On top of this gate is the figure of a bird, exactly as in the Japanese *torii*. To right and left are the figures of serpents, sometimes heads and, in rare cases, even human beings. Formerly there were also gates crowned by the figure of a serpent or of a ship. Permission to erect them was given only after the successful termination of a head-hunting expedition. I have never heard, however, that skulls were hung upon it. This was always stubbornly denied. However, a slave had to be buried under the gate, though this ceremony was often omitted. People walked through the gate in times of sickness, failure of the crops, miscarriage, or war.

A peculiar privilege was the permission to enlarge the ancestors' graves. For this ceremony, a certain number of buffaloes had to be slaughtered and a number of heads severed. Every time the grave was enlarged, a certain title was conferred and a higher rank assigned in the next world. Here is the most primitive form of the religious custom observed by more cultured races (Hindus, Egyptians) of enlarging their shrines and so acquiring magic power.

In Lampong and Kroë are also found weavings with pictures of ships, figures of people, animals, trees, etc. Recently Dr A. Steinmann has devoted considerable study to this subject.[1] The writer sees in these portrayals the death ship with the world tree and various other cosmic symbols. We merely make this assertion and try to justify it by various facts. In minor details some difference of opinion may be possible, but one interpretation need not exclude the other.

And so we believe that there is a close relation between these weavings and the *pepadon* system. Not only are these cloths draped around the stone when the *pepadon* is mounted, and carried at the head of the procession, but the foremost attribute of the feast, the wagon, is in the form of a ship. It is really an enlarged copy of the *pepadon* itself and is sometimes called *perahu pepadon*.

There is no doubt that the ships on some of these cloths

---

[1]Les tissus à jonques du Sud de Sumatra, Revue des Arts asiatiques, 1937.

represent *pepadon*; they either contain a *pepadon* or represent a scene from the *pepadon* feasts. We see people sitting on elephants and naturally think at once of the elephant *pepadon*.

That we are concerned here not with a Javanese custom but with a ceremonial which has been observed for thousands of years is evidenced by the prehistoric elephant images with their human figures, from Pasemah. But at the same time, we have here evidence that the images of Pasemah are related to feasts of rank and that they were erected as a memorial to the *pepadon* ceremony. No doubt they were dedicated with a great deal of ritual. Around them were set up the poles with birds (as in Timor at the present time), the mythical trees with beads, the death dolls, etc., all this to create the illusion of the mystic boat. And this boat must originally have been the place of initiation, where the candidates sat under the tree of knowledge, where they were introduced to the mystical totem animal, monster of the initiation, and where they beheld the ritual contest between the two *phratri* (symbolized by the quarrelsome clowns).

The final climax of this initiation was the ship, symbol of the waxing and waning moon, of life and death, light and dark, good and evil.

In later times it was regarded principally as the death ship, on which the tribal chief journeyed to the spirit world with all the attributes of his power—*pepadon*, trees, animals, images of the dead, etc.

Representations of this kind are also found on mats and in beadwork patterns. In Lampong, brass bowls are made in the form of a ship (for *sirih* and for blackening the teeth). On the fore side is the head of a bird, a deer, or a buffalo. Apparently these objects were inspired by models from the Bronze Age, but in this case the ship form has no deeper significance.

Bengkulu

In Bengkulu, on a low hill near the sea, still stands Fort Marlborough, which was built by the English between 1714 and 1720, after they had left Fort St. George for reasons of health. The building is not beautiful; indeed, what fort is beautiful? But it is a solid construction and will resist for centuries the tooth of time.

Properly speaking, it is only imposing and tragic. Imposing as a symbol of the enormous courage and spirit of enterprise of the English people, and tragic on account of its great loneliness on this distant and desolate shore, which lies white, gleaming under the merciless sun. In one of the corner towers there is still a gun, overlooking the endless Indian Ocean, that extends from here to the polar ice. That gun gazes in the direction of England like a magnetic needle to a mysterious current. It stands there loyal and attentive, unable to believe that the great days of the Company are passed, as if it will still always fire on the wicked foes of its country, who in quick ships sail into the bay of Bengkulu. Sometimes one hears its boom at night; then it spits flashes of green fire out of its bronze muzzle; then it blazes against the ghosts of the past. . . .

O England, how loyally the gun of Fort Marlborough looks after you; how many of your sons slumber under its shadow forever. . . . There are still some tombstones, which record their names; when one sees those heavy blocks, one cannot believe that so many young corpses are hidden under them.

Here follows some inscriptions:

Here Lyeth interred the Body of Capn. James Cuney. He departed this Life February ye. 7th. 1737 Ao. Aetatis 36.

Here lies interred The Body of Henry Stirling late of Council at Fort Marlborough on this Coast. He was ninth son of James Stirling of Keir Esqr. and the Honourable Mrs. Marion Stuart of the Kingdom of Scotland and Departed this Life on the first day of April 1744 Aged 25 Years.

George Shaw Son of Mr. Thomas Shaw of London Merchant; after he had served the RT. Honbl. Company as Factor in Fort St. George for some time; came over in the Year 1699 Second of this place. In which Station he continued until he was removed by death, April ye. 25th 1704. Aetatis 28.

All three were then young men. Shaw came here already in his twenty-third year and remained five years long on this comfortless, lonely outpost. Five of his most beautiful and gay years scorched in the singeing heat of this empty, wretched land. When one closes one's eyes for a moment, one sees the tragedy of his short life.

Perhaps he was poor, perhaps he did not behave properly. His father then said: go to the Indies, there the gold grows on the trees! Young George danced and exulted and was envied by all his comrades. On a shining summer morning, he boarded a sailing-vessel and sailed down the Thames; his mother and his sweetheart waved to him with tears in their eyes.

Full of illusions, he arrived at Bengkulu and became clerk at Fort St. George. The first days were quite nice, but then came a night in which he felt lonely. Then many of such nights followed. Moths and butterflies were playing around the candelabrum, and the heart of the young knight of fortune grew heavy; his thoughts flew out to merry old England, but whenever he looked out to sea, he felt nothing but the warm, moist nightwind on his face.

One day he was no more alone; a nice, brown girl did his cooking, mended his clothes, and stroked his fair hair.

And suddenly, one night, death came and carried away the young Englishman. Over his lonely grave crashed a salvo and unravelled a faded Union Jack.

There is yet another inscription, which is still more touching:

Here are deposited the Remains of Charles Murray Esqr. Assistent [sic] to the Resident of Fort Marlborough. His Bravery arrested the sanguinary Progress of the Band of Assassins on the Night of the 27th December 1807, when Thomas Parr Esqr. Resident of Bencoolen & Representative of the Government fell by their misguided Fury. His human Care preserved the Life of the Widow of his Friend, wounded in continued Effort to shield her Husband from the Daggers of the Assassins. Disease induced by anxious and unceasing Exertions in the zealous Discharge of his public Duty during a Season of Danger and Alarm, terminated this Life on the 7th of January 1808 Aged 21 Years. In Memory of the brave and humane Conduct and his public Service The Right Honourable Lord Minto Governor in Council ordered this Monument to be erected.

Here slumbers then an unknown hero of 21 years, perhaps one of those empire-builders, who have written England's name in the stars: a name which never will pass away as long as greatness exists in the world. The young bodies of these paladins lie scattered, forlorn and forgotten, in all parts of the world. Let them sleep; their lives were not easy.

Resident Parr was murdered while he was lying ill in bed. His gravestone lies in the fort. 'The rare and estimable qualities, the pure and mild virtues which in private life adorned The Individual are recorded in the Affections of the Afflicted Friends who have survived him.' The hill on which his house stood, is called Mount Felix.

The finest man who ever lived in Bengkulu and who was overwhelmed here by much sorrow, was Thomas Stamford Raffles.

He was born in Jamaica in 1781. His father was captain of a merchant vessel trading between London and the West Indies. After having been at a boarding-school for two years—the sole education he ever enjoyed—young Raffles became clerk in the East India House in London. He received only a small salary and was always in difficult circumstances. Yet he succeeded in learning the French language and in acquiring some knowledge of natural history. He read also everything he could lay his hands on.

'This was, however, in stolen moments, either before the office hours in the morning, or after them in the evening; and I shall never forget the mortification I felt when the penury of my family once induced my mother to complain of my extravagance in burning a candle in my room.'

These were difficult years; no wonder that the feeble boy sometimes overworked himself.

In his twenty-fourth year, he was appointed under-secretary in Penang. He had applied for this office because it enabled him to improve his financial situation. In April 1805 he departed, after having married a widow ten years older. A life of quick and great successes began.

In Penang, he immediately applied himself to the study of Malay, and after half a year he could read and write this language perfectly. Surprised at the working faculty and accurateness of the new official, the Honourable Company appointed him secretary in 1806.

For some years he lived quietly, probing more deeply into Malay problems and situations. From all sides he collected information on the morals and customs of the people, on the religion, the plants, the animals, the geography, etc. His simple ways and kindness enabled him to learn from the mouths of the

Malays themselves many particulars. He understood their character
excellently, and it is striking to hear the very Christian man say:

> I respect the religious of every persuasion, and am sorry my experience
> draws from me a wish that Christians did as much justice to their
> Redeemer as Mahometans do to their Prophet. Of the Christian religion I
> fear there is more said than done, and therefore shall not add to the
> numerous useless and foolish remarks upon it. I ever considered it as
> the simplest religion on earth, and for that reason the best. But of the
> Mahometan religion, on the contrary, as much, if not more, is done than
> said. We are here surrounded with Mussulmens, and I find them very
> good men, and by far more attentive to the duties and observances of
> their religion than the generality of Christians.

In Penang, he also made the acquaintance of Dr Leyden, who
became his most intimate friend and supported him strongly in his
study.

In June 1810, Raffles went to Bengal and drew the attention of
Lord Minto to Java; he pointed out to him the great strategical
and commercial interest of this island and advised him to conquer
it for England. 'On the mention of Java, his Lordship cast a look
of such scrutiny, anticipation and kindness upon me that I shall
never forget.' Seldom has a Governor ever accepted from so
young an official such bold advice. Minto immediately approved
and appointed Raffles agent to the Malay States.

So he removed to Melaka and began with feverish industry to
prepare the enterprise. Of course many competent authorities,
beginning with the admiral, declared his scheme impracticable. At
all times mediocre specialists have thwarted genial dilettantes. But
nothing speaks so much for Raffles' greatness as his blind self-
confidence in these critical months. Large provisions of victuals,
horses, and guns were imported from India; their destination was,
however, kept a strict secret.

From this time, we possess a fine description of Raffles by his
secretary, Abdullah:

> He loved most to sit in quietude, when he did nothing else but write or
> read; and it was his usage, when he was either studying or speaking, that
> he would see no one till he had finished. He had a time set apart for each
> duty, nor would he mingle one with another. Further, in the evenings,
> after tea, he would take ink, pen and paper, after the candles had been
> lighted, reclining with closed eyes, in a manner that I often took to be
> sleep; but in an instant he would be up, and write for a while, till he went
> to recline again. Thus would he pass the night, till twelve or one, before
> he retired to sleep.

Outdoors, the full moon will have stood above the cocos-palms, and the rustling of the waves in the dark bay of Melaka will have lulled asleep the weary man.

Sleep well, Raffles. Tonight you are still unknown, but tomorrow you will sail to the south-east, where fame and honour await you on the other side of the equator, where the rays of the moon are falling no longer on the water and where glamour and sorrow are inseparable.

In May 1811, Lord Minto came personally to Melaka and on 3 August, the whole fleet lay before Batavia. Without much fighting, Java fell into the hands of the English. Minto returned to Bengal and appointed Raffles Lieutenant-Governor of the island. Raffles was then 30 years old, the youngest ruler ever to govern Java.

We need not delay over the numerous reorganizations that he introduced in the government in such a short time. Still less at the excellent manner in which he collected scientific data from all sides. He went everywhere himself to study personally monuments and curiosities and to get a knowledge of local conditions. He was the first European who ever saw the famous temple of Borobudur.

His work in Java has given him a place of honour in history. But, for this honour, destiny made him sacrifice heavily. Some weeks after arrival on the island, his friend Leyden ('more indeed than my right hand') died, and three years later, his wife. Especially the loss of the last he felt deeply; how often had he found solace in the 'hours that were beguiled away under the enchanting spell of one of whom the recollection awakens feelings which I cannot suppress'. Her death did not stand alone among domestic afflictions, for about the same time he lost in quick succession the children she had borne him.

After the fall of Napoleon, Java was returned to the Dutch. In vain did Raffles protest against it. He was appointed Lieutenant-Governor of Bengkulu, but his health was so bad that the doctors advised him to return immediately to Europe.

In March 1816, he undertook the homeward voyage 'as a lonely man, like one that has long since been dead'. The charges, which General Gillespie had uttered against him in London, sat heavily upon him. Lord Minto had also died; the man to whom he was indebted for his political career, the mighty and influential friend, who could have protected him so well in London.

In St. Helena, he encountered Napoleon.

In England he wrote in a short time his masterly *History of Java*.

He was knighted and was in touch with all sorts of leading people. There even seem to have been plans to appoint him Governor-General of India. He also succeeded in revoking the charge of Gillespie. He visited, too, old Warren Hastings, a statesman with whom he had many points in common, both in his career and in his character. Alas, the conversation between these two remarkable men has never been recorded.

In 1817 Raffles married for the second time, made a journey across Europe, and departed at the end of that year as Lieutenant-Governor to Bengkulu, where he arrived in March 1818. A period of great exertion, great successes, and still greater sorrows began. One cannot do better than to quote his letters:

> This is without exception the most wretched place I ever beheld. I cannot convey to you an adequate idea of the state of ruin and dilapidation which surrounds me. What with natural impediments, bad government, and the awful visitations of Providence which we have recently experienced in repeated earthquakes, we have scarcely a dwelling in which to lay our heads, or were withal to satisfy the cravings of nature. The roads are impassable; the highways in the town overrun with rank grass; the Government House a den of ravenous dogs and polecats. The natives say that Bengkulu is now dead land (tanah mati). In truth, I could never have conceived anything half so bad. We will try and make it better.

His very first acts were the emancipation of the slaves and the closing of all gaming-houses. Already soon his passion for travelling awoke, and he made a trip to Pasemah, where no European had ever been before. The naturalist Arnold accompanied him. On this trip an enormous flower was discovered, the now famous *Rafflesia-Arnoldi*.

Shortly afterwards, he visited Minangkabau and discovered the first Hindu-antiquities in Sumatra. Half a year later, on 29 January 1819, he hoisted the British flag at Singapore, his most famous deed. If he had passed away then, he would have died in full glory, and friends and enemies would have acknowledged unanimously his merits. But death is a grace which destiny usually bestows too late upon men.

A dark time began for Raffles. In 1820 he annexed Nias and abolished slavery there. 'The whole island is a sheet of the richest cultivation that can be imagined, and the interior surpasses in beauty and fertility the richest parts of continential India, if not of Java,' he exulted. But in the same year, his eldest son died, followed by two other children half a year later.

'To these severe and trying afflications I have to add the loss of nearly all our best and tried friends in this country, and that both Sophia and myself have suffered most seriously from long and alarming illnesses.'

And then came those touching words, spoken by a severely ill, yet world famous man, who in solitary confinement on the south-west coast of Sumatra, looked out with feverish eyes to the scorching Bay of Bengkulu: 'My heart has been nigh broken, and my spirit is gone: I have lost almost all that I prided myself upon in this world.'

He wanted to return to England. 'We never were very covetous of affluence, and riches are now of less value to us than ever. Under existing circumstances, I prefer an honourable retirement to a longer perseverance, to the complete ruin of our health and future comfort.'

In the same year, his friend, Salmond, died, and in 1823 his fourth child was buried. 'How is it that all we love and esteem, all those whose principles we admire, and in whom we can place confidence, are thus carried off.' But then he resigned himself to his fate and sought consolation in his work; but melancholy returned by fits and starts.

'I could lay me down and cry and weep for hours together, and yet I know not why, except that I am unhappy '

On 2 February he boarded the *Frame* and sailed for Europe. But a few hours after sailing, the ship caught fire through the careless-ness of the steward going with a naked light to draw off brandy from a cask. There was barely time for those on board to escape before the ship's gunpowder exploded.

All this passed much quicker than I can write it. We pushed off, and as we did so, the flames burst out of our cabin-window, and the whole of the after part of the ship was in flames. The mast and sails now taking fire, we moved to a distance sufficient to avoid the immediate explosion; but the flames were now coming out of the main hatchway.

The boats were many hours before reaching shore; the fugitives had neither food, water, nor clothes.

The loss I have to regret beyond all, is my papers and drawings,—all my notes and observations, with memoirs and collections, sufficient for a full and ample history, not only of Sumatra, but of Borneo, and almost every other island of note in these seas; my intended account of the establishment of Singapore; the history of my own administration; Eastern grammars, dictionaries, and vocabularies; and last, not least, a grand map of Sumatra, on which I had been employed since my arrival here, and on which, for the last six months, I had bestowed almost my whole undivided attention. This, however, was not all; all my collections in natural history, my splendid collection of drawings, upwards of two thousand in number, with all the valuable papers and notes of my friends Arnold and Jack; and, to conclude, I will merely notice that there was scarce an unknown animal, bird, beast, or fish, or an interesting plant, which we had not on board; a living tapir, a new species of tiger, splendid pheasants, etc., domesticated for the voyage; we were, in short, in this respect, a perfect Noah's Ark.

The very next morning, after the return of passengers and crew, Raffles gave one more proof of his perseverance, by commencing a fresh sketch of the map of Sumatra, and by taking steps to form a new natural history collection. Some delay took place in obtaining another ship; and it was not until 10 April that Raffles finally sailed from Bengkulu on board the ship *Mariner*.

He lived for another two years; dark clouds seemed to have enveloped him and obscured the peace of his mind. One day they found him dead at the bottom of the staircase of his house. It was 5 July 1826, in the morning at 5 o'clock—his forty-fifth birthday; the sun was not yet up, but already a new day was dawning and the dew lay sweetly over the field.

Thus died the man, who made England's name great on distant shores. He was a hard, intelligent worker, a great and many-sided scholar and, above all, a bold and resolute statesman. His character was mild and friendly; most of his subordinates liked him. His simple ways made it possible for the Javanese and Malays to repose their trust and friendship in him. But deep in this kindly disposed man slumbered a hard and obstinate will, which without pity would break every resistance. And the same will urged this feeble body on bold expeditions through unknown territories. There never reigned a finer nor a more civilized ruler in Java or Sumatra.

He was buried in Hendon Parish Church, but owing to differences with the vicar, a member of a slave-owning family, no monument was erected at the time, and the actual site of the grave has not been ascertained.

So is the will of destiny. The graves of Thomas Dias, Raffles, Tongku Tambuse and numerous other unknown heroes lie scattered throughout the world, in seas and in forests, on mountains and on distant shores, where the wind and the waves call to each other, over which the clouds pass by and over which at night the ancient constellations shed their mysterious light.

Appendix I

THE MEGALITHIC CULTURE OF ASSAM

BY

CHRISTOPH VON FURER-HAIMENDORF, PH.D.

WHILE megalithic cultures dating back to neolithic times still flourish on several islands of the Malayan Archipelago, there is only one area on the Asiatic mainland, where, in its full form, a megalithic culture has been preserved up to the present day. This area is the mountain districts of Assam, particularly the Naga Hills. There primitive tribes have lived for thousands of years, comparatively undisturbed by the influence of higher civilizations, and ancient customs and forms of ritual, long perished in other parts of Asia, are still in full practice.

The megalithic culture of the Naga Tribes is recognized as representing a particularly ancient form of the megalithic complex so widely spread over South-Eastern Asia; a form only found in a similar state of development on the small island of Nias and perhaps on Luzon in the Philippine Islands.[1] It is evident, therefore, that an understanding of the megalithic ritual of the Nagas can throw considerable light on the early forms of Asiatic megalithic culture as a whole. During a stay among the Naga Tribes in 1936 and 1937, I was able to collect information on their megalithic culture, which supplements to some extent the material already published by T. C. Hodson,[2] J. H. Hutton,[3] and J. P. Mills.[4]

The richest form of megalithic ritual is found among the Angami Nagas. Approaching their villages, one finds the paths lined for a considerable distance with great numbers of monoliths of various size and shape. They are usually erected in pairs, in groups of four or in double rows; of two menhirs standing side by side, the one is almost invariably smaller than the other. Sometimes they are erected over a platform built of smaller stones, but more often the menhir rise directly from the ground. Monoliths and stone-platforms are also found within the villages, standing either in front of the houses or on open spaces.

[1] R. Heine-Geldern, L'art prébouddhique de la Chine et de l'Asie du sud-est et son influence en Océanie. Revue des Arts Asiatiques, XI, 4, 1937, pp. 177, 178.—B. A. G. Vroklage, Das Schiff in den Megalithkulturen Südostasiens und der Südsee, Anthropos XXXI, 1936, pp. 738–41, 753–7.

[2] The Naga Tribes of Manipur, London, 1911.

[3] The Angami Nagas, London, 1921.—Carved Monoliths at Dimapur and an Angami Ceremony, Journal Anthropological Institute, LII. 1922.—The Use of Stone in the Naga Hills, Journal Anthropological Institute, LVI, 1926.

[4] The Rengma Nagas, London, 1937.

The significance of these menhirs is not always identical. The Western Angamis erect menhirs both as monuments to the dead and as memorials of the social accomplishments of the living. Rich men put up menhirs in the course of great Feasts of Merit, by which they gain in social prestige and in rank. Even when a menhirs is erected in honour of a dead man, a Feast of Merit must be held by his son 'in the name' of the deceased parent. The higher stages of the Feasts of Merit, however, are performed solely and entirely in the honour of the donor. An essential feature of these feasts is the sacrifice of oxen, buffaloes, and mithan (Bos frontalis); with their meat and large quantities of rice-beer, the giver of the feast entertains the members of his clan or even the whole village. According to the custom of Kohima a man must give five preliminary feasts before he may erect menhirs. At the fifth feast a forked post is carved, dragged once round the whole village, and finally set up in front of the house of the donor. After this feast, a man may decorate his house with the carved barge-boards known as 'house horns'. At the sixth feast, two menhirs are put up, one representing the donor and the other his wife. Bachelors are not allowed to give Feasts of Merit. The stone-pulling may be repeated thrice: at first with two stones, then with six, and finally with eight; of these stones, one half is always set up for the man and the other half for his wife. A man may not, until he has worked through the whole series, proceed to the two highest feasts. These highest feasts are connected with the building of water tanks and stone circles. For a long time, no man in Kohima has been rich enough to afford the two highest Feasts of Merit, and in the village of Khonoma, several generations have passed since the last water tanks and stone circles were built. These stone circles have generally a basis of stone-work and are lined with squared stone-seats, sometimes painted with such fertility symbols as drinking horns or mithan heads. It is said that some of these stone-circles, mostly used as dancing places, contain the graves of men of renown.

The Eastern Angamis, in contrast to their western neighbours, do not erect menhirs for deceased persons, but solely to enhance the prestige of the living. Here, too, the wife of the giver of the feast plays an important rôle in the erection of the menhirs. When a man has completed all the preliminary feasts and has collected enough wealth, he calls together his friends and tells them, 'I have not become rich through my own efforts, but because the spirits blessed me. Our fore-fathers dragged stones and I am going to see if I cannot drag stones too.' It is believed that a man who has announced his intention of holding a stone-dragging feast, will have an extra large harvest. All his clansmen help him in carrying in his harvest and in cutting wood.

After bringing home the harvest, the preparations for the feast begin, during which time the donor and his wife must observe many taboos. His friends set about looking for suitable stones and finally select two stones standing near together. The donor then, touching the stones, says:

'I want to drag you, you come with me and be friendly, you don't give me trouble, you give me nice dreams.' In the following nights, he must have a lucky dream or else new stones have to be found.

When all the preparations are completed, the feast begins; on the first day, cattle and pigs are killed and all the villagers entertained with their meat, rice, and rice-beer. On the next day the men of the village, in their ceremonial dress, drag the two chosen stones on wooden sledges to where two holes have already been dug near a path. They allow the stones to slide slowly into these holes, raising them with cane ropes so that they stand upright. As soon as the menhirs are erected, the donor of the feast and his wife sprinkle the blood of a bull on their respective stones, pronouncing a formula, which is most illuminating as to the meaning behind the erection of menhirs. They say: 'May my meat increase, may my shares of meat increase, may my crops increase, may my food not be finished quickly.' This establishes the character of the ceremony beyond all doubt as that of a fertility rite.

Rich men may repeat the stone-dragging feasts ten times, each time with an increasing number of stones, but in case they should wish to give yet more feasts, they must begin again at the very bottom of the whole series with the preliminary feasts. Among the Western Angamis, such a man must lie in a winnowing basket like a newly born child and cut his hair like that of a child; a new belt must be made for him and a new cloth. The idea is evidently that he must be reborn and start a new life in order to commence once more the series of the Feasts of Merit. Similarly, a Lhota Naga, who wants, after having completed the full series, to continue to give Feasts of Merit, must enter the bachelor's hall again and live there like a boy.

The question arises, why the Nagas believe that the erection of menhirs increases the fertility of the fields. Their phallic shape—though never emphasized by carving of the stone, an art foreign to the Nagas—may originally have been connected with this belief. I do not think, however, that the idea of the menhir as a phallic symbol is foremost in the mind of the present Nagas. Yet, there is the widespread belief that stones should only be set up in pairs and the Kacha Nagas, who erect menhirs combined with dolmens, state clearly that the upright stone is male and the dolmen female.[1]

The beneficial influence of the menhirs on the fertility of the crops seems to lie in their function of establishing a connection between the living and the dead, rather than in their phallic character. The magical 'virtue' inherent in a man of exceptional wealth, is believed to emanate from him and to enter the stones he sets up, dwelling there even after his death and benefiting the whole community by increasing the fertility of

[1] J. H. Hutton, The Meaning and Method of the Erection of Monoliths by the Naga Tribes, Journal Anthropological Institute, LII, 1922, p. 243.

all the crops. This underlying idea explains also the custom of the Angami Nagas of burying their dead along the paths to the fields or in front of their houses. The graves consist of low plaforms of stone and are often used as resting places. However, apart from these tombs, stone platforms are also erected as cenotaphs.

Other elements of the megalithic culture of the Angamis are stone sitting-places, sometimes consisting of several ascending rows of seats and frequently associated with tanks or springs, and great truncated pyramids built of rough stone. Most of these are said to contain the graves of clan ancestors, but they are sometimes built purely in order to raise the prestige of the clan.

Paved avenues, stone steps leading up to the villages and stone fortifications of great strength complete the picture of the most flourishing megalithic culture on the Asiatic mainland.

Megalithic monuments are also erected by the Mao or Maram Nagas and the Lhota and Rengma Nagas. But it is curious that their neighbours to the north and north-east, the Aos and Semas, perform elaborate Feasts of Merit without setting up stones. They substitute wooden forked posts for the menhirs and their erection is invariably connected with the sacrifice of *mithan* or buffaloes. During a tour through the unadministered and partly unexplored area between the Naga Hills District and the Burma frontier, I saw similar Y-posts in the villages of the Sangtams, Changs and Yimsungr.[1] The significance of these posts corresponds to that of the menhirs. This becomes evident in the Eastern Angami village of Iganumi, where I saw instead of menhirs large Y-shaped wooden posts, with the ends of the two forks carved in the semblance of human heads. They are set up with the same ceremonies, that in other Angami villages accompany the erection of menhirs, and the two heads represent the donor of the feast and his wife.

The Ao Nagas have developed the simple forked posts into more elaborate carvings, which they set up during the higher stages of their Feasts of Merit. Some of these are carved and painted to represent hornbill tails, a favourite motif in Ao art. The Aos also set up squat, round posts which are probably phallic symbols, though they never describe them as such.[2]

The same forms in stone, huge phalli and Y-shaped monuments, are found in the ruins of the old Kachari capital of Dimapur. We have no historical documents concerning the Kachari culture and the true significance of the monoliths of Dimapur is therefore still obscure. Yet it seems that here, exactly as in certain areas of Indonesia, primitive megalithic forms have been taken over and developed by a higher civilization.

[1] Cf. C. von Fürer-Haimendorf, Through the Unexplored Mountains of the Assam–Burma Border, The Geographical Journal, XCI, March 1938, p. 215.

[2] J. P. Mills, The Ao Nagas, London, 1926, p. 260.

A peculiar variation of the megalithic complex is to be found among the Konyak Nagas, a tribe that represents the oldest cultural stratum in the Naga Hills. Here, only the chiefs give Feasts of Merit and the sacrificial animals, buffaloes and *mithan*, are tied to forked posts and there slaughtered. It seems worth noticing, that no posts are ever set up for the sacrifice of pigs, though the Konyaks value pigs in many ways more highly than cattle. Only a chief (*Ang*) who has given Feasts of Merit is considered a 'Great *Ang*'; such feasts are extremely expensive, since about forty *mithan* have to be killed. A carved post, the top carved in the shape of a hornbill, is set up in front of the *Ang*'s house. On the day of the setting up, the *Ang* and his wife of chiefly blood hide in their house; the young men carrying the carved post sing the same song as they sing when carrying the coffin containing the corpse of an *Ang*. This suggests that the carved post represents the *Ang*, who has—symbolically—to die (and therefore hides during the ceremony) and to be reborn.

No stones are set up during these feasts, but many of the sacred chiefs of the Konyaks possess thrones of stones, consisting of a flat seat on a base of smaller stones. Fairly large menhirs stand behind some of these thrones on which only the *Ang* and their sons of chiefly blood are allowed to sit. The same privilege applies to the big wooden seats in the *Ang*'s houses. They are cut out of a single piece of wood and have the form of a broad bed; carvings of hornbill heads, usually ten or twelve in a row, adorn both their ends. Similarly carved, in the form of hornbill heads, are the ends of the wooden coffins of men of *Ang*-clan. These coffins are then placed on platforms before which two carved figures, representing the deceased and one of his followers, are set up.

Stone circles are found in front of many men's houses of the Konyaks; in the centre, there generally stands a menhir on which, after a successful head-hunting raid, the basket containing the head is hung. The erection of such menhirs is not connected with Feasts of Merit.

In most Konyak villages, a stone is erected for each head brought in, the tongue and ears being cut off and buried under the stone. On three occasions when I was present at this rite, the stone slabs were so small that they could be carried by as few as two men. In the village of Hungphoi, on the other hand, I saw a menhir taller than a man, which had been erected only a few weeks previously at the bringing in of a head. Such stones are usually set up under a tree in front of the chief's house or on a small hill overgrown with Eucalyptus; the Konyaks associate the Eucalyptus in a similar way with head-hunting trophies as other Nagas associate the Erythrina, used as a 'head-tree' by Changs and Kalyo-Kengyus.

Though the stone-monuments and the wooden forked posts are the most conspicuous elements of 'megalithic culture', they are by no means the only characteristic features of this complex, so widely spread over South-Eastern Asia. It has been mentioned already that the typical Feasts

of Merit and the sacrifice of cattle are closely associated with the erection
of monoliths. The Feasts of Merit invariably entitle the donor to special
ornaments for his own person and that of his wife, as well as for his
house. There is among the Thangkhul Nagas, the belief that men, who
have given Feasts of Merit, will have a better fate in the next world and
though such an idea is not very pronounced among other tribes, I believe
that it has also a place in the spiritual basis of megalithic culture.

Another typical feature of the megalithic complex is the strong sym-
bolism of its art and particularly the importance of the buffalo or *mithan*
horn motif. This motif, also found in many parts of Indonesia,[1] is very
prevalent among the Nagas. Village-doors, house posts and planks,
sacrificial Y-posts and stone seats are decorated with carved or painted
heads of cattle, *mithan* or buffaloes, the exact species represented being
sometimes doubtful. These carved heads are not merely ornamental, but
commemorative of animal sacrifices and thus their value is not only
aesthetic, but definitely symbolic.

I believe that R. von Heine-Geldern is correct in ascribing this symbolical character to the art of the early megalithic culture of South-Eastern
Asia as a whole.[2] It is very clearly pronounced in the woodcarvings and
paintings of the Angami Nagas representing human heads, captured in
war, women's breasts as symbols of fertility, pigs' heads as signs of
wealth, and other lucky symbols such as the sun and the moon. The style
of both the carvings and paintings is severe and monumental; simplicity
of form, rectilineal contours, and an almost complete lack of ornamentation are their outstanding characteristics.

The art of the Konyak Nagas, though also mainly symbolical, is less
severe and shows a more naturalistic tendency. Carving in the round is
much more favoured by them, than by the Angamis and human figures
as well as animals are represented in movement. From a purely aesthetical
point of view, Konyak carvings stand on a far higher level than those of
any other Naga Tribe,[3] but since the megalithic complex is so much
more fully developed among the Angami Nagas, it seems that their
severe, massive, and conventionalized style is more characteristic of
megalithic art than the naturalistic style of the Konyaks.

The megalithic culture of Assam is not only confined to the Naga
Hills. A few hundred miles to the east we find an overwhelming number
of megalithic monuments set up by the Khasis, a tribe with an Austro-
asiatic language of the Mon-Khmer type. The hills near Shillong are

---

[1] W. Hough, The Buffalo Motive in Middle Celebes Decorative Designs, Proceed. United States Museum, LXXXIX, 1932, p. 29.

[2] Op. cit., p. 177.

[3] Cf. C. von Fürer-Haimendorf, The Morung System of the Konyak Nagas,
Journal of the Royal Anthropological Institute, LXVIII, 1938, Plates XXII and
XXIII.

covered with monoliths; their most common grouping is that of several menhirs with a small dolmen in front. The menhirs struck me as being very similar to those of the Nagas; yet they have no connection with Feasts of Merit, but serve as resting-places for the souls of the dead. The Khasis burn their dead and dispose the bones in small stone-cists at the family's burial place. When a clan increases in numbers, a large bone-repository is built, to which the bones of all its members are removed from their individual cists. Since some clans are widely scattered, the bones have frequency to be carried over considerable distances to the clan-repository. On these journeys, which are accompanied by many ceremonies, including the sacrifice of cattle, menhirs in groups of three are erected on the way, in order to serve the souls following their bones as landmarks and resting places. On the middle menhir is hung the head of a bull.

Rich families, in addition, set up huge stone monuments in honour of their deceased ancestors. These consist of an uneven number of menhirs and a dolmen or table-stone lying in front. Since the Khasis have a matrilineal organization, they set up these memorials for the clan-ancestress and her brothers. The menhirs are considered as male and represent the maternal uncles, while the dolmen represents the clan-ancestress. In contrast to the Naga monoliths, many of the Khasi menhirs are carefully worked with well-rounded tops.

While the megaliths of the Nagas are mainly erected in the course of Feasts of Merit, it appears that those of the Khasis are intimately associated with the cult of the dead. Yet, both aspects of megalithic ritual, the gaining of prestige for the living and the establishment of connection with the souls of the dead, are in different degree, to be found in both areas.

The same ideas seem to lie at the root of the megalithic cultures of Indonesia and thus suggest a unity of the megalithic complex extending from the Naga and Khasi Hills over Nias and Sumatra to Flores, Ambon and Ceram.

Appendix II

The crippled tiger (see p. 136). The belief in the magic power of lame animals and gods is spread over the whole world. The Chinese believe that the owl, To Fei, is a bird with a human face and only one leg; during the summer he conceals himself and only in winter he may be seen. The man who wears his feathers need not to be afraid of the thunder. The bird, Pi Fang, also has a human face and only one leg; in his beak he carries fire. Where Pi Fang comes, inflammations arise. The Dyaks in Borneo say that their rice-bird formerly was bitten by the king of animals and since that time has only one good developed leg. The Torajas of Celebes know the constellation of the cock with the lame wing; the people of India, the constellation of the lame cow (*Srawana*); the inhabitants of Bali, the slanting house (*gubug penceng*); those of Java the leaky eel-basket (*wuwu bolong*). The Davaos of Mindanao say that the constellation Marara is a one-legged and one-armed man who sometimes causes cloudy weather at planting time so that people may not see his deformities.[1] In Samosir, one knows a protective ghost, who has a lame left leg, because 'the evil is always on the left'.

These examples may be easily increased. We will confine ourselves to a special aspect of this theme, viz. the crippled master-smith.

The most renowned smith in Javanese mythology is Menak Jingga, a dwarf with a prone forehead and a lame leg, who ruled in Balambangan, East Java. He was invincible because he possessed a javelin of yellow iron. Once, he even marched up against the mighty city of Majapahit in order to carry off a beautiful princess. He married Retna Rasa Wulan, the moon-wife. Cripple demons must be connected with the waning moon which is wounded by the sun. A similar figure is the priest Durna.[2] He possesses the magic knowledge of weapons and has power over the fire. His brother-in-law, Krepa, likewise is a great connoisseur of arms and

---

[1] No doubt the famous Javanese *batik*-motif *parang rusak* (broken knives) is connected, too, with religious mutilation. Originally it may have been worn only by persons who had passed a full initiation, in which they had been heavily mutilated.

[2] He, too, is a lunar figure, closely related to Agastya and his Buddhist pendant, Bharada, the great magician. Bharada is stopped on his voyage through the air by a tamarind-tree, just as the monkey Sugriwa, the waning moon, is caught by this tree. Bharada makes the tree small by his cursing; Sugriwa and Rama do the same in the Malay stories (cf. Zieseniss, Die Rama Sage, pp. 32–3). In Ceylon, the tamarind-tree is regarded as the dwelling of the devil—during the night it spreads a fatal smell; in Bengal, its shadow is thought to be pernicious.

smith of divine battle-cars; meanwhile, the best friend of Durna, Drupada, is perfectly skilled in the knowledge of weapons and possesses an arrow, which makes fire. The same formidable Durna, however, is a cripple; he has a broken arm, a broken nose, and only one eye.

He is more or less the pendant of the deformed clown, Semar, who in some stories appears as a priest skilled in warfare. Durna and Semar die at the same moment and are in a mystic way identical; their sons, Aswatama and Petruk, are the only ones who succeeded in following their fathers through the gate of heaven. Semar's son, Gareng, has, like Durna, a lame foot and a deformed arm.

In the story (lakon) 'Murwakala', that is recited to exorcise calamities, there appears a deformed gamelan-player, Panjak dalang Klungkungan; the word 'panjak' signifies smith's helper.

Besides cripple magicians, there are in Javanese mythology cripple witches, too. In the story 'Petruk is king' (Petruk dados ratu), we hear how the holy letter Kalima Sadat is robbed. The cunning Petruk succeeds in getting the letter back. On his journey home, the sorceress Bittibitti follows him and takes the letter from him. Petruk now changes himself into a Jambu-tree, and Bittibitti, tempted by the delicious fruits, puts the letter on the ground and climbs the tree. Then the jester suddenly retakes his true form, catches the letter, and runs away. The witch is unable to follow him, because in falling down from the tree, she was crippled.

It is possible that a remembrance of her is to be found in the kraton-dance Diyu dengklik, which is performed by a female demon with a deformed leg. In the Ethnographical Museum in Berlin is an ancient bronze cup from Java with the picture of a cripple god; see Tijds. Batav. Gen. 64, Fig. 17, opposite p. 2.

The Chinese god of literature, Kuei Hsing, is lame. Between the lame rice-bird of Borneo and the Chinese fire-bird, the emblem of smiths, there exists some coherence. The lame smiths in China and in Java are in a near relation to each other; the link between them is found in Champa. There a story is told about two demonic smiths, who fought for Nai Bala, the moon-wife and the protectress of the home, the pendant of the Javanese Ni Towong.

We are not competent to state an opinion about the Chinese data, but we trust that a careful research will throw light on the Javanese data.[1]

One example: The Javanese krises usually consist of 5 sorts of iron, representatives of the 5 tribal parts and the 5 ancestors. The wooden handles and the metal blades, decorated with an eagle and a snake, symbolize fire and water, male and female. The conformity of the Chinese conception is striking. Before making a sword, the sword-

---

[1]The kayon or gunungan, the figure of a mythical tree or mountain, is derived from China, too. One finds it already pictured with a house and two snakes on reliefs from the Wei-period.

wright has to unite himself with a woman; then he takes care that the elements, fire and water, are proportionately represented in the weapon. '*Une épéé n'était précieuse que si les cinq couleurs composantes se composaient parfaitement et si le cuivre et l'étain, intimement combinés, formaient un ensemble indissoluble*' (Granet).

Resuming, we arrive at the following result:

1) In Indonesian mythology, there appear mutilated persons and animals; they possess magic powers. Mostly they are crippled, blind, with one eye, or only with half a body.

2) Often, they are smiths or jesters. In Burmese mythology is a blind smith.

3) Originally they represented the demon of initiation or the sponsors of the candidates.

The best known jester is Semar, in Java. He is older than the world and more powerful and wiser than the gods. His character is very erotic; he inaugurates young people in the magic science of love; the most popular love-amulets are called Semar Messem, 'the Smiling Semar'. During some pilgrimages to the summits of volcanoes, one has to call on him and has to crack vulgar jokes; otherwise, one will meet with an accident. Semar is the particular protector of the dynasties; he dwells in a crater of a volcano, the house of smiths.

His son, Petruk, is lame. A legend narrates that he has been king for only one day. Formerly, in some parts of Java, one made, during the planting of rice, a statue of this jester and did homage to it as to a king. After one day, however, this statue was thrown away. This ceremony would make a rice-field very fertile.

Semar and Petruk appear very often in the shadow-play (*wayang*) at the end of a dramatic scene. They annihilate with their jokes the black magic, which is awakened by the drama. Sometimes they accompany the souls to the hereafter and are thus connected with the dead. In Celebes, one narrates that a cripple smith keeps watch at the entrance of the land of the dead and stops all wicked souls.

In many Indonesian myths, there appears a half human body (in Java, Lalang Sejiling, in Samosir, Si Aji Bahirbahir), often the first being on earth, at the same time an initiator and an initiate. Like the lame smith, he sometimes creates the world, but at the same time he suffers under this task. Only through his mutilation or death the plants, animals, etc., arise. The smith and the clown are both aspects of the culture-hero. Let us call to mind also the one-eyed Vulcanus, the cripple Hephaistos, the dwarf who forged the sword of Siegfried, etc.

Superhuman and phallic clowns are to be found in the mythology of some Indian tribes in America, whilst originally the European jesters, too, possessed magic powers. King Carnaval is not only similar to the mock-kings of Java and Cambodia, but is also connected with the dead and the resurrection of life. His festival is celebrated at the return of the new year and his conflagration is nothing else than a fertility rite. A special study of the part of the clown in ethnology would supply very interesting information.

A variation of the mutilation is the scar on the forehead of the progenitor of the Kalangs in Java. One remembers the holy crocodile of Palembang with the scar on his head. Probably these scars are ethnological remnants of mutilations which were inflicted on the boys during the initiation.

For a moment we shall return to the Chinese fire-bird, the emblem of smiths. Mr Moens in Yogya possesses a prehistoric bronze axe whereon is represented this bird, holding an axe, the symbol of fire, in his beak. This piece must be connected with the culture of Dongson in Tonking.

In Chinese mythology, birds are spoken of with three and more legs; the same bird is to be found in the stone bird-images in Nias, which are often provided with four legs.

Appendix III

Rice-pounding blocks (see p. 101). It seems useful to collect a few facts about the magic meaning of rice-mortars in Indonesia.

1. The rice-block indicates the social position of the owner. The mightier he is, the more holes are to be found in his mortar. In the Batak country one finds rice-blocks of wood and of stone with beautiful ornaments, sometimes with a lizard, the protector of the grain-depository, or with a human face.

2. It is regarded as a boat; there are various Javanese stories wherein is narrated how people went across the sea on a rice-block. Often the rice-blocks are made in the shape of a boat.

3. One believes that it is able to cause rain or inundation. In the Batavia Museum is a mortar from Sumatra; in former times, people made offerings to this block in order to get rain. The water that assembled therein was considered to have medical powers. This mortar now and then disappeared, which was an omen of bad growth or scarcity.

In China, too, some people believe that a rice-block causes inundation.

4. It is supposed that the goddess of rice dwells in it. Sometimes one places flowers and sacrifices near it and prays for a good harvest.

5. The rice-block is regarded as a woman and the pounder as a man. The Malays use a particular saying for a woman showing coquetry: 'The rice-block is seeking the pounder' (*lesung mencari alu*). In Timor, it is not allowed to step over a pounder, because by doing so, one gets a pain in the breast; one never sits down on a rice-block. That block, one says, looks like a person without a head, and if one sits down on it, one will perish in war and lose one's head.

If a Javanese woman is to be delivered of a child, it is desirable that her husband be present by the bed. This promotes the confinement, it is said, because the child longs for his father. When the father has passed away, he is represented by a rice-pounder, the end of which is wrapped up with a head-cloth.

6. It is very peculiar that the rice-block sometimes has a demonic character. In an Indian fable, a rice-block kills a jackal. Among the Parigi in Celebes, a rice-mortar is said to go out and cut off heads. A Japanese fable tells how a rice-block and a pounder killed a troop of monkeys. In the Batak country, I heard a story about a mortar that stole fruit from a tree. In Java exists a play, *adu lesung*, whereby a priest lets dance a rice-block and a pounder at full moon; in this play, various mortars fight against each other, too.

7. The rice-block brings luck. In the story 'Tau Karita' in Sumba is told how a fisher receives a golden rice-block from the god of waters; this present makes him rich.

8. One pounds in rice-blocks during eclipses of the moon and when receiving eminent guests.

9. The rice-block plays a part at social and at religious feasts. In Halmahera there exists a play that only is executed during the great feast of the dead. It is played by young men and women, who walk singing around the great rice-block; each couple holds a decorated pounder which is filled with rattling small stones. A similar feast is also celebrated in South India. The Angami Nagas pound grain on special occasions, dressed in festive attire (see Hutton's book, pp. 194, 198 and 231–3).

10. In Java, there exists a play in which rice is pounded in a mortar that stands on a human body. The man must try to free himself. Probably this is a remnant of an old initiation-rite.

Literature.

Besides the literature mentioned in my book, The Archaeology of Hindoo Sumatra, and in Loeb's Sumatra, I used articles of Neumann and Wellan in Tijdschrif van het Aardrijkskundig Genootschap 1887 and 1934, of Pieters in De Tropische Natuur 21, of Gramberg and De Haan in Tijdschrift Bataviaasch Genootschap 24 and 39, of Knebel, of Overbeck in Journal Malayan Branch Royal As. Soc. 12, and of Hoven in Bijdragen tot de Taal, Land en Volkenkunde van Nederlandsch Indie 82 and Koloniaal Tijdschrift 1925. Further, The Life of Sir Stamford Raffles by Boulger and the Jaarboeken van het Bataviaasch Genootschap. Also, De Heiligdommen van Palembang by Prof. Krom, 1938.

PLATES I–XL

1. Large Buddha in Palembang.
Granite, ht. 3.60 m.
Made in the sixth century.

Photo Van Ronkel

2. Stone terrace at Sintuo in Minangkabau. On the west side is an altar of
rough stones, on which lies a pierced stone (*batu bertikam*). Pierced stones are
worshipped in many parts of the world as a symbol of feminity.

Bronze Kuwera from Mount Seguntang near Palembang. In the left hand is a money-bag with a marten's
head, in the right, a lemon; before him, an overturned
jewel pot. Kuwera is the god of wealth. Ht. 7.5 cm.

Bhairawa from Sungai Langsat at the Upper Batang Hari River, in the heart of Sumatra, ht. 4.41 m. Probably a portrait of the Minangkabau ruler, Adityavarman, or the Javanese king. Krtanagara, and made in the fourteenth century. He is standing on a man, who is lying on his back with legs folded under the body. In the right hand, the Bhairawa holds a knife; in the left, a skull. In his hairdress sits Aksobhya, the Buddha of the East. A flaming halo encircles his head.

Amoghapasa in Rambahan, brought in 1286 from Java to Sungai Langsat and consecrated again in 1347 by King Adityavarman. The head is surrounded by a halo; left, the sun; right, the moon. Originally the image had eight arms. Left, Syamatara and Sudhanakumara; right, Hayagriwa and Bhrkuti. Eight little images of Buddhas and Taras sit on lotus flowers. Underneath appear a horse, a hurling-disc, a queen, a jewel, a minister, a general, and an elephant. Ht. 1.63 m.

PLATE V

MIDDLE SUMATRA

The Maligai Stupa of Muara Takus is perhaps the grave of a royal personage. Malays say that the Hindu ruler was transformed into an elephant, and for this reason, great herds of elephants regularly visit the ruins to do homage to the spirit of their departed ancestor. Since time immemorial the stupa court has been their favourite playground, where they walk about and disport themselves all night long by the light of the moon. English readers will remember the charming story of Toomai and the Elephants by Kipling.

1. Dancing elephant and bull from Pulo on the Panei. According to a popular superstition in Sumatra, the elephants assemble in the jungle to dance in the full moon. In the temple dances of Tibet, a bull appears as the servant of Yama, the god of death.

2. Base of a stupa in Si Joreng Belangah. On four sides, *yaksa*—half human, half divine beings—are portrayed. All these figures have the hair puffed, wide-open eyes, large ear studs, and a short hip garment. Related to South Indian art.

Photo Arch. Survey

1. Bahal I. Garlands surround the roof. On both sides of the entrance to the room are hewn out two life-size men, the upper part of the body being destroyed. Near the second steps stand small demons. Two large demons and elephant heads are visible near the lowest staircase.

2. Inscription at Padangbujur, announcing the name of Raja Soritaon. The two lizards are supposed to entice all the lizards in the neighbourhood and urge them to weep for the dead.

Wonderful bronze plaque from Bara, the back support of
some image, plainly South Indian in style. In the centre is a
round disc with lotus border, the inner part of which is
defined by a band of pearls. Below, two *makara* with tails
spout a flaming halo, which terminates in a *kala* head. Under
the latter are two small elephant heads. Ht. 56 cm.

PLATE IX

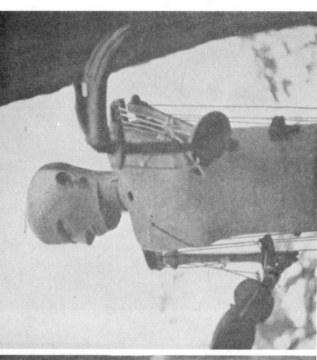

Si Galegale, a wooden doll with jointed limbs, which is made to dance at some feasts of the dead, in order to placate the spirits of the departed. No one who has seen it dancing and weeping in the green mists of Samosir, in a night filled with stars and silence, will ever forget it.

PLATE X

SAMOSIR

Photos V, Coenraad

Si Galegale, a jointed doll, which is mounted on a long chest with wheels. In front of it is a little doll, with folded hands, which are raised in salute when the large doll dances. The woman on the left wears brass ear-rings.

PLATE XI

SAMOSIR

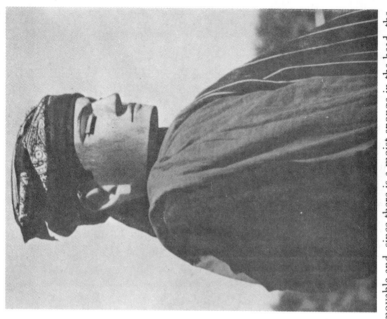

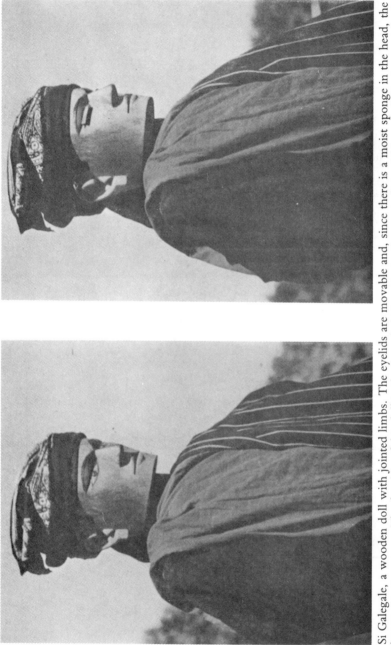

Si Galegale, a wooden doll with jointed limbs. The eyelids are movable and, since there is a moist sponge in the head, the image can even weep. The dancing of this doll in the moonlight is an imposing spectacle, making an indelible impression on all observers. The figure is dressed in costly garments and wears a head kerchief, formerly a horsehair wig with the head of a hornbill.

PLATE XII

SAMOSIR

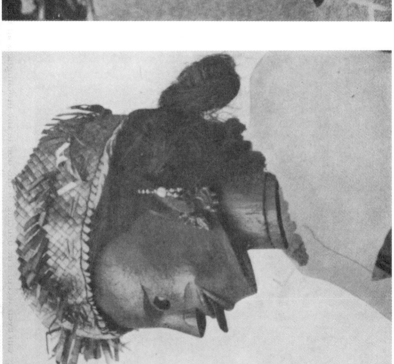

Si Galegale or Mejan, an almost life-size wooden doll with jointed limbs, which is mounted on a long chest with wheels. Some dolls can move their eyes and put out their tongue. Formerly some of them bore a mask.

Photo V. Coenraad

Mask from Simalungun, east of Lake Toba.

PLATE XIV

NORTH SUMATRA

House in Uluan, on the south-eastern coast of Lake Toba. The front is adorned with carved buffalo's heads, woman's breasts and lizards. The ship-formed rice-mortar is clearly visible.

PLATE XV

WEST SAMOSIR

On a hill at Siriaon (near Urat) lies a broken stone sarcophagus, which is partly sunken into the earth. It contains eight skulls; on the back sits a headless female image. Holy *hariara*-trees grow near it. The chest belongs to the *Marga* Sinaga and is five generations old. Pallopuk has made it and Pangarambang is the still living possessor.

PLATE XVI

Sarcophagus for skulls at Naingolan, more than 3 m long, looking to the east. On the head a long, curved point, an ancient head-dress of Batak chiefs, which is still found in some wooden images of Nias. On the back sits a woman with a small bowl in her hands.

Sarcophagus for skulls at Pangambatan Parsingguran, length 4 m, height 2.50 m, looking to the north. Made by Oppue Batu Koling and containing 300 skulls. The great monster head has a gentle, inquisitive smile and an expression of deep resignation. This image is one of the greatest and noblest works of art ever produced in Sumatra. The wooden prototypes of such chests must be sought in the Pakpak Lands, where big chiefs are interred in decorated ships, which are placed on the fields. Often, however, one keeps such wooden chests in the house.

1   2

3   4

1. Sarcophagus at Huta Paung, on the south-western coast of Lake Toba. On the head, a long point with a buffalo's head.
2. Sarcophagus at Huta Bagasan, on the south-eastern coast of Lake Toba.
3. Sarcophagus at Tangga na Godang, near Tarutung.
4. Large rice-mortar in Lumban Pangaloan, on the western coast of Lake Toba. In the background, an enormous stone-wall; and left, a part of a sarcophagus.

1. Tolping I.

2. Tolping II.

3. Pancur (western coast of Samosir).

Photo Ypes

4. Pangambatan Parsingguran (south-western coast of Lake Toba).

Urns containing skulls.

5. Tolping III (eastern coast of Samosir).

1. House-ornaments in Uluan, on the south-eastern coast of Lake Toba. On the left an elephant's head in Lumban na Bolon. Formerly, one could apply such ornaments only after having hunted a human head.

Photo Dr P. Voorhoeve

2. Model of a stone sarcophagus in Aek Godang, on the south-western coast of Lake Toba. Sarcophagi in animal form are to be found in Nias, the Batu- and Hinako-islands, Bali, and Sumba, too. Also, they are depicted on some weavings with pictures of ships in South Sumatra. East of Lake Toba, in Simalungun, are sarcophagi with heads of hornbills, also among the Lhota Nagas in Assam.

Hoda-hoda are men disguised as hornbills, who dance at the burial of a *raja*. They represent the bird, which brings the soul of the deceased to the hereafter. Sometimes they are ritually killed by a buffoon and afterwards raised to life again as a symbol of resurrection and eternal life.

Photos V. Coenraad

In Toba, the *Hoda-hoda* are men disguised as horses, wearing a wooden horse-head or a horse-mask. They represent the horses, which formerly were killed on the grave of a *raja*. Funeral horse-dances were known in Pamir and Turkestan, too.

Mushroom-shaped stones (*niogaji*) in Tetegewo, made for the wives of important chiefs, and erected after birth or marriage. Each woman has the right
to expose her golden ornaments on it; the stones are thought to get magical
potence by it. The wives perform dances on these stones. Each *niogaji*
produces a musical sound when struck with the flat of the hand. Clearly
visible are the discs with the heads and tails of animals, which commemorate
feasts of merit.

Photo Prof. J. P. Kleiweg de Zwaan

Youth for the chief's house in Bawomataluwo.

Photo General A. Kruisheer

1. Feast.

Photo J. C. Lamster

2. Dragging a stone.

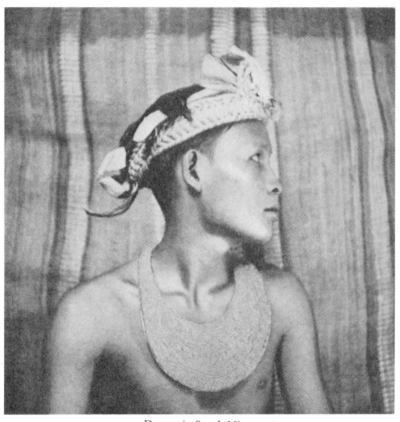

Dancer in South Nias.

Warrior.
In the rattan ball are kept objects, which bestow magical virtue.

PLATE XXVII

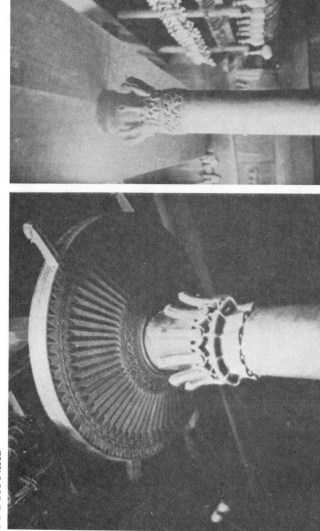

Interior of the chief's house in Bawomataluwo. One sees long rows of pigs' jaws, which must keep in the house the souls of the slaughtered animals. Underneath, beautifully carved cunning hooks in the shape of birds, volutes, and phalli. Further, bottles and flat baskets with plates.

Photo R. Bonnet

Interior of the chief's house in Bawomataluwo.

Photo H. Sundermann

At certain feasts of merit the tribal chief and his wife have the right to be carried in an *osaosa*, a sedan chair in the shape of some fantastic animal, for which formerly severed human heads were required. Under the chair is often the image of a slaughtered slave. Such carrying down in a litter is found among the Lushei Kukis, too.

Buying of ranks is typical for Kafiristan and the New Hebrides.

Photo R. Bonnet

Interior of the chief's house in Bawomataluwo. From the ceiling hang bottles and flat baskets with plates. In the centre arises a pillar which unfolds into a flower, cleverly carved and of wondrous beauty.

1. Pillar with hornbill, which has female breasts and four feet.

2. *Osaosa* indicates a wooden disc with the head of an animal. At certain feasts, the chief and his wife have the right to be carried in it. Stone *osa* are erected in commemoration of these feasts, one-headed specimens for men and three-headed specimens for women.

1. Unfinished stone sarcophagus in Hilisimaitano. The head of the deer has horns and a beard of gilded tin, which are fastened with iron wire.

2. Left: The chief's house in Cudrubaho (Idano Tai) has a pillar with a necklace, breasts, and two upraised arms. Completely human pillars are still found in some Toba Batak villages. Right: Crocodile in Botohilitano.

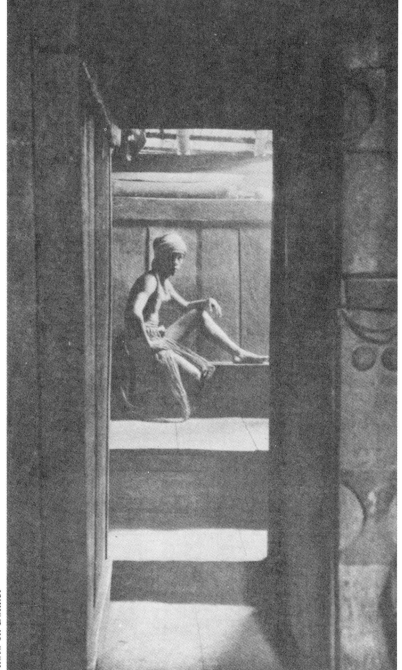

Photo R. Bonnet

Entrance of a chief's house in South Nias.

1. Images (*behu*) at Olajama near Soliga. Before it, one sees dolmen (*awina*), dancing-stones for women; formerly they covered skulls. The little standing stones (*fao gana'a*) commemorate feasts, in which were made golden ornaments.

2. Pyramids containing skulls of important chiefs in Holi. Under these skulls lay severed heads of slaves.

1. Dancer wearing a mask with the head of a hornbill.

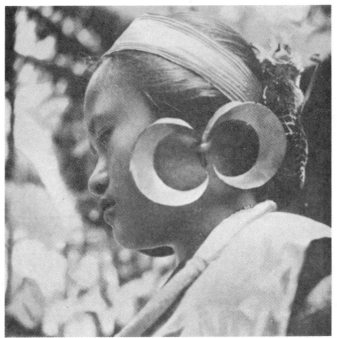

2. Maiden in festive dress. On the head, a finely chiselled band of gold. In the ears, large golden ornaments. Lawalawaluwo.

1. At the left side of this large elephant kneels a warrior with a pointed helm on his head. Around his neck is a bronze ring; in his girdle, a great sword, and on his back, a drum. His legs are encased in rings, the predecessors of our modern puttees.

Photo H. W. Vonk

2. Large relief at Air Puar. Two men with pointed helms each hold a buffalo by a rope, while together they hold a drum. Under the drum appears a dog; a crocodile bites him in the leg.

1. Bronze bowl. (Collection A. van Doorninck).

2. Bronze bell. (Collection A. van Doorninck).

Photo Ethnogr. Museum, Rotterdam

1. Weaving with picture of a ship.

Photo Ethnogr. Museum, Leiden

2. Model of a ship on wheels, in which the tribal chief and his wife are brought to the festal ground. Formerly dead bodies were set down in these ships, after which they were hurled into a deep ravine. The Bataks of Padang Lawas had also such boats on wheels.

1. Heads in the high bank of the Selangis River.

Photo H. W. Vonk

2. Dolmen at Muara Pajang.

Gravestone of a Muhammadan Javanese in
Kebanagung, near Pageralam.